St. Mary Parish, Louisiana, Heirship Series
Vol. I
Annotated Abstracts of the Successions, 1811-1834

Compiled by Mary Elizabeth Sanders

PELICAN PUBLISHING COMPANY
Gretna 2013

Copyright © 1972
By Mary Elizabeth Sanders

First Pelican printing, 2002
Second Pelican Printing, 2013

The word "Pelican" and the depiction of a pelican are trademarks of Pelican Publishing Company, Inc., and are registered in the U.S. Patent and Trademark Office.

ISBN: 978-1-56554-923-4

Printed in the United States of America
Published by Pelican Publishing Company, Inc.
1000 Burmaster Street, Gretna, Louisiana 70053

DEDICATED

TO THOSE HEARTY AND COURAGEOUS PIONEERS WHO SETTLED ST. MARY PARISH, CARVED A CIVILIZATION OUT OF THE WILDERNESS AND BECAME OUR ANCESTORS.

JARED YOUNG SANDERS I
1791 - 1862
Fourth sheriff of St. Mary Parish, 1818-1821
[See Est. #181]

RACHEL NIXON HULICK
1798 - 1872
Wife of Jared Young Sanders I
[See Est. #96]

TABLE OF CONTENTS

ACKNOWLEDGEMENTS v

PREFACE viii

SOURCES xiii

HISTORICAL INTRODUCTION xviii

MISSING SUCCESSIONS 1

ABSTRACTS 34A

ADDENDA SECTION 164

SUPPLEMENTARY ADDENDA SECTION . . . 184

INDEX 185

SUPPLEMENTARY INDEX 230

ACKNOWLEDGMENTS

It has been said, and truly so, that no man is an island unto himself. This has never been better demonstrated than in the publication of a work such as this. In a sophisticated and cynical world such as we are said to live in, it is refreshing to find that people are not merely <u>willing</u>, but <u>eager</u>, to share. Perhaps it is in the hope that these records and relationships will be correctly preserved. At any rate, right up until the day typing of the Index itself began, information from those who had already worked on these families came in. And it was so gratefully received! This necessitated rewriting many pages, and this also accounts for some of the blank spaces in the manuscript.

This work really has a co-compiler. Mrs. Clyde Alpha of Franklin, who has worked many hours in the St. Mary Parish Clerk of Court's office and knows the people and history of the parish better than most, has made possible this work in its more complete form. She has identified many of the first missing successions; she has loaned me books, microfilm, and records; she has given unstintingly of her time. Persons interested in preserving these loved memoirs and relationships owe Mrs. Alpha much; and I thank her greatly.

Mr. Sidney L. Villere, another dedicated coworker in New Orleans who is also a collateral descendant of some of these early St. Mary families, has also helped immeasureably. In discussing our work, I mentioned some of my problems to "Mr. Sidney." He suggested that I jot down some he might be able to help solve. And help he did! He helped identify the missing

Olivier successions. He located in Orleans Parish the will of the Rev. Charles Mynn Thruston, whose family apparently came to Attakapas after his death in 1812. And he helped me identify members of families he has worked on - Olivier de Vezin, Verret, Cantrelle, etc.

My much-loved cousin, Addie Sublette (Mrs. M. A.) also of New Orleans, so freely shared background material and concrete data on her Kemper family to furnish a more complete record of Nathan Kemper, his background and descendants.

My dear friend, Mrs. Bertrand Haralson of St. Francisville, very kindly put me in touch with relatives of "my" Feliciana people. Mrs. Sarah Towles Reed of New Orleans and Mr. James Leake Stirling of St. Francisville so eagerly helped with information on their ancestors, Dr. John Thomas Towles and Alexander Sterling, respectively. Mrs. Mabel Martin of St. Francisville helped me obtain a copy of the will of Alexander Sterling, who was a resident of Feliciana and whose will was probated before West Feliciana Parish was created. The will is now recorded there.

Mrs. Jacqueline Vidrine of Ville Platte and Glenn R. Conrad, Director of Archives at the University of Southwestern Louisiana in Lafayette, both graciously responded to calls for help in identifying some of my "missing links," as did my good friend, Pearl Segura, head of the Louisiana Department at Dupre Library, the University of Southwestern Louisiana, respond to a plea with regard to translating a French document.

Otis Hebert's roots go deep into Attakapas, as do mine. He formerly taught American History at Louisiana State University in Baton Rouge. As he is a native of the Attakapas area [Abbeville] and knows it and its people so well, he is especially qualified to give the historical introduction. I will always be grateful to him for taking time from his very busy schedule as Director of our state's Archives and Records Service to write it. I am also grateful to his "girl Friday," Mrs. Alberta Ducote, for her ever-cheerfulness and eagerness to help.

I am especially grateful to the Attakapas Historical Association for permission to quote from their three special publications, as noted in the Source List on page xv.

Genealogists would be in a perpetual state of "limbo" without the co-operation of the Clerks of Court and their staff members. We have been particularly blessed in Attakapas. Mr. Benny Blakeman in St. Mary Parish and Mr. M. A. Barras in St. Martin Parish and Mr. Barras' lovely wife have all co-operated in every possible way, as have their courteous staff members. My grateful thanks are due all of them.

I also wish to thank Huey Henry Breaux, a Lafayette attorney with whom I discussed legal aspects of this compilation, and **Dr.** and Mrs. James F. Bassett for their help. Mr. **Breaux** is an avid genealogist also and very kindly loaned me material, especially on the Provost family, which contributed much to the value of the book. Dr. and Mrs. Bassett took time from their busy lives as a member of the Education faculty at the University of Southwestern Louisiana and homemaker, respectively, to read the compiler's Preface. Their suggestions have made that part of this work clearer and more understandable.

The interest and help of all these people are deeply appreciated.

                            Mary Elizabeth Sanders

Lafayette, La.
February, 1972

PREFACE

In some respects Louisiana is a genealogist's paradise; its records date back two and a half centuries and in many cases they are complete, having escaped the ravages of time, fire, war, flood, negligence. On the other hand, records frequently are incomplete, due to negligence, flood or fire. In a few cases, courthouse fires have entirely destroyed their precious records. Such a fire was experienced in the 1880's at the Vermilion Parish courthouse, Abbeville, in the Attakapas area.

St. Mary Parish has been fortunate in retaining its records. Mr. Benny Blakeman, Clerk of Court, is to be highly commended for his timely actions towards preserving the records which have survived.

Even so, St. Mary Parish has not wholly escaped loss. Segments of the earliest records are missing -- including the earliest civil suits and some of the early successions. Several theories have been advanced as to what happened to these "missing links." One theory is that an early fire destroyed them; another, that a flood literally engulfed them. Indeed, there are watermarks on some of the early records examined in compiling this work. However, the most plausible explanation would seem to be that the missing records were victims of the Civil War.

New Orleans fell to Northern forces in late April of 1862. Before the year was over the victors had spread as far west over south Louisiana as St. Mary Parish. In the effort to preserve the records, officials reportedly hid them. They probably were shifted from place to place -- and it seems likely that some were misplaced in these shiftings. It is a fond hope that some day they will turn up in an old trunk in someone's attic.

Another reason Louisiana can be a genealogist's "Garden of Eden" is the structure of its law, which preserves a woman's identity and allows a **married** woman's maiden name to be known in almost all cases. Also under this law, when a succession involves minor children [under 21 years of age], family meetings must be held in the minors' behalf. These family councils are composed of 5 persons over 21 years of age. Generally, the minors' closest relatives, either blood or by marriage, where such relatives reside close enough to the minors to do so, participate in these "family meetings." Usually the exact degree of kinship of these persons to the minors is shown. However, where there are no relatives available, friends are substituted and their status is so stated.

In order more fully to understand this work, the reader should be familiar with the following paragraphs.

A person who has died is referred to as the decedent. A person writing a will is called the testator. When a decedent has written a will, he is said to have died testate; when he has not written a will, he is said to have died intestate.

Louisiana recognizes several types of wills. Only two are involved in this work. By far most numerous are olographic wills: those written by the testator in his own handwriting. Under Louisiana law this type will does not require witnesses. When it is probated [proved to be genuine and legal, or valid], 3 or more witnesses are required by the court to testify that the will is indeed written in the handwriting of the testator.

The other type will found in this work, of which there are only a few, is nuncupative by public act. This will is written by a notary public for the testator, who signs it in the presence of at least two witnesses domiciled in the same parish as the notary. This is a self-proving document.

When a person dies in Louisiana, an <u>originating petition</u> is filed on behalf of the **heirs**, thus initiating the succession. If a will has been found, it is <u>probated</u> [or proved] at this time. It was not unusual in "olden days" for a will to be located after the originating petition had been filed with the court. The originating petition usually names all the known heirs, also usually sets forth their exact relation to the decedent.

If the known heirs were not present or were "at odds" among themselves, the decedent's personal effects were sealed by authority of the court. A justice of the peace could perform this sealing. The seals would then be "lifted" or "raised" with the authority of the court in the presence of at least one of the heirs or a representative. This practice is no longer in vogue.

Children under 21 years of age are <u>minors</u>. Minors under puberty who had lost one or both parents had to have a <u>tutor</u> and an <u>undertutor</u>. Unless there were extenuating circumstances, a surviving parent would be **confirmed** as <u>natural tutor</u> or <u>tutrix</u>, in the case of the mother. A non-relative was frequently appointed undertutor.

Minors over the age of puberty were called <u>adult minors</u>. These older children had to have two curators - one called a <u>curator ad bona</u> and one called a <u>curator ad litem</u>. Usually the adult minors were consulted as to their preference of curators.

According to Louisiana law, the age of puberty was "about 14 years of age." It is no longer the law in Louisiana that adult minors have curators; all minors now have tutors and undertutors unless emancipated.

A few words of caution. This work is intended as a <u>guide only</u> to the successions of St. Mary Parish. Only those parts of the successions are

x

abstracted which indicate heirships. The reader should bear in mind that every document is <u>not</u> included. It has been the compiler's task to judge which are the important ones as to heirship. Relationships given in quoted sources are also given as <u>guides</u> <u>only</u>, and compiler can not assume responsibility for their accuracy. In all cases, those seeking substantiation must turn to the records themselves for it.

A few pertinent documents in French have been merely noted; no effort has been made either to translate them or have them translated by another.

The French are notorious for the inconsistency in what they call themselves. Sometimes their entire names are inverted in the records. Frequently the surname is followed by a reference to an individual's home. A classic example is the Olivier family. One prominent branch of this family is known as "Olivier De Vezin" or simply "De Vezin."

Which brings us to spellings. The reader must bear in mind that many of the Attakapas pioneers were completely illiterate. Unable to write their own names, they were unable to tell officials how to spell them. Likewise, many of the officials themselves were hardly literate. There is also the question of different languages -- French, Spanish, and after the Louisiana Purchase in 1803, English -- officials had to cope with.

Thus mutations in the spellings of names were frequent. The compiler spelled names in the abstracts as they appeared in the document under consideration, and consolidated them in the Index. It was necessary to combine surnames with similar spellings, such as "Prevost" and "Provost," simply because it is impossible to follow individual spellings in the records.

The Index in the Clerk of Court's office to the Successions includes those which are missing. It is problematical as to when the Index was compiled. It seems likely that it might have been reconstructed from memory after the records were lost. It shows many initials rather than given names. Many of these missing ones were identified at least tentatively herein and decedents' heirs given. In this work, these "reconstructed" successions are placed immediately ahead of the abstracts. They are Successions No. 1-93. One number is assigned to more than one succession in several instances.

Successions marked with an asterick [*] before the decedent's name at the heading of the abstract have additional genealogical information in the "Addenda" Section, immediately behind the abstracts. This is information which was obtained after the abstract was typed and ready for the printer. These names are included in the Index to this work. There is also a "Supplementary" Addenda Section and also a "Supplementary" Index.

The reader should become familiar with the sources listed on the following pages. These sources document genealogical data herein.

Despite errors which undoubtedly may creep into this work, it will still be a useful guide to the early settlers of St. Mary Parish.

SOURCES

A bibliography is usually placed in the back of a scholarly work. But this source list is so situated that the reader will know it is extant before he gets into the body of the work. This work is fully documented; that is, every statement not actually taken from the records themselves, is accounted for. It is important that the reader know the sources in order to evaluate the data given more intelligently.

Original Sources

Interviews and personal notes as indicated.

Unpublished Records

Church

Baptism, Marriage, and Death Records, St. Martin of Tours Catholic Church, St. Martinville, La.
Baptism and Marriage Records, St. Louis Cathedral, New Orleans, La.

Federal

Third Census of the United States, Schedule I (Free Inhabitants of the Parish of Attakapas [St. Martin], Territory of Orleans), unpublished returns, 1810. [Shown as Federal Census of 1810.]
Fourth Census of the United States, Schedule I (Free Inhabitants of the Parish of St. Mary, State of Louisiana), unpublished returns, 1820. [Shown as Federal Census of 1820.]
Seventh Census of the United States, Schedule I (Free Inhabitants of the Parish of St. Mary, State of Louisiana), unpublished returns, 1850. [Shown as Federal Census of 1850.]
American State Papers, Public Lands, Vols. II and III. [In 1832 the Congress of the United States began publication of governmental

legislative and executive documents. The
documents were divided into 10 classes, one
of which was Public Lands. Many courthouses
and larger libraries have copies of these
volumes, which are of course long-time out
of print.]

Local

Attakapas Militia Census [1792], St. Martin Parish
Original Acts, Book 14, folio 142.

Brand Book for Opelousas and Attakapas Districts,
1739-1888. [The original is housed in Dupre
Library, University of Southwestern Louisiana,
Lafayette. It has been microfilmed and the
original is no longer available for research.
Microfilm copies may be searched. Individual
books are housed in some courthouses in the
Clerk of Court's office.]

Franklin, La., Planters' Banner [weekly newspaper]

Franklin and St. Martinville, La., cemeteries.

Kentucky Gazette. See G. Glenn Cleft under "Printed Materials."

St. Martin Parish, La., Original Acts [designated
as "OA" followed by book-folio numbers],
Marriage Records and Successions, Office of
the Clerk of Court, St. Martin Parish, St.
Martinville, La.

St. Mary Parish Civil Suits, Marriage, Probate
Court, Conveyance Records and Successions,
Office of the Clerk of Court, St. Mary
Parish, Franklin, La.

St. Mary Parish taxpayer list for 1813, Franklin,
La., Planters' Banner, 6 Apr. 1848, page 6,
cols. 4 and 5.

Printed Material

Winston DeVille, Marriage Contracts of the
Attakapas Post, 1760-1803 [designated as
"DeVille"] and

Jane Guillory Bulliard and Leona Trosclair David,
[Annotated] 1774 Census of Attakapas [desig-

nated as "1774 Census"], Special Publication No. 1, Attakapas Historical Association (St. Martinville, La. 1967).

George A. Bodin, Selected Acadian and Louisiana Church Records, Vols. I and II, Special Publications 2 and 3, Attakapas Historical Association (St. Martinville, La., 1968 and 1970). [Designated as "Bodin" showing volume and page number.]

[References from these 3 works are used by special permission of the Attakapas Historical Association, P. O. Box 107, St. Martinville, La.]

Clarence Edwin Carter, (Ed.), The Territorial Papers of the United States, Vol. IX, The Territory of Orleans, 1803-1812 (U. S. Government Printing Office, Washington, 1940).

G. Glenn Cleft, Kentucky Marriages, 1797-1865 [includes "Kentucky Gazette."]

Winston DeVille and Jacqueline Olivier Vidrine, Marriage Contracts of the Opelousas Post, 1766-1803 (1960, n. p.). [Designated as "DeVille, Opelousas Marriage Contracts."]

Walter Prichard, F. B. Kniffen, and Clair A. Brown (Eds.), "The Journal of James Leander Cathcart" in the Louisiana Historical Quarterly (Vol. 28, No. 3, July, 1845). [James Leander Cathcart and James Hutton as Navy Agents and John Landreth as surveyor made a journey on behalf of the Federal government reserving certain public lands containing timber suitable for Naval construction. This journey in early 1819 carried the party along the Bayou Teche. Evan Bowles acted as pilot. Cathcart kept a daily journal of this adventure, in which he mentioned many planters along his route and gave interesting tid-bits of information about them. The original is deposited in the

National Archives in Washington. It remains a major period source for Attakapas history and genealogy. References herein to this source are designated as either "Prichard" or "Cathcart".]

Mary Elizabeth Sanders, Records of Attakapas District, La., Vol. I, 1739-1811 (1962) and Vol. II, St. Mary Parish, La., 1811-1860 (1963). [Calendars only. Both republished 1970. References to certain individuals appearing in these 2 works are indicated by merely showing "Vol. I" or "Vol. II".]

Biographical and Historical

Stanley Clisby Arthur, Old Families of Louisiana (New Orleans, 1931).

―――, The Story of the West Florida Rebellion (St. Francisville, La., 1935).

Biographical Directory of the American Congress, 1774-1961 (U. S. Government Printing Office, Washington, 1961). [Designated "Cong. Dir."]

Eliza Haddon McClure Brevoort, Gullicks and Allied Families, 1653-1948 (Evansville, Ind., 1948).

Kennell Philip Brown, M. D., A Record of the Descendants of Nicolas Provost (Jeanerette, La., 1957).

Margaret Ann Buckner, Early Virginians (Fredericksburg, Va., n. d.). [Designated as "Buckner."]

Henry E. Chambers, A History of Louisiana (3 vols., Chicago & New York, 1925).

Daughters of the American Revolution, Mississippi State Society, Family Records: Mississippi Revolutionary Soldiers (n. p., 1956). [Designated as "Miss. D. A. R. book."]

Irene S. and Norman E. Gillis, Biographical and Historical Memoirs of Mississippi (n. p., 1962).

Lucile Barbour Holmes, Oaklawn Manor (Franklin, La., 1968).

William Henry Perrin, Southwest Louisiana Biographical and Historical (New Orleans,

1891, and Baton Rouge, 1971). [References to "Perrin" in all cases refer to the biographical section.]

Also recommended:
Glenn R. Conrad, "The Teche Country Fifty Years Ago" [from <u>The Southern Bivouac</u>, January, 1886] in the <u>Attakapas Gazette</u> (published quarterly by the Attakapas Historical Association, Vol. VI, No. 4). [This very interesting and informative source was published after this work was completed.]

HISTORICAL INTRODUCTION

St. Mary Parish was originally part of the Attakapas country. During the French regime of Louisiana's colonial history, many Frenchmen settled in the area who came directly from France. Among these families were the Bienvenus, Oliviers, Sigurs, DeClouets, and Darbys. After Spain acquired Louisiana, Spaniards with names such as Navarro, Moras and Romero settled in the area. These Spanish settlers were among the first to start plantations in the area. Also during the Spanish period Acadian refugees -- Broussards, Thibodeauxs, LeBlancs, Landrys, etc. -- settled in the Attakapas region. After the American Revolution a considerable number of British and American settlers migrated to the Attakapas country. Among the Anglo-Saxon family names who came were the Garrets, Yanceys, Footes, etc.

In 1811 the legislature of the Territory of Orleans, the name given to that part of the Louisiana Purchase territory which later became the State of Louisiana [with West Florida added to it], passed an act providing for the division of the County of Attakapas into two parishes -- St. Martin and St. Mary. Attakapas was one of the original 12 counties created in 1805; it was St. Martin Parish, when parishes were formed in 1807. St. Mary Parish was to be that part south of a "line running east from the upper line of the plantation of Francis Boutte, on the Bayou Teche, to the great lake [Grand Lake], and west from the said Francis Boutte to the mouth of the bayou of the petite Anse of the Bay [Vermilion]." Other parishes created out of the County of Attakapas were Lafayette (1823), Vermilion (1844), and Iberia (1868).

When the parish of St. Mary was formed, Franklin, the oldest town in the parish, became the seat of government. The town had been founded about 1808. In 1818, according to James

L. Cathcart and James Hutton, surveyors for the United States government who were in the Bayou Teche region in search of live oak and red cedar timber suitable to construct naval vessels, Franklin was the only town in the parish and had 15 or 20 homes and 120 to 150 inhabitants.

The recorded history of St. Mary Parish dates back to approximately 1800. By that date there were perhaps a dozen families who had settled and were establishing farms in the lower Bayou Teche region. Perhaps the first settler in the region was Joseph Berwick, who was settled in the wilderness around Berwick Bay as early as 1790. Cathcart said, "Mr. Berwick is the son of the man who gave the name of the bay . . . . He was born on this spot, is unlettered, but civil and intelligent." They also commented on four 30-foot Indian mounds then standing near the present town of Berwick which were in full view of the Berwick house for thirty years. The report also stated that the Berwick plantation produced 150,000 pounds of cotton in 1818.

Other early settlers of the area included James Sanders of South Carolina, who apparently settled on Bayou Sale around 1800; Octave de la Houssaye, a sugar planter near Jeanerette; and William Peter Kemper, son of Nathan Kemper, born about 1802 and one of the first white children born in the parish.

The relative late development of the Attakapas country area is easily understood considering the inaccessibility of the region. Between St. Mary and New Orleans, which was founded in 1718, lay two swamps -- the Des Allemands swamp and the Chacahoula swamp -- about eighty miles wide. The journey around these swamps by way of Donaldsonville or Plaquemine took as long as two weeks. A longer but more easily accessible route was by way of the Atchafalaya River.

Still by the time of the Louisiana Purchase in 1803 the population of the Attakapas country was 1,447, half of whom were white. The people were scattered from Berwick Bay to the Mermentau River and from the Gulf of Mexico to Opelousas. By 1810, the first official United States census in Louisiana, the population had increased to 7,369.

During the early decades of the 1800's, Bayou Teche became a busy waterway. One, two, and three-mast sailing vessels plied the river mostly to and from New Orleans through the bayous and lakes to Plaquemine and Donaldsonville. Some of the larger two and three-masters sailed the Gulf Coast to Galveston and other ports. And some even sailed around the Florida peninsula to New York and Boston. The steamboat made its appearance on Bayou Teche in 1835 by Watson McKerall.

In 1857 the New Orleans, Opelousas, and Great Western Railroad reached Brashear City [now Morgan City], coming through the heretofore impassable Des Allemands and Chacahoula swamps. In the 1870's work was begun on a bridge across the Atchafalaya, a great engineering feat for its day, and was completed before the end of the decade. The first train to make the trip from New Orleans to Houston over the railroad was in 1881.

The next major advance in transportation occurred in 1926 with the building of U. S. Highway 90 paralleling the railroad across the swamps and a highway bridge across the Atchafalaya the following decade.

A. Otis Hebert, Jr.
Director, State Archives
and Records Commission

Baton Rouge, La.
October, 1971

#1. JOSEPH CARLIN - 1810. Decedent died in late December of 1809, for he was buried on 30 or 31 December 1809 on the plantation of Honore Carlin, his son. [Death Register, St. Martin of Tours Catholic Church, St. Martinville, La.] There is a double entry of this burial in the record, giving conflicting burial dates. Age at time of death is not given. The following information pertaining to this family is from photostatic copies of material in the St. Louis Cathedral, New Orleans, in the possession of Mrs. Clyde Alpha, Franklin, La., who kindly permitted me the use of them.

Joseph Carlin, resident of Bayou des Allemands, born in Nantes, France, legitimate son over 21 years of age of Joseph Carlini of Lombardy, Italy, and Marie Zerbinati of Rome, Italy, married Francoise Lange, born in Toulouse, France, legitimate minor daughter of Pierre Lange of Toulouse and Marie de Richebourg of Paris, France, on 6 May 1774, by Father Dagobert in New Orleans. They had been legitimately married previously by Judge J. LeBlanc of St. John the Baptist Parish. Jean Baptiste Bauvelin, Pierre Sauve, and Jean Baptiste Lange were witnesses.

There is apparently no record of the exact date of the birth of Joseph Carlin or his wife, but the Militia Census of 1792 for Attakapas [see Vol. I] lists him as 50 in that year, which would place his birth at about 1742, making him about 67 at the time of his death. Francoise Lange Carlin was buried 13 Sept. 1815 [Death Register, St. Martin of Tours Catholic Church, St. Martinville, La.] Her age is not given at the time of her death, but she was several years younger than her husband, as she was shown to be a minor at the time of their marriage. She must have been born in the late 1740's. Her succession is probably St. Mary Est. #43, opened in 1815 in the name of "F. Carlin," one of the missing records.

This couple had at least 7 children, 5 sons

and 2 daughters. Civil suit #158, St. Mary
Parish, Heirs of Carlin vs. Joseph Provost alias
Collet, filed 22 Mar. 1817, concerns a land grant
to Joseph Carlin dated 4 Feb. 1794 from the
Spanish government. Most of these children are
named therein.

  1. Denis was the oldest. There is no exact
date of his birth, but from the 1792 Militia
Census (which is not accurate for those in this
family for which we do have records) we know that
he must have been born sometime in late 1767 in
St. Charles Parish. He married Suzanne Labaterie,
daughter of Jean Labaterie and Marthe Dizlande
[Bodin I 217], probably in the late 1780's in St.
Martinville. His succession is Est. #108. The
date of his death is not given therein. The
Estate Index lists this estate as having been
opened in 1825, but it does not appear to be
complete. His wife's succession was opened in
1830, Est. #213. They had at least 14 children.
See their successions for their family.

  2. Celestin was the second son. He was likewise baptized by Father Dagobert. His birth was
7 June 1768 in St. Charles Parish. His godparents
were Jean Baptiste Lange [possibly his mother's
brother] and Therese de Bore. On 13 Nov. 1793 he
married Marie Therese Provost, widow of Pierre
Provost, in St. Martinville. For details of her
background, see Est. #61, which is probably hers.
His succession is Est. #242, opened in 1833.

  3. Alexis, the third son, was born 5 Dec.
1773 [Bodin II 113], apparently in St. Charles
Parish, and married Genevieve DeRouan in St.
Martinville 26 Jan. 1795; she was a daughter of
Joseph DeRouan and Genevieve Hebert [Bodin I 134].
Alexis Carlin's succession was opened in 1838,
Est. #386.

  4. Honore, the fourth son, was born 12 Mar.
1774 in St. Charles Parish, though his age is
given in the 1792 Militia Census as some 3 years
older. He was baptized by Father Dagobert. His

godparents were Celestin Carlin and Marie Anne
Bourgeois. This Celestin Carlin must have been
his uncle and indicates that Joseph's sons may
have been given family names. On 14 May 1794 he
married Marguerite Bourgeois of Bayou des Allemands. She was born 14 June 1773 at sea, a
daughter of Jacques Bourgeois and Marie Anne
Sauvagin of Bayou des Allemands, natives of
Bordeaux, France; her grandparents were Jean
Marie Bourgeois of Dijon, France, and Marguerite
de Montigny of Paris, France; and Jean Baptiste
Sauvagin of Bordeaux and Francoise de Marigny of
Paris, France.

His obituary is listed in the Franklin, La.
Planters' Banner of 3 Jan. 1846, stating he died
in Dec. of 1845. His succession is Est. #576,
opened in 1845.

These 4 sons were residents of St. Mary Parish.

5. Eugene Carlin, the youngest of the sons, was
born in March of 1775, probably in Attakapas [Bodin
I 113]. He was a resident of New Orleans in his
adulthood and he probably married there.

There were at least 2 daughters.

6. Dorothea or Dorothy, married Evan Bowles.
For their family see Ests. #228, opened in 1832;
#263, 1833; and #885, 1855.

7. Therese, married Pierre Bonvillain, whose
age in the 1792 Militia Census was given as 20,
11 Feb. 1794 in St. Martinville [Bodin I 114].

Est. #32, opened in 1814 in the name of "H.
Carlin" might be the succession of a brother of
Joseph Carlin. Had it been that of a son, the
son would probably have been listed in the 1792
Militia Census along with the father and other
sons. It is apparently neither that of a
daughter or daughter-in-law of Joseph Carlin.
Since a Celestin Carlin was godfather of Honore
Carlin in 1774, and the baby's brother Celestin,
second son of Joseph and Francoise, was only 6
years of age at the time, it seems probable that
the godfather Celestin was Joseph's brother and
that his sons were given family names. It is
possible that he may have had a brother Honore.

Further research on this family may reveal that
"H. Carlin" of the 1814 St. Mary estate was that
of a brother of Joseph.

#2. ------

#3. E. NOBAN - 1811. Inventory & appraisement.

#4. C. EUMEL - 1811. Could be Hymel or Himel.
Charles and Christopher Himel, Hymel, appear in
St. John the Baptist church records. [Bodin I 212]

#5. W. MC FHADON - 1811. Inventory &
appraisement.

#6. PHILO NORTON - 1811. [Vol. I.]

#7. J. LOURI - 1814. Date is out of context. Jeanne Loiret married Edmond Meuillon.
[Bodin II 159]

#8. T. DAVIS - 1811. A Thomas Davis purchased a horse from David Choat in 1805. [St.
Martin Original Acts] Possibly this is the same
man.

#9. J. B. SENETTE - 1812. Probably Jean
Baptiste Senette. [Vol. I & II.] Footnote 162
in Cathcart's Journal concerns this family.
See Est. #99A, Eugene Senette, 1817.

#10. B. PROVOST - 1812. Probably Baptiste
Provost. [Vol. I.]

#11. J. B. HEBERT - 1812. Possibly the
Jean Baptiste Hebert who married Rose
Thibodeaux 27 Sept. 1760 in St. Martin Parish
[OA 2-112]. [Vol. I & II.] There is much Hebert
material in Bodin's 2 volumes.

#12. J. GARRETT - 1812. Probably Joshua
Garrett. One of this name appears in the St.
Martin Parish records before St. Mary Parish was
created. On 20 Sept. 1805 Joshua Garrett sold
to his 2 sons, William Garrett and John Joshua
Garrett. Joshua's wife was Rachel Garrett.
Bodin [II 102,103] tells us that Joshua Garrett
(Garrot) was from Virginia and his wife was
Rachel Melon. Their son William married
Agatha DeRouen at St. Martinville 27 Apr. 1802.
Their daughter Celeste was married to John
Stein. John Joshua Garrett died in St. Mary
25 Aug. 1849. He was 66. His birth date was

3 Sept. 1783 [Planters' Banner, 30 Aug. 1849, page 3, col. 2]. His succession [Est. #682] was opened in St. Mary Parish in 1849. He married Phoebe Armstrong 13 Mar. 1812 [St. Mary Parish Marriage Book 1, page 8]. See her succession, Est. #592, opened in 1846. Numerous references to this family are in Vol. I and Vol. II. See also Est. #172. See page 96.

#13. C. OLIVIER - 1812. St. Mary Parish Probate Suit #11, Charles Olivier De Vezin vs. Jules Villere, filed 13 Nov. 1826, tells us that Charles Olivier Devezin [De Vezin] married Celeste Mathilde DeBlanc of Attakapas in St. Martinville in April of 1798.

Celeste Mathilde DeBlanc was born at Natchitoches on 15 July 1783, daughter of the Chevalier Louis Charles DeBlanc and his wife Elizabeth Pouponne d'Erneville. He was Commandant of the Fort Saint Jean Baptiste des Natchitoches.

Charles Olivier De Vezin and Celeste M. DeBlanc had 6 children:

1. Marie-Perle, born 31 Mar. 1800, married ca. 1820 Jules Gabriel Villere, son of Gov. Jacques Philippe Villere and Jeanne Henriette de Fazende, born at "Conseil Plantation" in St. Bernard Parish on 11 Dec. 1794. She died 4/27/1878.

2. Pierre Charles, born 22 Jan. 1802; died 5 Sept. 1812.

3. Celeste Mathilde, born 10 May 1804, married (1) a Pellerin (2) St. Cyr de la Houssaye of St. Martin Parish.

4. Joseph, born 6 July 1806; a midshipman in the U. S. Navy in 1826. Nothing further known of him.

5. Elina, born ca. 1808, married Joseph Marcel Ducros; died 23 Apr. 1896.

6. Laure, married Octave de la Houssaye of St. Martin Parish.

Celeste Mathilde DeBlanc Olivier died 10 [or 19] Sept. 1811. I believe this estate to have been the succession of Celeste Olivier, wife of

Charles Olivier, son of Charles Honore Olivier. It is unusal at that time for a woman to be shown in legal records with her husband's name, but there are other instances where this was done. An examination of church records and family records such as I could find lead me to this conclusion.

Charles Barromee Olivier De Vezin, born in 1777 and died 1862, married (2) 15 Mar. 1812 Anne Wilhelmina Perrault, daughter of Jean Baptiste Perrault and Anne Marie Madeleine LeCann. They had at least 12 children. For more information on his background, see his father's succession, Est. #50. The above information is from Probate files of St. Mary Parish, church records of St. Martin of Tours Catholic Church, St. Martinville, and most especially from the records of Mr. Sidney Villere of New Orleans, who kindly granted me permission to use this information from his personal files.

#14. J. L. HEBERT - 1812. Probably Jean Louis Hebert [Ebert]. See Vol. I.

#15. J. BAKER - 1812. The Mississippi D. A. R. book [page 12] tells us that Joshua Baker was born in Berkeley Co., Va. [now West Virginia], 11 Mar. 1763; that he married 2 June 1790 in Mason Co., Ky., Susannah Lewis, daughter of Isaac Lewis, born in Newcastle, Del., 13 Sept. 1768, died 24 Nov. 1813; and that he died in Mississippi 14 Mar. 1816; that he served as a private in Capt. Evans' Co., 9th Va. Regiment in the Revolution; and that he came to Wilkinson Co., Miss., in 1804.

Arthur tells us in <u>The Story of the West Florida Rebellion</u> [page 58] that Joshua G. Baker was an officer of the Mississippi Territorial Militia and was sent in the summer of 1810 as the personal representative of Gov. Holmes of that Territory into West Florida, his duties being to ascertain the real views of the leaders of the then-brewing rebellion against Spain, as well as the views of the inhabitants themselves. Like so many others in the Feliciana-Natchez area during this time, he also made his way on to the Attakapas area.

He was apparently not in Louisiana prior to 1810. He is not listed as having Louisiana land in <u>American</u> <u>State Papers</u>, but he was included in the 1810 Federal Census of St. Martin Parish and he was a St. Mary 1813 taxpayer. The firm of Baker & St. Jones [St. Julien or St. John?], in which he was probably a principal, was also listed as an 1813 St. Mary taxpayer.

Thus Joshua Baker seems to have been alive after 1812, the date given for this succession. It is a fact that he owned a great deal of land in St. Mary Parish, and his succession would have had to be opened in the parish. There is no other record of it, so it must be concluded that this was indeed the succession of this prominent citizen. Since the records are lost, it is possible that the Index was compiled after the loss, and the date thus became confused.

An act of sale in Mortgage Book B-4, page 361, dated 14 Aug. 1824, from Lewis Baker to Isaac L. Baker tells us they were brothers. It tells of Lewis Baker selling land to Isaac L. Baker, "being 1/9 of a certain tract or portion of land inherited from his father, Joshua Baker, Sr., deceased." So we know from this that Joshua Baker, Sr., had 9 heirs at the time of his death.

An act of sale the previous month recorded in the same book, page 144, from Joshua Baker to Isaac L. Baker tells of Joshua Baker likewise selling "land belonging to the heirs of Joshua Baker, Sr., inherited from his said father." So we have 3 of the 9 heirs of Joshua Baker, Sr., established by these 2 acts of sale: 1. Joshua Baker, Jr., 2. Lewis Baker, 3. Isaac L. Baker.

4. Anthony W[ayne] Baker, Est. #183, opened in 1830, was a 4th son. No specific heirs or relationships are given in this succession, but close relationship to both Joshua and Isaac L. Baker is indicated.

The succession of Lewis Baker [Est. #168, opened in 1828] gives us another of the heirs of Joshua

G. Baker, Sr., for in addition to showing Isaac L. Baker and Joshua Baker as paternal uncles of his 2 minor children, a family meeting for them shows Alexander Porter, Jr. [the builder of beautiful Oaklawn Manor, near Franklin] as paternal uncle by marriage. St. Mary Parish Marriage Book 1, page 70, gives the marriage of Evalina Baker to Alexander Porter, Jr., then of the Parish of St. Martin, on 24 Aug. 1815. She was of the Parish of St. Mary. Thus,

5. Evalina Baker, wife of Alexander Porter, Jr., is the fifth heir of Joshua G. Baker, Sr.

Lucile Barbour Holmes tells us in her splendid booklet, Oaklawn Manor [Franklin, 1968, page 1], that Alexander Porter, the builder, was born in the County of Donegal, Ireland, 24 June 1785, a son of James Porter, executed by the English during the Irish Rebellion of 1798. Shortly after this, he came to America with his younger brother, James, and their uncle, Alexander Porter, for whom he was no doubt named. They settled first in Nashville, Tenn., about 1801. Young Alexander became a lawyer and came to Attakapas about 1809. This couple had no surviving issue. See page 75 also.

A power of attorney in Conveyance Book F-1, Folio #5212, St. Mary Parish, dated 26 Dec. 1843, gives us 3 other heirs:

6. Sarah W. Baker, wife of James Metcalf;
7. Mary Baker, wife of John Kerr; and
8. Susan E. Baker, wife of Henry L. Conner, all then "of Adams Co., Miss." The power of attorney was written in Concordia Parish, La., where they apparently had plantations, with townhouses in Natchez, and conveyed their power of attorney to Joshua Baker. I am indebted to Mrs. Clyde Alpha of Franklin, who had found the above conveyance reference, for pointing it out to me in order that we might have this record of the heirs of Joshua Baker, Sr.

The Mississippi D. A. R. book gives full information on the above individuals and the final heir of this decedent [pages 12 and 13]:

Isaac Lewis Baker, born Mason Co., Ky., 14 Nov. 1792, died St. Martinville, La., 9 Aug. 1830, married twice: (1) 3 May 1820 to Charlotte Lewis; (2) 25 Sept. 1828 to Margaret Henry Crozier. [See page 178 for his only known surviving child.] His succession is Est. #207, opened in 1831.

Sarah Williams Baker, born Mason Co., Ky., 26 Mar. 1796, married St. Martin Parish, La., 2 Oct. 1817 Dr. James Metcalfe.

Evalina Baker [this source lists the name of the wife of Alexander Porter as Amelia Villers Baker; in the St. Mary Parish Marriage Records it is clearly Evalina Baker], born Mason Co., Ky., 22 Sept. 1797, died 30 Oct. 1819, married Alexander Porter, Jr., St. Mary Parish, La., 24 Mar. 1815 [this date is given in the Marriage Records as 24 Aug. 1815; see preceding page.] There was no surviving issue of this marriage.

Joshua Baker, Jr., born Mason Co., Ky., 23 Mar. 1799, married 25 Nov. 1824 Frances A. Steele; see her succession, Est. #282, opened in 1834 in St. Mary Parish; they were married in St. Martin Parish.

Lewis Baker, born Mason Co., Ky., 27 July 1801, married 25 May 1823 Lucy Myswonger; see his succession, Est. #168, opened in St. Mary Parish in 1828.

Mary Howard Baker, born Mason Co., Ky., 13 Jan. 1803, died 14 Oct. 1862, married 5 Mar. 1820 Dr. John Ker, son of David Ker.

Anthony Wayne Baker, born Wilkinson Co., Miss., 26 July 1804, died on U. S. Frigate "Constellation" 14 Sept. 1825. See his succession, Est. #183, opened in St. Mary Parish in 1830.

Susan E[valina?] Baker, born Wilkinson Co., Miss., 15 Apr. 1807, died 14 Nov. 1858, married 25 May 1824 Henry Conner.

And the ninth heir of Joshua G. Baker, Sr.:

9. Louisa Russell Baker, born Wilkinson Co., Miss., 16 Sept. 1809, married 1833 William Norton, possibly related to George Flowerdew Norton,

husband of Sarah A. Thruston. [See Ests. #136 and 140.]

John W. Baker [Est. #145, opened in St. Mary Parish in 1826] left "3 sisters and 1 brother" yet living in Kentucky. These individuals are, unfortunately, not named in this succession. While John is not a son of this decedent, he must surely have been closely related - perhaps a younger brother or a nephew.

#16. M. BUFORD - 1812. This succession and #22, below, both listed as "M. Buford", are probably the successions of Warren Buford and his wife, Mary Buford, who died in Concordia Parish. See Civil Suit #144, Heirs of Williamson vs. Warren and James Buford, filed 17 Oct. 1816. This suit states that Mary B. Williamson, wife of James Ellison; Elizabeth Williamson, wife of Robinson Baird; Ann N. Williamson; and Esther A. Williamson, all of Adams Co., Ohio, are the legal representatives and children of their mother, Catherine Buford, late wife of William Williamson of Ohio and that their mother was the lawful daughter of the late Warren Buford who died at

Concordia in Louisiana and of Mary Buford, wife of said Warren. Warren Buford and James Buford of St. Mary Parish are among "other heirs." Also "amongst other heirs" was the plaintiffs' deceased brother Thomas Buford, due "to a seventh part". Apparently their uncle Thomas had no issue and they were claiming their right to his "seventh part" of his father's and mother's estate. This "seventh part" would seem to indicate that Warren and Mary Buford left seven heirs at the time of their decease.

A note of William Buford for $88.35 is included in the inventory of Warren Buford's estate which is shown in the Civil Suit. He may have been a 5th child of this couple. A Henry Buford who is listed in the 1810 St. Martin census may have been a 6th child. The inventory is dated 16 Dec. 1808, Parish of Concordia, La. This succession may be extant there in the Clerk of Court's records. The courthouse is located in Vidalia, La.

#17. M. PELLERIN - 1812. Probably Marie-Joseph Pellerin, wife of Alexander Frere, married 14 Jan. 1805, St. Martinville [Bodin II 101]. She was a daughter of Gregoire Pellerin and Cecile Prejean. Gregoire Pellerin was born in 1724, a son of Bernard Pellerin and Marguerite Gaudet; Cecile Prejean was a daughter of Charles Prejean and Catherine Broussard. Gregoire and Cecile Prejean were married 10 Jan. 1752. [74 Cen., 41-42.] For complete list of their children, see this reference.

See Civil Suit #385, Frere et al vs. Frere & Pellerin. Marie Pellerin died 21 Jan. 1811. She and Alexander Frere had 2 children: Marie Elizabeth J. Frere, a minor above the age of puberty 3 Oct. 1822 when this suit was filed, and Joseph Alexander Frere. On that date she was the wife of Gabriel Fuselier and her curator ad hoc was Theodore Fay.

Alexander Frere was a son of Rene Frere and Anne Couart of Paris, France. He remarried 7 Aug.

1812 at St. Martinville Catherine Hennen [Bodin II 101]. See Est. #59 in the name of Catherine Hennen opened in 1817. His third wife was Louise Pecot [Mar. Book 1, page 114; also see her succession, Est. #379, opened in 1838]. See his succession, Est. #452, opened in 1841.

#18. G. B. RAMAY - 1813.

#19. D. SMITH - 1813. Undoubtedly David Smith, who was included in the 1810 Federal Census of Attakapas. There is much in the early records about this family. He was the first husband of Ann Tinker, later wife of John M. Watson [Est. #62, 1818] and then of William Finch. See her succession, Est. #104, opened in 1819. David and Ann Tinker Smith were the parents of two boys, David and James.

#20. J. GARRETT - 1813. See Est. #12, above. This is probably an extension of Joshua Garrett's succession, possibly the succession of his wife, Rachel Melon.

#21. M. J. LEGNON - 1813. This is the first of several multiple listings for one estate number. This is probably the succession of Marie Joseph Thibaud, wife of Louis Legnon. See his succession, Est. #81, opened in 1819, for their family.

L. MOORE - 1813. (Petition) Since this is indicated as a petition only, it may not be a succession. Possibly it has to do with the community Lewis Moore, Sr., had with his first wife. See his succession, Est. #202, opened in 1831.

L. TURELLA - 1813. "Turreya" is a surname included in Bodin I [see page 388].

#22. M BUFORD - 1813. See Est. #16, above.

#23. E. SENETTE - 1813. (Will) This is probably the filing of the will by the decedent Eugene Senette, Est. #99A, opened in 1817. It was not uncommon for wills to be filed during the testator's life-time. Though there is a will included in the later succession and there is no mention of an earlier filing, it might have been a later will. See also Est. #9, J. B. Senette, opened in 1813.

#24. McG. KER/KERR - 1813.

#25. J. COOK - 1813. A John Cook was listed in the 1810 Federal Census, as was Samuel Cook.

#26. LLOYD WILCOXON - 1813. This may have been the father, of the same name, of the individual of that name who was active in St. Mary Parish in the early years. This family is thought to have been from Virginia.

#27. J. EVANS - 1813. John and David Evans were listed in the 1810 Federal Census. See Est. #237, opened in 1833 in the name of Cornelia S. Evans. Cornelia and John Evans may have been this individual's children.

#28. J. HOWE - 1813. A Jean Houry had cattle brand registrations listed, probably one in the 1780's and one in the 1790's. It is probable that this was in fact John (or Jean) Henry. It seems likely that this succession was that of John Henry. See Civil Suit #175, Heirs of John Henry vs. William Moore et al, filed 26Sept. 1817. Hannah Henry, wife of Martin Lenore; Margaret Henry, wife of Alexander [probably Alexander Louis] Gacher; and Elizabeth Henry, wife of Jacques [Jacob] Gacher, all of St. Mary Parish, 3 of the legal heirs of (Catherine) Margaret [Marguerite] Nopper, deceased, their mother and wife of John Henry of the Parish of St. Mary, were plaintiffs in this civil suit. It is stated therein that she left 6 children. It is also stated that his estate included a tract of land granted John Henry, their father, in the year 1786 by an order of survey of the Spanish government dated 11 Feb. that year. Elizabeth Henry was born in Dec. of 1796 [Bodin II 128], married Jacob Gashe 10 Sept. 1816 [St. Mary Marriage Book 1, page 104]. Margaret married Louis Gashe 26 Feb. 1816 [St. Mary Marriage Book 1, page 80]. The succession of Eliza Henry, Est. #611, opened in 1846, states she was the wife of Jacob Gashe.

Bodin tells us [II 128] that Jean Henry was born in Germany, a son of Martin (Adam) Henry and Marie Barbe Ofman; that his first wife was Catherine Marguerite Nopper and his second wife, whom he married 1 Aug. 1799, was Marie Richard. Jean or John Henry was on the 1779 militia list for the Attakapas district, but was not included in the 1792 militia census.

Bodin also gives us 2 other of the 6 heirs of Jean Henry and (Catherine) Marguerite Nopper:

4. Marie Rosalie Henry, married (1) Joseph Ring [II 128], Est. #52, opened in 1816, and (2) Jean Baptiste Miller [I 211], Est. #182, 1830, and Est. #266, 1834.

5. Jean Baptiste Henry, born 18 Aug. 1778, married 1 Aug. 1798 Marguerite Sonnier [II 128].

#29. J. G. MORRIS (DR.) - 1814. Dr. James Morris is listed as a St. Mary 1813 taxpayer. His middle name was Gardner.

#30. R. PATTEE - 1814. There was a Pattee in business with a Rigues, which firm (Rigues & Pattee) figured in early court records. See court minutes. This is probably the estate of Roland Patti. See Mortgage Book B-A, page 97: Roland Patti et al to John Merriman, 22 Oct. 1813; Rigues & Pattie to John Merriman, sale of a negro. The page has disintegrated. Only fragments remain, but the left-hand margin indicating headings remains. Bodin tells us [II 187] that Marie Patte married Andre Rigues. No date or place is given. She could be the daughter of Roland Pattie. Jean A. Rigues, their son who was born in Kentucky, married Carmelite Martin 30 Jan. 1834 at St. John's Catholic Church in Lafayette. [Bodin II 203]

#31. JOHN DITCH - 1814. (Will) John (Jonathan) Ditch was a son of John Ditch of Maryland and Catherine Miller. He was in the Attakapas area by 1807, when he registered a cattle brand in St. Martin Parish. He was married to Louise Jackson. They had at least 4 children:

1. Marie Louise, born 15 Sept. 1798 in Kentucky, married Martin M. Campbell 1 June 1813

[St. Mary Marriage Book 1, page 25]. She died a year or so later without issue, for Martin M. Campbell married (2) Drusilla Highfield, widow of Montfort I. Perriman [Est. #49, 1815], 20 Mar. 1817 [Marriage Book 1, page 111].

2. Louise, born 4 July 1800 at Cape Girardeau, Ill. Most of the above information is from Bodin I 135.

Rebecca apparently was also a daughter. She may have had a double name and been the Louise mentioned above. Rebecca Ditch married Alexander Renton 13 June 1816 [Marriage Book 1, page 93]. Her mother gave written permission to marry. The signature is difficult to read; it begins with an "L" and could very well be "Louise" or "Louisa." Her succession is Est. #432, opened in 1840. She was apparently survived neither by husband or children. Rosella Senetier [Rosaline Seniker, below], apparently decedent's sister-in-law, petitions in behalf of her children. No relationships are mentioned. Evidence indicates this Rebecca to have been a daughter of John Ditch and Louise Jackson.

3. At least one son of this decedent was John Ditch, who married (1) Julie Prevost 2 Feb. 1820 [Marriage Book 1, page 188], (2) Rosaline Seniker 6 May 1828 [Marriage Book 1, page 414]. His succession is Est. #275, opened in 1834.

I am indebted to Mrs. Clyde Alpha of Franklin, who has done much research on this family, for sharing her information on this family.

#32. H. CARLIN - 1814. See Est. #1. This may have been the succession of a brother of Joseph Carlin.

#33. Z. BOUTEE AND M. A. DECUIR - 1814. Undoubtedly husband and wife. Bodin [I 71] shows a marriage (no date or place given) between Francois Zenon Boutte and Marie Aspasie Decuir, daughter of Francois Decuir and Marie Labbe. Vol. II, page 132, places the marriage of the latter couple in St. Martinville. It seems likely that this succession might be for the above-mentioned couple.

#34. I. OR J. BEEKLEY - 1814.

#35. LENO, FREE MAN OF COLOR - 1814.

#36. A. ETIE - 1814. Bodin tells us [II 94] that Pierre Etier [also spelled Etie, Elie, Elier, Ethier], native of Bordeaux, France, married to Catherine Baudoin, had 2 sons: Pierre, who married Victoire Borel (see his succession, Est. #110, opened 1821); and Antoine, who married Julie Provost, daughter of Pierre and Marie Therese Provost, 23 Apr. 1805 at St. Martinville [II 197]. [Marie Therese Provost married (2) Celestin Carlin after the death of her first husband. See her succession, Est. #61, opened in 1817 in St. Mary Parish].

Est. #25 in St. Martin Parish, opened 9 July 1808, was the succession of this Antoine Etier. An inventory was listed on that date. It was not until 5 Apr. 1811 that the succession was opened in earnest, however. On that date another inventory was taken and at that time it was stated that Julie Prevost was the widow of decedent and natural tutrix of Antoine Etier, Jr., "her son by her said deceased husband and sole surviving heir of said decedent. A daughter, Julie Antoinette Etier, also survived her father but has died since his death." Pierre Etier, "uncle of said Antoine Etier, Jr." was undertutor.

Since this succession was opened on the eve of the formation of St. Mary Parish from St. Martin Parish and they probably resided in the newly-formed political unit, it is probable that it was reopened or transferred there at a later date.

Julia Etier married Ursin Provost, son of Nicolas Provost and Marie Jeanne Provost [see Est. #95], 29 Nov. 1813 [Marriage Book 1, page 31]. It is possible that this is Julie Provost, widow of Antoine Etier. His estate might have been reopened due to her remarriage on account of her minor son, Antoine Etier, Jr. At any rate, this is probably a continuation of the succession of the deceased Antoine Etier. See Addenda, #95.

*#37. L. THIBEAU - 1814. A Louis Thibeau had cattle brands registered in St. Martin Parish as early as 1793 and a Louis D. Thibeau had one registered probably in the first decade of the 1800's.

#38. J. J. SUMNER - 1814. Inventory and appraisal. Joseph J. Sumner was an 1813 St. Mary taxpayer and he was summoned to serve as juror in the November, 1813, term of court. [See Est. #45.] On 4 Apr. 1814 Dorothy Sumner, Tutor to John Sumner and William Henry Sumner, minor children and heirs of Joseph John Sumner, deceased, sold land to Washington Jackson of Natchez, Territory of Mississippi, and Donelson Caffery [Mortgage Book A-B, page 145, #221]. On 17 Feb. 1814 Dorothy Sumner sold in her own name to the same. Since she is not named as the widow, it is thought she might have been decedent's sister. [Mortgage Book A-B, page 132, #204].

On the same date, 17 Feb. 1814, Exum Sumner of Tennessee sold land by his special agent, Duke William Sumner [Mortgage Book A-B, page 131, #203]. Exum could have been the father of Joseph John, Dorothy, and Duke William Sumner.

*#39. LOUIS VERRETT - 1815. A Louis Verrett registered a cattle brand in 1809 in St. Martin Parish and an individual by that name was listed in the 1810 Federal Census for Attakapas [St. Martin Parish]. Bodin tells us that Louis Verret was married to Marie Patin of Pointe Coupee [I 391]. They were the parents of Marie Verrett, who was born 17 Jan. 1788 and married John Labarthe. See her succession, Est. #70, opened in 1818. See also #117, page 171.

#40. P. JOHNSON - 1815. A Patrick Johnson is listed in American State Papers [see Vol. I] in connection with land claims. Est. #298 was opened in this name in St. Mary Parish in 1835. The latter decedent may have been the son of this decedent.

#41. T. GATES - 1815. See Est. #106, Dr.

James Hennen, opened in 1820. This must be the
succession of Thomas Gates, described in some
early records as being "of New Orleans." He was
married to Eliza Hennen, daughter of Dr. Hennen.
At that time both Thomas and Eliza were deceased.
They were survived by one daughter, Eliza H[ennen?]
Gates. They were married 8 Feb. 1814 [Marriage
Book 1, page 37]. Since the record plainly states
he was "of New Orleans" and Eliza R. Yates was
the daughter of James Hennen and Anne Hennen and
his succession (Dr. Hennen's) plainly states that
Eliza Hennen, his daughter, married Thomas Gates,
it must be concluded she had previously married
a Yates, by whom she apparently had no issue.

#42. WILLIAM L. BRENT (DR.) - 1815. See
footnote 142 in "Cathcart's Journal." A William L.
Brent was an 1813 St. Mary taxpayer and was listed
in American State Papers [see Vol. I] in connection
with a land claim. The doctor was probably the
father of the lawyer of the same name, prominent
in the early days of St. Mary Parish. This
family came from Maryland. The tombstone
inscription of the latter is included in a D. A.
R. compilation of St. Martinville tombstones,
on page 7, which copy was checked in the St.
Martin Parish Library:"William Leigh Brent, 20
Feb. 1784 - 3 July 1848. Represented Louisiana
in the U. S. House of Representatives for 3 terms,
ending March 1827." The Congressional Biographical Directory of 1961 gives this information [page
594]: "BRENT, William Leigh (nephew of Richard
Brent), a representative from Louisiana; born at
Port Tobacco, Charles County, Md., February 20,
1784; studied law and was admitted to the bar;
moved to Louisiana about 1809 and commenced
practice; appointed by President Madison as
deputy attorney general for the western district
of the Territory of Orleans; . . . died in St.
Martinsville, La., July 7, 1848; interment in St.
Martin's Catholic Cemetery."

On the preceding page is the listing for his

uncle, Richard, also a Member of Congress, from Virginia: "BRENT, Richard (uncle of William Leigh Brent and nephew of Daniel Carroll), a Representative and a Senator from Virginia; born at "Richland" on the Potomac River, at Aquia Creek, Stafford County, Va., in 1757. . . member of the Virginia House of Delegates from Stafford County in 1788 and from Prince William County in 1793, 1794, 1800, and 1801. . . died December 30, 1814; interment in the family burial ground at "Richland," on the Potomac River, at Aquia Creek."

Of Daniel Carroll [page 666], the same reference says: "(uncle of Richard Brent, cousin of Charles Carroll of Carrollton and Charles Carroll, 'Barrister,' and great-grandfather of Charles Hobart Carroll), a Delegate and a Representative from Maryland; born in Upper Marlboro, Prince Georges County, Md. July 22, 1730; . . . Member of the Continental Congress 1780-1784, signing the Articles of Confederation on March 1, 1781; appointed a delegate on May 26, 1787, to the convention that framed the Federal Constitution; member of the first State senate of Maryland. . . died at Rock Creek (Forest Glen), near Washington, D. C., May 7, 1796; interment in St. John's Catholic Cemetery, Forest Glen, Md."

The foregoing rather lengthy excerpts are included as aids in identifying the individual whose succession was opened in St. Mary Parish in 1815. There are other Carroll connections of this family who served in Congress, of a lesser degree of kinship. These are in the direct line.

#43. F. CARLIN - 1815. Undoubtedly Joseph Carlin's widow, Francoise Lange. See Est. #1.

#44. J. W. ADDISON - 1815. Probably Julia W. Addison, wife of William Addison. See Civil suits #185, 186, and 187, all filed 16 Sept. 1818. Julia Addison, deceased, was the second wife of William Addison. By a former marriage with Jonathon Smith of East Baton Rouge Parish, also deceased, she had:

1. Jonathan and 2. George Smith of St. Mary Parish; 3. Daniel Smith of the state of Indiana; 4. Lebanon Smith of East Baton Rouge Parish; and 5. Julia, 6. Jacob, and 7. John Smith, the last 3 named being minors. Jonathan Smith of St. Mary Parish was married to Mary Ann Kershaw, daughter of John N. Kershaw, Jr. See Est. #134.

#45. D. SUMNER - 1815. Sale of property. Probably Dorothy Sumner, as tutor to the minors of Joseph John Sumner. As such she was involved in several early civil suits. See the index to the suits, #64 and 65. These suits are missing; only the index is extant. Or this could be the estate of Dorothy herself, Duke Sumner or on behalf of Exum Sumner. See Estate #38.

#46. D. W. IRWIN - 1815. A Joseph Irwin was a St. Mary taxpayer in 1813.

#47. W. J. & J. HIGGINS. - 1815. This might be the succession of John Higgins, who appears in the early records of St. Mary Parish.

A. BULLE - 1816. Double listing. Lewis Buelly registered a cattle brand in St. Martin Parish in 1811.

#48. D. ALLEN - 1815. Probably David Allen. A David Allen was summoned for jury duty at the November, 1814, term. See Court Minutes.

P. H. BERNARD - 1816. Multiple listing. Pierre Hiacinthe Bernard of Marseilles, France, son of Francois Xavier Bernard and Marie Anne Treullier, married Catherine Laurendiny [Bodin I 37]. Pierre Bernard was 30 in the 1792 Militia Census, which places his birth ca. 1762. A cattle brand was registered in this name in 1806, he was in the Federal Census of 1810, and was involved in land claims listed in American State Papers [see Vol. I].

Cattle brands were also registered in 1805 in the name of Pierre Hervillien Bernard and in the name of Hervillian Bernard in 1811. Hyacinth Bernard was an 1813 taxpayer in St. Mary Parish, was listed in American State Papers in connection with a land claim and was listed in the 1820 St. Mary Parish Federal Census.

Est. #93 is undoubtedly that of Catherine Laurendiny, wife of Pierre Hyacinthe Bernard.

ACHILLE BERARD - 1816 (Partial). See abstracts.

#49. MUNFORD I. PERRYMAN - 1815. Inventory & appraisement. [Vol. II.] On 28 Apr. 1814 decedent married Drusilla Highfield [Marriage Book 1, page 43]. See Civil suit #326, Martin M. Campbell, Tutor, vs. Mrs. Miriam Parquin, Curatrix, filed 27 Mar. 1822: Martin M. Campbell, tutor to Hariett and Alfred Perryman, minor children under the age of puberty of Montford J. Perryman, deceased. Drusilla (Highfield) Perryman married (2) Martin M. Campbell 20 Mar. 1817 [Marriage Book 1, page 111]. See Estates #31 and 67.

#50. C. A. OLIVIER - 1815. Pierre Francois Marie Olivier, Sieur de Vezin, was the first of the name in Louisiana. He came as a French nobleman to French Canada, where he directed the first iron foundry in North America. He came to Louisiana as the secretary of Governor Pierre Rigaud, Marquis de Vaudreuil. Later he was appointed the Surveyor-General of Lower Louisiana, and during the Spanish administration he was ranked as a high official of the Cabildo. He briefly returned to Canada to marry on 14 June 1749 Marie-Josephine Gatineau Duplessis. Their eldest son Hugues Charles Honore Dugue Olivier De Vezin, sometimes called "St. Maurice" after the iron foundry of the same name, was born in New Orleans on 8 June 1751. He served under Galvez during the American Revolution, and was married to Marie Madeleine De Marigny de Mandeville in the St. Louis Cathedral in New Orleans. They were the parents of 4 children:

1. Francoise Emelie Olivier DeVezin, born 3 Feb. 1777.

2. Charles Borromee Olivier DeVezin, born in 1777 or 1778; married (1) in April of 1798 in St.

Martinville Celeste Mathilde DeBlanc. See Est. # 13 for her background and their children. She died in 1811 and he remarried 15 Mar. 1812 Anne Wilhelmina Perrault, daughter of Jean Baptiste Perrault and Anne Marie Madeleine LeCann. They had about 12 children. He died in 1862.

3. Pierre Olivier Duclozel DeVezin, born 30 Apr. 1782 and died 30 Oct. 1840; married (1) Jeanne Aspasie Devince Bienvenu, daughter of Alexander Devince Bienvenu and Louise Felicite Henriette de Latil de Timecour, born in 1785 and died in St. Martinville 27 Nov. 1810; he married (2) Marie Josephe Latiolais, daughter of Joseph Latiolais and his wife Francoise Nezat, born 20 Mar. 1790 and died 16 Oct. 1829. They were married 15 Mar. 1812.

4. Adelaide Dugue Olivier DeVezin, born 22 Oct. 1785, married 4 Nov. 1800 Louis Charles Cesaire Marie DeBlanc, son of Louis Charles DeBlanc and Elizabeth Pouponne d'Erneville, brother of Celeste Mathilde DeBlanc, first wife of Adelaide's brother, Charles, #2, above.

The Estate Index lists this Estate as that of "C. A. Olivier." Charles Honore Olivier de Vezin, as he generally called himself in his latter days, died 24 Apr. 1815 at the age of 65 years and was buried on his plantation on the New Iberia side of Bayou Teche. [Death Register, St. Martin of Tours Catholic Church, St. Martinville, La.] Since this estate was opened at the time of his death, it is felt that it was surely his and that the "H" was misread as "A" in writing the index. This must surely be the succession of this prominent citizen, who certainly had to have his succession opened.

See also Est. #13. For the background of Pierre Francois Marie Olivier, Sieur de Vezin, see Stanley C. Arthur, <u>First Families of Louisiana</u>, page 411.

I am indebted to Mr. Sidney Villere of New Orleans for the above history of this branch of the Olivier family. Mr. Glenn R. Conrad, Director of Southwestern Archives, University of Southwestern Louisiana, Lafayette, La., and Mrs. Drouet W. Vidrine of Ville Platte, La., also shared with me their knowledge of this family in identifying these two Olivier successions.

* <u>J. CHAREL - 1816</u>. Double listing. Possibly Jacob Cheret, Sr., found in early St. Mary Parish records. Jacob was father of Margaret, who married Francois Gashe 29 Sept. 1817 and Mary, who married James McMurtry 11 Oct. 1821 and possibly of Jacob, who married Adelaide Nopper 15 Oct. 1827, daughter of John Nopper. See Est. #154.

<u>#51. M. L. HAYME - 1816.</u> Martin L. Hanie was an 1813 taxpayer. See Civil suits 202 and 203: Andrew Skillman and wife vs. Jesse E. Lacey, filed 9 July 1819. Andrew Skillman's wife was Ann Sterling, widow of Martin L. Hanie, deceased, of the Parish of Feliciana. These combined suits contain information pertaining to the succession of Martin L. Hanie in Feliciana. [Early Feliciana records are in the courthouse at St. Francisville, seat of West Feliciana Parish, or Clinton, seat of East Feliciana Parish. The Parish of Feliciana was divided into East and West Feliciana in 1824]. See also Est. #100. This must be Hanie's succession.

<u>#52. J. RING - 1816</u>. The succession of Joseph Ring, sometimes spelled Ringuet(t)(e). Joseph Ring married Mary Rosalie Henry 25 June 1804, St. Martinville [St. Martin OA 22, entry # 131; listed incorrectly therein as Mary Ropela Amy]. See Vols. I and II. Bodin tells us (II 204) Joseph Ringuet was a son of Andre Ringuet and Marie Anne Bishof. See Est. #266 in the name of Jean Baptiste Miller, opened 1834. It is shown therein that there was one minor daughter of this marriage, Rosalie, still a minor 4 Sept. 1828. Mary Rosalie Henry was a daughter of Jean Henry and Catherine Nopper. See his succession, Est. # 28, opened in 1813, for details of his family.

<u>#53. F. POMEL - 1817.</u> Very likely this is the succession of Francois Pomet(t)(e), active in early St. Martin affairs, who married Marie Borel,

daughter of Pierre Borel and Catherine Toupart,
[marriage contract signed 18 July 1787, St.
Martin OA 5, entry no.34, Deville, page 16]. He
must have died a few years later, for as the Widow
Pomet she married (2) Jean Baptiste Bourgeois,
son of Jacques Bourgeois and Marieanne Sauvagin on
28 Feb. 1794 [Bodin I 70 and Deville, page 23].
Francois Pomet was a native of Toulan in Provence,
a son of Jean Baptiste Pomet and Francoise Barraillez.

Marie Borel died 21 Dec. 1851. Her succession,
opened early in 1852, is Est. #753. There do not
seem to have been any Pomet children involved.
This succession could have been in connection
with her husband's estate, even though he must
have died a quarter of a century earlier. It
could have been a son who bore his name.

#54. A. AUKMAN - 1817. Undoubtedly Andre
(Andrew) Aukman. See Civil suit #231, Aukman vs.
Renton, filed 12 July 1820. Mary Aukman of the
Parish of Iberville, widow of the late Andrew
Aukman of St. Mary Parish, sued Alexander Renton.

J. DE LA COURET - No date shown. Double
listing.

#55. J. BOREL - 1817. Undoubtedly Joseph
[Francois] Borel, Sr. Joseph Borel, Sr. and Jr.
are both involved in land claims in American
State Papers. See Vol. I. One claim is for
"Heirs of Joseph Burell" - undoubtedly this same
individual. Evidence seems to indicate that this
succession was that of the eldest son of Pierre
Borel and Catherine Toupart. His full name
seems to have been Joseph Francois Borel, Sr.
All the heirs are listed in the succession of
his son, Pierre, Est. #376, opened in 1838,
who died without issue. His heirs were his
brothers and sisters:

1. Benjamin, who married Rosela [Emilia?] Andrus.
2. Joseph Francois, who married 8 July 1815
Modeste Bourgeois, his cousin, daughter of Jean
Baptiste Bourgeois and Marie Borel.

3. Louis.

4. Hilaire, who married 12 Apr. 1814 Hortense Provost. See his succession, Est. #125, opened 1823.

5. Eugene, who married 27 Jan. 1818 at St. Martinville Hortense Bourgeois, his cousin, daughter of Jean Baptiste Bourgeois and Marie Borel, born 29 Oct. 1802 [Bodin I 70].

6. Elizabeth/Lise, second wife of Joseph Andrus, son of Solomon Andrus/Andrews and Sarah _____, second wife of Louis Moore, Sr. They were married 2 May 1825 Marriage Book 1, page 298. His succession is Estate #436, opened in 1840. See his mother's succession, Est. #135A, opened in 1824.

7. Mary Eurasie, wife of Reuben Doty.

8. Pelagie, wife of Thomas B. Kershaw, son of John N. Kershaw, Sr. See his father's succession, Est. #134, opened in 1824. Pelagie Borel's succession is Est. #476, opened in 1842.

A daughter, Louise, born 1 Oct. 1798, was also a daughter of Joseph and Elizabeth Andres, as is shown in Bodin II 27. This may have been #8, above, Pelagie; she may have had a double name.

At least a ninth child of Joseph and Elizabeth Andres was, of course, Pierre Borel, above decedent. A Benjamin Borel also married Emilia Andrus. See her succession, Est. #722, opened in 1850.

Elizabeth Andres, wife of dececedent, born in Carolina, was daughter of Benjamin & Marie Hargrave.

For further study of this family, see Bodin I 51 and II 27, as well as other references in these two volumes. See also Bodin II 3.

#56. JOSHUA ROWLAND - 1817. Joshua Rowland registered a cattle brand in 1811 in St. Mary Parish; Josiah Rowland was listed in the Federal Census of 1810 for St. Martin [Attakapas] Parish; and Josiah Rowland married Modist LaGatrie 12 Dec. 1814 [Marriage Book 1, page 56]. Very likely these are one and the same individual and this is probably his succession.

#57. J. PHILIPS - 1817. Apparently this is not a succession. See Mortgage Book B-A, pages 253 and 257. Syndics of creditors of the late firm Wellman & Phillips of the City of New Orleans sell property belonging to the firm, composed of A. W. Wellman and John Phillips. The firm may have gone out of business, may have gone into bankruptcy, or one of the principals may have died. Further information can probably be found in Orleans Parish.

#58. J. SORRELL 1817. See Est. #98, Joseph Sorrel, opened 18 Mar. 1817, entirely in French. Both these estates are probably segments of the same succession. Joseph Jacques Sorrel, or Jacques Joseph Sorrel, was early in the St. Martin Parish area. A cattle brand was registered in the name of Joseph Sorrel in 1758. He is listed as Lieutenant of the First Company in the Militia Census of 1792; but as such his age is not given. The annotated Census of 1774 tells us (page 39) that he was a bachelor, who in 1793 had a brother, Francois Sorrel, living at Havre de Grace, France. He seems also to have been known as "Santiago." There are other references to this individual in Vols. I and II, as well as in "Cathcart's Journal," footnote 371, and Territorial Papers, Orleans Territory. C. J. (Contamine) Sorrel, Est. #83, opened in 1820, the only other of that surname in the early period, may have been a nephew, possibly a son of the brother, Francois, mentioned above.

#59. CATHERINE ERMAN AND A. FRERE - 1817. Beyond a doubt Catherine Hennen and Alexander Frere. See Est. #106, the succession of Dr. James Hennen, opened in 1820. Catherine Hennen was a daughter of Dr. James Hennen and his wife, Ann. She was the second wife of Alexander Frere. They were married 7 Aug. 1812. See Est. #17. They were the parents of one only daughter, Caroline. Catherine Hennen was deceased at the time her father's succession was opened in 1820. Alexander Frere's third wife was Louise Pecot, whom he married 17 July 1817 [Marriage Book 1, page 114]. Catherine Hennen Frere probably died a few years earlier and her succession was opened at the time of his remarriage on account of their minor daughter; hence his name being included in the index, for he was certainly not deceased at this time.

#60. T. H. LANAWAY - 1817. Probably Thomas Lanaway. See Civil suit #21, Court Minutes. The early suits are missing.

#61. T. PROVOST - 1817. Receipts. This is probably the succession of Marie Therese Provost, wife of Celestin Carlin (see Est. #1 and #242, opened in 1833). She was born 14 Jan. 1766, a daughter of Nicolas Provost, dit Blondin, and his wife Marie Francoise Quebedeau. She married (1) on 19 Feb. 1786, Pierre Provost, son of Joseph Provost, dit Collete, and his wife, Jeanne Daublin. After his death she married (2) Celestin Carlin in November of 1793, with whom she signed a marriage contract in 1794. She died 16 Oct. 1806, and was buried "on Honore Carlin's property on the lower Bayou Teche because her body could not be transported to the parochial cemetery." [Death records of St. Martin of Tours Catholic Church, St. Martinville, La.] See 1774 Cen., p.55.

Est. #9, St. Martin Parish, opened in the name of Celestin Carlin 10 Sept. 1807, is entitled "Settlement with the heirs of Pierre Provost." It states: "Inventory of goods and chattels, Lands and tenements belonging to Mr. Celestin Carlin and his deceased wife, Therese." It is further stated that she was survived by 11 children, 3 of which were her children by Pierre Provost:

1. Julie Provost. Married 23 Apr. 1805 Antoine Etier. See his succession, Est. #36, above. This is probably the Julie Provost who married Ursin Provost 29 Nov. 1813, St. Mary

Parish [Marriage Book 1, page 31]. See Bodin II 197.
   2. Eugenie Provost.
   3. Lucille Provost. May be the one who married Lufroy Provost 1 Oct. 1812 [Marriage Book 1, page 13]. See Est. #121, opened 1822.

For decedent's 8 children by Celestin Carlin, see his succession, Est. #242, opened 1833. Since this succession was opened before St. Mary Parish was formed, and the St. Mary Parish estate is marked "receipts," it is felt that as a convenience, the legal action was opened in the new courthouse; therefore, this estate is surely a continuation of her previously opened succession.

   #62. JOHN M. WATSON - 1818. John M. Watson was the second husband of Ann Tinker, widow of David Smith (Est. #19, 1813, above). They were married 23 Oct. 1815 [Marriage Book 1, page 76]. Information in the marriage records tells us that he was born in Accomack County, Va., lawful son of Zorabel Watson and his wife, Susan Watson. See her succession for her background (Est. #104, opened in 1819). From her succession we learn that this couple had no children.

   #63. A. DURRI - 1818. It is possible that this succession name was misread; it could be for Azariah C. Dunn. See Conveyance records, 16 Apr. 1813: 5 arpents purchased by this individual from William L. Brent.

   #64. P. GUENON - 1818. Possibly Pierre Guenon. See Mortgage Book B-A, page 246, 12 Mar. 1817: sale of slave from Pierre Guedon to Louis Hiliare Boutte [in French].

   #65. MICHEL/MICHAEL HARGROIDER - 1818. This individual is listed in Vol. I in connection with a land claim in American State Papers. He also registered a cattle brand in St. Mary Parish in 1815, in the name of Hergroider.

   #66. T. JONES - 1818. Thomas and Samuel Jones were brothers of Feliciana Parish. They figured in early parish records.

   #67. J. M. PERRYMAN - 1818. Probably some

part of the succession of Mon(t)ford J. Perryman. See Est. #49, above.

*#68. R. TROUSDALE - 1818. Appointment of Curator to Mary Walker. Robert Trousdale was apparently appointed curator to Mary Walker. Robert Trousdale died in St. Mary Parish on 29 Oct. 1853, aged 75 [Planters' Banner, 3 Nov. 1853, page 3, col. 3]. A Mary Walker, relict of Gideon Walker, is mentioned in the Original Acts of St. Martin Parish in a document dated 21 Dec. 1805. Bodin tells us that Gideon Walker was married to Mary Fork [Faulk]. They had at least one child, Sarah, who married Jacques Hardgrave [James Hargraves]. See Est. #77, concerning Sarah Walker, opened in 1819. This could be the estate of the widow, Mary Walker, mentioned above, who in her old age could no longer take care of her own property and had to have a curator appointed; thus it would not be a succession.

#69. M. L. DECUIR - 1818. Possibly Marie Lucile Decuir, wife of Louis Hilaire Boutte, son of Andre Claude Boutte and Francoise Bodin. [74 Census, page 44]. See also Est. #158.

#70. MARIE VERRETT, WIFE OF JOHN LABARTHE - 1818. Bodin tells us Marie Verrett was born 17 Jan. 1788, a daughter of Louis Verrett and his wife, Marie Patin, of Pointe Coupee [I 391]. She married John Labarthe 1 Dec. 1808 at Donaldsonville. He was born in France, a son of Jacques Labarthe and Marie Giraud. She probably died a year or so prior to the time her succession was opened, because John Labarthe was married 7 Oct. 1818 [Marriage Book 1, page 155] to Hyacinth Carlin, born 26 July 1798, a daughter of Alexis Carlin [see Est. #1] and Genevieve DeRouan [Bodin I 113, 217].

#71. J. W. ADDISON - No date. See Est. #44, above. No doubt part of the same succession.

#72. M. HIGH - 1819. Undoubtedly Michael High. See Civil suit #148, Dempsey Snipes, Curator of the estate of Michael High, deceased,

vs. Lewis & Henry Sterling, filed 2 Dec. 1816.
John High of New Orleans was brother of Michael.

L. SMITH - 1817. Double listing. Undoubtedly Lucius Smith. A Lucia Smith was in the Federal Census of 1810 for St. Martin Parish. There was a sale of property 6 Oct. 1818 by Jehu Wilkinson, Parish Judge, belonging to the absent heirs of Lucius Smith, deceased, to Jared Y. Sanders. A true copy of this sale is in the compiler's possession, and the sale is recorded in the St. Mary Parish clerk of court's office.

#73. **E. EMAR - 1817.** Himel, Hymel?

M. A. G. DETRAVAME - 1819. Double listing. Very likely Marie Adelaide Guerne deTravane, wife of Joseph Charpantier [Bodin I 135]. They had at least one child, Charles Michael Charpantier, who married Marguerite Clarisse Verret on 13 Jan. 1819 [Bodin I 118, 169].

#74. **S. JONES - 1819.** A Samuel Jones has several land claims in *American State Papers* [Vol. I]. On 31 Dec. 1814 he made a sale to Joshua Baker. This is probably the succession of the same individual. See also Est. #66, above.

*#75. **S. KNIGHT - 1819.** Probably Solomon Knight. He married Rachel Hamilton 25 Feb. 1814 [Marriage Book 1, page 35]. See Civil suit #286, Alexander Lewis of the State of Tennessee vs. Widow & Heirs of Solomon Knight, filed 26 Mar. 1821. Unfortunately, the heirs of Solomon Knight are not named in this suit.

Genealogical note from Mrs. Clyde Alpha. Abel and Solomon Knight applied for certificates 7 June 1742 from Buckingham monthly meeting Quakers, Bucks Co., Penna., to go to Orange Co., Va. Certificates signed 6 July 1742. On 1 Aug. 1742 Abel and Solomon Knights' certificates were received at Alamance Co., N. C. Obviously these are not the individuals who came to Louisiana, but almost surely they are of the same family, if not in the direct line.

#76. **R. PAMPTON - 1819.** See Civil suit #256,

Finch & Thompson vs. Alfred Thruston, filed 4 Mar. 1820; this suit concerns the estate of Robert Pamphleu, deceased. This must be his succession.

#77. SARAH WALKER - 1819. See Est. #68, above. Sarah Walker, daughter of Gideon Walker and his wife, Mary Faulk, married Jacques Hargraves, but she seems to have been alive and still producing children after this date. See Bodin II 119-120. This could have been an estate in connection with her father or mother's succession, which would have been in her name but not her succession. Sarah Walker's full name seems to have been Sarah Celeste Walker. Jacques James Hargrave[grove (s)] married Sarah Walker 2 Feb. 1802 at St. Martinville. He was a son of Benjamin Hargrave[grove (s)] and Elizabeth Goultenetyt [Galtney, Waltney?] of Virginia. See Bodin II 119. Further study of this family will probably solve these questions.

#78. J. WILLIAM BASTINE - 1819.

#79. HENRY LYON - 1819. See Mortgage Book B-A, page 136, 18 Apr. 1814: Alexander Lewis of Nashville, Tenn., sells 2 lots to Henry Lyon of St. Mary Parish. Same book, page 254, 28 Sept. 1817: Henry Lyon leases one lot to Peter White of St. Mary Parish.

*#80. F. THURSTON [THRUSTON] - 1819. Pritchard tells us in "Cathcart's Journal" that Frederick Conrad moved to Louisiana from Virginia between 1813 and 1819. He and Frances Thruston, his wife, had a large family, at least 7 children:

1. Charles Mynn Conrad, born at Winchester, Va., 24 Dec. 1804, and moved with his father to Mississippi, thence to the Teche country in Louisiana. He died in New Orleans 11 Feb. 1878 and is buried there in Girod Street Cemetery. He was elected United States Senator from Louisiana in 1842. [Biographical Directory of the American Congress, page 731]. He married Mary Eliza Angela Lewis. See her succession, St. Mary Est. #453, opened in 1841.

2. Sidney Ann Conrad, born 26 Oct. 1806 in Winchester, Va., and died 30 Mar. 1839 at Franklin, La.; she married William Taylor Palfrey. [Her tombstone, St. Martinville, La.]

3. Mary Clare Conrad, married (1) David Weeks [Marriage Book 1, page 164], the builder of "The Shadows" plantation home still standing in New Iberia; (2) Judge John Moore, in 1841, son of Lewis Moore, Sr., and his first wife, Rebecca Henshaw. See the father's succession, Est. #202, opened in 1831. She was married to David Weeks 31 Dec. 1818. [Marriage Book 1, page 164]

4. Ann Alexander Conrad, second wife of John Thomas Towles. They were married 24 Oct. 1818 [New Iberia, La., Sunday Iberian, 12 Sept. 1971, page 25]. See his succession, Est. #232, opened 1832. See also page 184.

5. Frances Elizabeth Conrad, married Winthrop Sargent Harding, son of Lyman Harding, 12 May 1828 [Marriage Book 1, page 418]. See his father's succession, Est. #107, opened in 1820.

6. Frederick D. Conrad, married a Hickey from East Baton Rouge Parish.

7. Alfred T. Conrad of New Orleans.

This is undoubtedly the succession of Frances Thruston Conrad. See also Est. #140.

#81. L. LEGNON - 1819. Undoubtedly the succession of Louis Legnon, an early settler in the Attakapas area. He registered cattle brands in St. Martin Parish in 1781 and 1794. According to the 1792 Militia Census (in which he was 30 years of age), he was born in 1762 in Canada. Bodin tells us he was a son of Francois Loignon and Marie Dubay. He was married at St. Martinville to Marie-Joseph Thibaud, probably ca. 1781 (at the time of his first cattle brand registration.) See Est. #21, opened in 1814; this may be her succession. They were the parents of at least 8 children. [Most of this information is from Bodin I 284 and II 159].

1. Marie Alexandrine Loignon [Legnon], married Henry Edelemer, no date or place given.

2. Marie Louise Loignon, born 29 Sept 1785.
3. Emilia, born 6 Nov. 1787, married Jacques Caffier [from the baptismal record of Louis Hamilton Wofford, St. Martin Church, 4 May 1812].
4. Eugenie, born 2 Nov. 1789. She married William Washington Wofford, recently arrived from Georgia, probably in 1807. He was born in North Carolina, a son of William [Nathaniel] Wofford and his wife Lucy Spradley. The Woffords had at least 3 children: (1) Celina E[ugenie?], born in 1808 [according to the Federal Census for Vermilion Parish, La., in 1850]. She received permission from her father to marry George Petry (born in 1801 in Germany, according to the same census), on 24 June 1828 [Marriage Book 1, page 426]. This marriage is not recorded in the St. Mary Parish courthouse, and the permission to marry is not indexed. This couple had at least 3 children: 1. Mary Petry, 22 in the 1850 census, 2. George Washington Petry, 15, and 3. Louis Petry, 13. Celina Wofford Petry died previous to 25 Oct. 1853, in that year. Her succession was opened 29 Dec. 1853. Most of her succession was destroyed in a fire in the Vermilion Parish courthouse during the 1880's. Her husband and at least the 2 minor children survived her. George Petry was their natural tutor. David M. Lyons was undertutor at one time. Another undertutor's last name was Hardy. A family meeting for the minors included Alexander Dartes, Jr. and Sr., Evars [?] Dartes, Henry Petry, Paul Toups, David Ly[ons?], all relations. Joseph J. or G. Gray was also probably related. These bits of information about the succession of Celina E. Wofford were taken from the burned scraps of her succession which remain, and they are included here mainly for posterity's sake and also because Celina Petry was a granddaughter of Louis Legnon. (2) William Washington Wofford, Jr., born 6 Feb. 1810, and died 26 Nov. 1842. George Petry of Lafayette Parish "by marriage a brother in law"

petitioned for letters of administration in this succession, which is Est. #502 in St. Mary Parish. (3) Louis Hamilton Wofford, the third known child of William Washington Wofford and Eugenie Legnon, was born 9 Aug. 1811 and died in the summer of 1842 in Lafayette Parish. His succession is Est. #500 in St. Mary Parish. Both were opened in 1843. Apparently neither of these Wofford brothers was married.[See St. Martinville Church records.]

Eugenie Legnon Wofford died between 1811 and 1815, for about the year 1815 William Washington Wofford, Sr., remarried this time to Nancy Alzira McMurtry, daughter of Samuel McMurtry and his wife Catherine Hyder, daughter of Benjamin Hyder of Rutherford Co., N. C. This couple are ancestors of the compiler. For their family, see her succession, Est. #493, opened in 1843.

5. Julie, or Julienne, Legnon, born in December of 1791, married (1) Peter Dartes(t), 29 Mar. 1814 [Marriage Book 1, page 40]. See his succession, Est. #165, opened 1828, and Civil suit #311, Julie Legnon, wife of Peter Dartest, vs. John Smith and Joseph Theall, filed 28 Aug. 1821. Her children by him are found in his succession. She married (2) John Hawkins of St. Mary Parish, probably around August of 1833.

6. Joseph Legnon, born in Feb. of 1794, married Eugenie Dartes at Charenton [Bodin II 159]. (No date given.)

7. Frederick Louis Legnon, born 25 July 1796.

8. Eugene Legnon. See the succession of Peter Dartest, #165, 1828: Eugene Legnon was uncle to the minor children of the deceased, husband of Julie Legnon, #5, above.

Arthemize Legnon, married to Alexander Dartest 25 Apr. 1816 [Marriage Book 1, page 84] may have been another child of Louis Legnon and Marie-Joseph Thibaud.

Most of the above information on this family is from Bodin I 284 and II 159 unless otherwise specified.

#82. C. THWAITES - 1820. Undoubtedly Charlotte

Tinker, daughter of Jeremiah Tinker and Miriam Thompson, his wife, and wife of _____ Thwaites. Charlotte Thwaites was survived by one daughter, Charlotte Frederica Thwaites, who married William G. Caulfield of the County of Middlesex, Kingdom of Great Britain. [See Conveyance Book D-7, page 92, entry no. 759, dated the year 1833.] See Est. #195.

#83. C. J. SORREL - 1820. See Est. #58, above, and Est. #98, below. Probably the succession of Contamine J. Sorrel.

#84. HECKALIAH/HACKALIAH THEALL - 1820. An early American settler who was in the area as early as 1808 at least, when he registered a cattle brand. His wife was Hannah Hughson. See her succession, Est. #425, opened in 1840. This family came from Dutchess Co., N. Y. See Est. #230. They had at least 3 sons and 1 daughter: John B., Joseph, and James F. Theall and Ann Theall.

John B. Theall married Frances Mixter. Their 2 children are named in her succession, Est. #965, opened in 1857: Ruffin and Henry Mixer/Mixter Theall.

Their second son was Joseph Theall. See his succession, Est. #230, opened in 1832. The third son of this couple was James F. Theall, who married Martha Lacy, daughter of Jesse E. Lacy [Est. #114] and Susan Andres/Andrews, married 1 Feb. 1827 [Marriage Book 1, page 362]. They had one daughter, Nancy, who married Malcolm A. Fraser 25 May 1843 [Marriage Book 3, page 38]. She died 26 May 1851 [Planters' Banner, 31 May 1851, page 3, col. 2]. Her succession is Est. #740, opened that year. Malcolm A. Fraser was a son of James Fraser and Anne Brownson. They were from Canada. See Planters' Banner, 24 Mar. 1853, page 3, col. 3. James F. Theall died in 1840. His succession is Est. #418, opened in that year.

Mrs. Alpha gives the information that the Thealls had a daughter, Ann, who married Benjamin M. Birdsall, who died 1 Mar. 1830, aged 45 [born

1785]. Ann Theall Birdsall died 15 June 1839, aged 59 [born 1780]. This information is from their tombstones in the Franklin Methodist Church cemetery, now destroyed but copied previously by Mrs. Alpha. This information is from her files.

#85. G. HENDERSON - 1820. Very likely George Henderson, in early records.

#86. A. HAMBLETON - 1820. The marriage license of Rebecca Hamilton and William Canbrough in 1821 reveals she was widow of Alexander Hamilton and natural tutrix of Eliz. R. Hamilton, her minor child by her marriage with said Hamilton. She prays for family meeting due to her intention to remarry; Alex. Renton is shown to be Elizabeth's uncle and only relation. Rebecca's maiden name was probably Renton, and it was probably Elizabeth's middle name. This is surely the succession of Alexander Hamilton.

#87. BLANK.

#88. Z. COCK - 1820.

#89. M. J. LELAND - 1820.

#90. F. CAMPBELL - 1820. Farquard Campbell was an 1813 St. Mary Parish taxpayer and was active in the affairs of the newly-formed parish. He was probably a brother of Martin M. Campbell. Mrs. Alpha, who has worked on this family, feels they might have been sons of John Campbell of Feliciana Parish, but this has not been proved. This is probably the succession of Farquard Campbell.

#91. L. JOHNS - 1821. See Mortgage Book B-A, page 93, 29 Sept. 1813: James Johns sells to Abraham Bird. This could be the same individual; the original initial may have been misread in compiling the index. Helve Johns, born in Georgia, was the wife of Resin Bowie [Bodin I 215].

#92. E. ROSE - 1821. Probably Edmund Rose, husband of Mary Hays, daughter of Malachi Hays and his wife, Elizabeth Treet, of Pennsylvania. Malachi Hays and his wife had at least 5 children: Michael, John, and David Hays; Mary Hays, wife of this decedent; and Elizabeth Hays, wife of (1) George Marsh and (2) William Dooley. Edmund Rose had 2 brothers, William P. and John Rose.

This information is from the files of Mrs. Clyde Alpha of Franklin, La.

#93. C. LAWIEDING - 1821. Almost assuredly Catherine Laurendiny, wife of Pierre Hyacinthe Bernard. See his succession, Est. #48, above.

My especial thanks go to Mrs. Clyde Alpha of Franklin, La., who gave so freely of her time in helping identify numerous of the above "missing links" in addition to those I have noted in the abstracts below.

ABSTRACTS

#48.(PARTIAL ONLY) ACHILE BERARD - 1816.

17 Nov. 1821. Petition of Hortense Boutte, wife of Benoist Baron Bayard. She was confirmed as natural tutrix of her minor children, Achile Berard and Achile Camille Berard, a previous family meeting having been held in consequence of her second marriage with the said Benoist Baron Bayard. Charles Olivier as surety prays for a family meeting to be composed of: Francois Cassar [Cezar] Boutte, Sr., uncle of said minors; Frederick H. Duperier, brother-in-law of said minors [apparently married to Hortense Berard, minors' sister]; Francois Cassar [Boutte?] fils, cousin of said minors; Jean B. Berard, brother of minors; and Joseph V. Boutte, cousin of minors. These are the nearest relations residing in the parish. Francois Cassar [sic] Boutte, who was undertutor and their grandfather, now deceased.[See his succession, Est. #158.]

14 Sept. 1832. Jacques Fontinette and Jean B. Perrett, residents and freeholders, appointed experts to appraise the landed estate that may be offered. Louis DeBlanc fils named undertutor to

Achile Berard and Achile Camille Berard, minor children and heirs of the said Hortense Boutte and Achile Berard, deceased. Jean Berard, also minors' grandfather, also deceased.

    Gen. note. For background of the Boutte family, see Est. #158, as noted above. Achille Berard, decedent, was a son of Jean Baptiste Berard and Anne Broussard. He married Marie Hortense Boutte at St. Martinville 7 July 1806. For further details of the background and children of Jean Baptiste Berard and Anne Broussard, see annotated Census of 1774, pages 53 and 54.

* #94. LOUIS DEMARET, DEC. 4 SEPT. 1815.

    Louis Demaret late of said parish lately died intestate. Donelson Caffery and Dennis Carlin appointed appraisers. Jacob Haifleigh, James Ferguson, John Moore and Winfrey Lockett signed inventory. Dennis Carlin appointed curator of Zaide, Alix, and Edgar, minor children of Louis Demaret, dec. Martin Demaret made oath pertaining to accuracy of inventory 12 Jan. 1816. At the time of Louis Demaret's death in 1815, Zaide Demaret was a minor over the age of puberty and Alix and Edgar were minors under the age of puberty. Witnesses to division of property among the heirs 5 Jan. 1816 were James Sanders, John Towles and Donelson Caffery. Heirs: 1. Clarice, wife of James Ferguson; 2. Adelaide, wife of John Moore of the Parish of St. Landry; 3. Marie Zaide, wife of Levi Foster [as of 4 Oct. 1822]; 4. Alix, wife of Jefferson Caffery [as of 27 Dec. 1824]; 5. Edgar; 6. Ursin; 7. Martin; and 8. Adelard.

    22 Apr. 1834. Alix Demaret and Jefferson Caffery both deceased, leaving minor children: 1. Ralph Earl, 2. Clarissa Mary, and 3. Jefferson Jackson Caffery under the age of puberty. James Ferguson their tutor. See their successions: his, Est. #180, opened in 1829; hers, Est. #255, opened in 1833.

    Ursin Demaret also deceased. His heirs are named in his succession, Est. #267, opened in 1834.

Gen. note. Louis George Demaret, this decedent, was a son of Andre George Demaret and Marie Jeanne Bourdon. His wife was Adelaide Blanco Navarre [Boudin II 74]. She was a daughter of Don Martin Navarro, a native of Spain who came to Louisiana in 1766 as treasurer of the newly acquired province. His wife was Adelaide Gayoso de Lemos, probably sister of the seventh Spanish Governor of Louisiana, Gayoso. [Chambers III 334.] Since decedent's wife is not mentioned in the succession, she must have predeceased him.

Ann Crow Demaret, wife of Martin F. Demaret, born 23 Oct. 1799, died 28 Mar. 1852. [Franklin Cemetery.]

Martin F. Demaret, born 12 May 1798, died 7 Oct. 1845. [Franklin Cemetery.]

Zeide Demaret Foster, born 10 May 1801, died 28 Mar. 1852. [Obituary, Planters' Banner, 3 Apr. 1852, page 3, col. 3.]

Marie Alix Demaret born 17 May 1810;

Edouard Demaret born 8 Dec. 1813; he married Marie Anne Brashear 3 May 1838 at Lafayette. [Bodin II 74, 75.]

*#95. NICOLAS PREVOST, DEC. 16 SEPT. 1816

Marie Prevost, widow. [She is mentioned as mother of all the heirs in Civil suit #337, Andre Gauffreaud & wife, Lucile Prevost, vs. Heirs of Nicolas Provost, deceased; filed 28 Mar. 1822.] The papers in this succession are not bound in order; the above date is the earliest I found.

Heirs: 1. Godfroi married 25 July 1809 at St. Martinville Anne LeBlanc [Bodin I 321] ; 2. Lenfroi; 3. Ursin [married 29 Nov. 1813, Marriage Book 1, p. 31, Julia (Julie) Etier, the widow of Antoine Etier, Est. #36]; 4. Nicolas [Phileman], sons and heirs of full and legal age as of 19 Oct. 1822; 5. [Celeste] Eleanor, born in January of 1789, [Bodin II 197], wife of Nicholas Loisel [she had apparently been married to Jacques Monnier; see Bodin II 197]; 6. Lucille, wife of Andrew

Gauffreau, daughters and heirs of full age; 7. Hortense, wife of Hilaire Borel; and 8. Hubert Pellerin, tutor of his minor children, all heirs of Julie Provost, deceased, his wife, daughter of decedent herein. Julie was alive when her father died, as she signed papers in connection with his succession in 1818. See Ests. #126 and 129 for her heirs.

Gen. note. Decedent was born ca. 1749, son of Nicolas Provost, dit Blondin, and his wife, Marie Francoise Quebedeau. He married Marie Jeanne Provost, born 28 Jan. 1768, daughter of Joseph Prevost, dit Collete, and his wife, Jeanne Daublin. They were married 1 Apr. 1785. [Annotated Census of 1774, pages 55 and 43.]

Godefroy, born ca. 1788; Hortance, born 15 May 1798; Leuphroy, born 7 Mar. 1792; Lucie, born 22 June 1795. [Bodin II 197]

#96. BARNET HULICK, DEC. 18 JAN. 1816

Will. Children named: 1. Rachel, 2. Eliza, 3. Caroline, 4. Julian, 5. Mary, and 6. Jesse. Jehu Wilkinson named executor. Sgd. 4 May 1813. Witnesses: Isaac Reed, James G. Morris, John Lees, Joseph H. Charpantier, Samuel Huntington. Pbt. 18 Jan. 1816. Appraisers were James Sanders and Isaac Reed. Witnesses to inventory: Samuel Wilkinson and Anson Stanbrough.

3 Feb. 1816. Buyers at sale of estate: Jehu Wilkinson, Joseph Charpantier, Samuel E. Scott, Farquhard Campbell, Samuel Wilkinson, John Reeves, Joseph Legnon, Matthew Nimmo, Celestin Carlin, Stephen Barabino, Antoine Walker, Lloyd Collins, Isaac Reed, Michael Charpantier, Clark Hardy, John Lees, Rigobert Verrett, Joseph Theall, James Sanders, Kentucky McClean, Andrew W. McClean, Alfred Thruston, Fils Fils Carlin, Warren Buford, Louis Legnon, Honore Carlin, _____ Carlin, Evan Bowles, Dartest.

3 Mar. 1817. Jediah Nixon, uncle, appointed tutor to Julia, Mary, and Jesse W. Hulick. James Sanders, Jesse Smith, Joseph Theall, J.

Charpantier, Thomas L. Ferguson signed. T. Thomas and William W. Wofford witnessed. Jediah Nixon and James Sanders are bondsmen same date.

6 Mar. 1817. Rachel N. Hulick picks uncle Jediah Nixon as her guardian. Eliza also picked uncle Jediah as her Curator ad bona. She and Rachel were adult minor children and heirs of Barnet Hulick.

18 Sept. 1818. Rachel, wife of Jared Y. Sanders, petitions for sale of land and settlement of estate.

7 Nov. 1826. Julianne now wife of Henry Nursen.

Gen. note. Decedent, Barnet Hulick, was a 5th generation of Dutch descent (Peter^4, Peter^3, Jochem^2, Hendrick^1), being descended from Hendrick Hulick, who came to New Amsterdam in 1653 from Holland. This family's genealogy has been published in the well authenticated GULLICKS AND ALLIED FAMILIES, 1653-1948, by Eliza Haddon Brevoort, as well as in other genealogical works. Barnet Hulick was a direct descendant of many early Dutch families, including Van Pelt, Van Sicklin, Wyckoff, Van Ness, Van Salee, Van Voorhees. He was born Barent Gulick 22 Jan. 1769 in Somerset Co., New Jersey, a son of Peter Gulick and Willemptige Johnson, daughter of Claes Barentse Janssen, alias Nicholson Johnson, and his wife, Antje Wyckoff. Barnet was called "Barent" in his father's will. As "Barnt Gulick" he served as a sergeant in the Whiskey Rebellion, later moved with his family to Dearborn Co., Indiana, where he served as a judge and as a captain in the militia, being listed in the latter as both "Barrent" and "Barnet". He removed his family to the Attakapas country about 1809, where he died in December of 1815 or early January of 1816. In Louisiana he was known consistently as "Barnet Hulick".

Barnet Hulick was married 12 Feb. 1797 in Middlesex Co., N. J. to Sarah Nixon, daughter of Robert Nixon and his first wife, Rachel --------. Sarah's younger brother and sister, Jediah and

Abbie Ann, accompanied her and her husband when they left New Jersey and on to Louisiana. She married James Sanders; Jediah Nixon seems to have not married; at least so far as is know he left no descendants.

Rachel Nixon Hulick, the Hulicks' eldest child, was born 16 Jan. 1798 in Middlesex Co., New Jersey; married Jared Young Sanders, I, 29 Apr. 1818; died in St. Mary Parish in 1872.

Eliza was born in July of 1801 in or near Elizabeth, N. J.; married William Peter Kemper on 27 Apr. 1825; died in St. Mary Parish in May of 1862.

Caroline Hulick apparently died in girlhood.

Julia Ann Hulick was born 30 Nov. 1806; married Henry Randolph Nursen in St. Mary Parish on 25 Oct. 1825; died in St. Mary Parish 18 Sept. 1867. See Addenda section for her children.

Mary Vance Hulick was born ca. 1808 in Dearborn Co., Ind.; married John Mills Bateman ca. 1830 in St. Mary Parish; died 5 June 1866 in St. Mary Parish.

Jesse W. Hulick was born ca. 1812 in St. Mary Parish; married Harriet Perryman 18 Nov. 1832, St. Mary Parish; died ca. 1845 in St. Mary Parish, apparently without issue.

Sarah Nixon Hulick is thought to have died shortly before her husband wrote his last will, on 4 May 1813.

Family correspondence indicates that Robert Nixon and Rachel, his first wife, had at least 3 sons besides Jediah. One, Robert, was a sea captain. The other two, whose first names are not known at this writing, apparently came to Louisiana and were both drowned. One of these latter apparently was the father of Emily Sophia Nixon, who married David Bell on 1 June 1829, St. Mary Parish; Caroline P. Nixon, who married William Porter Allen on 18 Feb. 1835 in St. Mary Parish; and Jackson Robert Nixon, who married Eliza Ellen Nimmo, daughter of Matthew Nimmo, in

St. Mary Parish on 17 May 1838. These 3 are known to have been brother and sisters. Thomas Robert Nixon and Henry R. Nixon are also associated with relatives in St. Mary Parish and may have been children of the other brother.

Joshua Nixon and Alexander Nexon had early land grants in the Attakapas area, and Woodson Nixon was in the 1810 Census for St. Martin Parish; they may have been sons of Robert Nixon. Joshua was married to Marie Choat, daughter of John Choat and Sarah Holstein Choat. They had one daughter, Ann, who married Noah Tevis 24 July 1811 in St. Martin Parish [OA 26, page 147]. Ann Nixon was born 6 Oct. 1795 in Louisiana. [Mr. Wade Hayes of Vidor, Tex., a descendant of Ann Nixon and Noah Tevis, supplied the date of her birth.] After his death, Marie Choat remarried John Carlyle 30 Apr. 1799. She is stated as being "of Natchez" [Bodin I 114, 120].

*#97. FRANCIS HUDSON, DEC. 28 FEB. 1817

Elizabeth (Patterson) Hudson, widow and late wife of Francis Hudson, decedent, petitioned. Basil Crow and George Royster were appraisers; John B. Theall, W. Buford, and Samuel E. Scott witnessed the inventory. George Royster appointed undertutor to Benjamin, Caroline, John, and Virginia Hudson, minor heirs of Francis Hudson.

7 Mar. 1817. Francis Turner Hudson and Elizabeth Hudson, adult minor children and heirs of Francis Hudson, deceased. Winfrey Lockett and Basil Crow witnessed. George Royster, Basil Crow, and John B. Theall bondsmen. W. Buford, & Martin Demaret witnessed.

11 Mar. 1817. Meeting of friends, the minors having no relations in the state: Basil Crow, George Royster, Anna Royster, Winfrey Lockett, and Rufus Nickelson signed minutes of meeting. George King and Thomas Makin witnessed.

11 Apr. 1817. Betty Patterson is spoken of as being the mother of the 4 younger children. This does not necessarily mean she was not also the

mother of the older 2.

#98. JOSEPH SORREL, DEC. 18 MAR. 1817

This succession is entirely in French. It was apparently opened on the date shown above. This and Est. #58, above, are probably segments of the same succession.

#99A. EUGENE SENNETTE, DEC. 17 JUNE 1817

Will. Wife, Charlotte Sennette. Children by marriage with the said Charlotte Sennette: Eugenie, Aurore, Eugene, Azelie, John Baptiste, Hugere Silvanie, and Charlotte Delphine Sennette (7). Wife appointed executor. Witnesses: Joseph Charpantier, Joseph A. Moore, Charles M. Charpantier. Signed: 15 Jan. 1817; probated: 17 June 1817. Appraisers: Martin Demaret & Dennis Carlin; witnesses to inventory: Celestin Carlin & Joseph Charpantier.

2 Aug. 1817. Pierre Arrieux undertutor to last 5 above named.

10 Dec. 1820. Pierre Oudum [?] appointed in his stead; Eugenie and Aurore Sennette declared adult minor children; named Pierre Arrieux their curator ad bona.

6 Jan. 1818. Stephen Brashear appointed curator ad bona of Aurore. Farq. Campbell witnessed.

31 Jan. 1823. Eugene Sennette declared to be an adult minor and chose Ursin Demaret as his curator ad bona; Eugenie Sennette now wife of Ursin Demaret and 21 years of age; Charlotte Sennette now "also Charlotte Calomal."

22 Jan. 1828. Eugene Sennette declared to be 21 years of age or upwards.

Gen. note. Decedent's widow, Charlotte, married Bartholemy Calumet [Calomel in succession paper, above] 21 Sept. 1822 [Marriage Book 1, page 245]. Eugenie Sennette married Ursin Demaret, son of Louis Demaret, Est. #94, above, 25 Aug. 1818 [Marriage Book 1, page 152].

#99B. HIRAM ALLEN, DEC. 15 DEC. 1818

Parish of St. Landry. William Campbell and Mary Ann Allen, wife of Drury Thompson of St.

Landry Parish, appoint Drury Thompson attorney in fact in Estate of Hiram Allen, deceased. Witnesses: James Ray & Joseph Tate. Sarah Allen, wife of William Campbell, is one of the heirs of Hiram Allen, deceased. Witnesses: John Thompson & John McDaniel.

15 Jan. 1820. Family meeting called for Rebecca Allen, aged 11 years; Nesbett Allen, aged 16; James Allen, aged 15; and Mary Allen, about 19 years of age. Drury Thompson appointed tutor to Rebecca and curator ad bona to other 3, these 4 being minor heirs of Hiram Allen, deceased.

21 Feb. 1820. Family meeting: Drury Thompson, step-father; William Campbell, brother-in-law; and in default of other relatives of the minors, family friends: John Thompson, Dennis McDaniel, and John McDaniel. Witnesses: Lewis Moore and C. M. Charpantier.

*#100. ALEXANDER STERLING, DEC. 20 MAY 1818

Under order of the Hon. John H. Johnson, parish judge and judge of probate in and for the Parish of Feliciana, Donelson Caffery & Isaac L. Baker ordered to make inventory. Witnesses: John Pattee & William Sterling. Ruffin Sterling petitions he is the legitimate descendant in the direct line of Alexander Sterling and Ann Sterling, his wife, both deceased, and one of the forced heirs; that he is entitled by law to 1/7 part of the estate. The name of Ruffin Sterling is not included among the children of this couple named in this petition; but he obviously is one of their children. See succession of Alexander Sterling, West Feliciana Parish, St. Francisville, La. Other children of Alexander and Ann Sterling: 1. Henry, 2. Lewis, 3. Alexander, 4. William M., 5. Ann, 6. John Sterling. [Ann Sterling is the wife of Andrew Skillman formerly wife of Martin L. Haynie, Est. #51]; John is a minor represented by James Perrie, his curator and guardian. Witnesses: Samuel Zadig & John Mead.

Creditors: William Finch, Alexander A. Sterling,

Jared Y. Sanders, Thomas Pugh, Jehu Wilkinson, Jones Shaw, John Lees, Lloyd Collins, Ruffin Sterling, Winfrey Lockett, James S. Johnson, John B. Theall, William Darling, William Whaley, Lewis Sterling, James Anderson, Peter ____ Rentrop, William Richardson (notation "paid by J. Wilkinson"), Joseph Theall, William L. Brent, Dennis Carlin, Perryman Foot [very faded], Pierre Etier, Sr., Pierre Etier, Jr., Ursin Carlin, Jesse E. Lacy, Nicholas Verrett, John H. Johnson, Louis Judice, Stephen Babarino, George Singleton, Daniel Clark, Richard Floyd, Evan Bowles, Anthony Walker, F. T. Hudson, Charles Harrington.

1 Feb. 1819. Beginning of sale of property belonging to the estate of Alexander and Ann Sterling. Purchasers: William Finch, Ruffin Sterling, Jared Sanders, Thomas Pugh, Jehu Wilkinson, Jones Shaw, Lloyd Collins, John Lees, Winfrey Lockett, James L. Johnson, John B. Theall, William Sterling, William Whaley, James Andres, Peter H. Rentrop, William Richardson, Samuel Andres, Joseph Theall, William L. Brent, Dennis Carlin, Berryman Foot, Pierre Etier, Ursin Carlin, Jesse E. Lacy, Nicholas Verrett, John F. E. Johnson [?], Louis Judice, Lewis Sterling, Stephen Babarino, William Sterling, George Singleton, John R. Dawson, Andrew & Ann Skillman, James L. Johnson, Daniel Sparks, Michael Hayes, Evan Bowles, Pierre Bonvillian, Anthony Walker, F. T. Hudson, Whaley & Lees, Joseph Theall, Charles F. Covington, Ursin Carlin. Witnesses: John B. Dawson & James Dupree [?].

Settlement not shown.

Gen. note. Alexander Sterling was born ca. 1760 in Scotland. He married Ann Alston of South Carolina. Was employed by the Spanish government to survey and lay out what is now the state of Louisiana. Henry Sterling was born ca. 1793 in Louisiana and married Mary Bowman; Lewis Sterling was born ca. 1800 in Louisiana and married Sarah Turnbull, daughter of John Turnbull and Catherine

Rucker. See Est. #232. [Biographical and Historical Memoirs of Mississippi by Irene S. & Norman E. Gillis, 1962, pages 586-7].

*#101. FRANCOIS PREVOST, DEC. 24 FEB. 1818
Decedent has lately died. Will [French].

6 Mar. 1818. Baptiste Berard [?] & Jacques Fontenette appointed to appraise property in St. Martin Parish.

9 Mar. 1818. Ursin Prevost, an adult minor son and one of the heirs of Francois Prevost, deceased, over 14 years of age, chose Ursin Darby his curator ad bona.

10 Mar. 1818. Madelaine Borel, widow of Francois Prevost, decedent. 7 heirs: 1. Julie, wife of Nicolas Hebert; 2. Manette, wife of Eugene Borel; 3. Francois [born 30 June 1795, Bodin II 197]; 4. Hyacinthe, wife of Ursin Darby [another husband of Hyacinthe is Zenon Bourgeois, perhaps a later husband. Bodin I 321]; 5. Ursin, born 24 Dec. 1798 [Bodin II 198], represented by his curator ad bona, Ursin Darby; 6. Jean Baptiste, [born 27 Apr. 1801, Bodin II 197], a minor represented by his curator, Ursin Darby; and 7. Eliza, minor child of Madelaine Prevost, represented by her father, her natural tutor, Joseph Prevost, Madelaine Prevost being deceased.

9 Mar. 1818. Fam. meeting for Eliza Prevost: Madelaine Borel, grandmother; Francois Prevost, undertutor [brother?]; Ursin Darby; Hilaire Borel; Pierre Etier; Nicholas Loisel; and Eugene Borel.

10 Aug. 1820. Fam. meeting for John B. Prevost, adult minor: Francois & Ursin Prevost, brothers; Eugene Borel, uncle; Hilaire Borel & Ursin Prevost, cousins. Madelaine Borel appointed curator ad bona. Some of this succession was impossible for the compiler to decipher.

Gen. note. Evidence indicates that decedent was married twice. He was a son of Joseph Prevost and Magdalen Mayeaux and was born 25 May 1752 in Pointe Coupee. He married (1) 29 Dec. 1774 Genevieve Bonin [Benoit], daughter of Antoine

Bonin and Marie Marguerite Sellier; (2) 17 May 1784, Magdelaine Borel [also called Madelaine], daughter of Pierre Borel and Catherine Toupart. Apparently the first two heirs named above were the children of the first wife. Bodin also shows a daughter, Marie, born 3 May 1777; this may have been Annette/Manette: she may have had a double name; or this may have been a child who did not live to adulthood. The other 5 named children, above, apparently were the children of decedent's second wife, Madelaine Borel.

The above information is from Bodin I 321 and II 197 and the annotated Census of 1774, page 43. Those interested in further information on these families are recommended to these sources.

Evidence indicates that Eugene Borel was brother of decedent's second wife, Madelaine Borel, and since Eugene Borel married his sister's step-daughter, his sister became his mother-in-law! See also Est. #252.

#102. JACOB KNIGHT, DEC. 29 NOV. 1819

Christina Horner, formerly wife of Jacob Knight, deceased, of the one part, and Elizabeth J. Brown, Henry Knight, William Knight, and Michael Knight, children and legal heirs of said Jacob Knight, all of full age, of the other part. Luke Bryan and James Muggah make petition on behalf of widow and heirs. Frederick Rentrop is a witness. Christina is referred to "as our mother" by the heirs. Elizabeth J. Brown's husband's name is not shown.

Gen. note. Bodin tells us [II 134] that Jacob Knight was a son of Philip Knight. He was deceased before 1809, when John Horner was already the husband of Christine Knight, decedent's widow.

6 Apr. 1814. Christine Horner and John Horner sell land to William Biggs, relinquishing all claims they have themselves and as heirs and representatives of Michael Infil [Enfeel]. [Book B-A, page 293, Entry #613. Recorded 25 Aug. 1818.]

His public land was next to the Knights' land.
Vol. I: Michael Enfile registered a cattle brand
in 1798; as Michael Infil, has a land claim in
American State Papers. Christine was probably
the daughter of Michael Enfeel.

25 July 1820. Elizabeth Brown, widow of the
late John Brown and daughter of Jacob Knight,
deceased, married Patrick Reels of St. Mary Parish.
Bond signed by William Knight. [Marriage Book 1,
page 49.] William Knight, son of Jacob Knight and
Christine Enfeel, was born in Ky. ca. 27 Apr. 1788
[Bodin I 134, 216]; married Catherine Russ,
daughter of William Russ and Winifred West of North
Carolina. [Bodin II 134]. Henry Knight married
Mary Madelaine Liquer [Siguer, Leguier, LaCour],
daughter of Jean Liquer and his wife, Marie Anne
Malbrou, 30 June 1804 [Bodin II 133, 159].
Michael Knight was born ca. 10 June 1790 [Bodin II
134]; married Charity Hamilton 1 Apr. 1813
[Marriage Book 1, page 19]. See also Est. #75
and 86. Mrs. Clyde Alpha of Franklin shared much
of the above information with the compiler.

#103. GEORGE DOHERTY, DEC. 23 OCT. 1819
Levi Foster petitions for settlement, stating
decedent died intestate. This is a vacant estate.
Decedent seems to have been in farming partnership
with Andrew McClain. George Royster and John
Towles participated. No heirship shown.

#104. ANN FINCH, DEC. 4 DEC. 1819
Mrs. Ann Finch recently died intestate leaving
2 minor children, legal heirs to her estate:
David Smith and James Smith, by her marriage with
David Smith, deceased [Est. #19]. The former is
an adult minor residing at this time in Scotland
and the latter is a minor under the age of 14
years residing in St. Mary Parish. Donelson
Caffery and James Ferguson appointed appraisers.
Witnesses: J. Brashear and Evan Bowles. William
Finch is the surviving husband of decedent.

6 Dec. 1819. Marianne Parquin, wife of Louis
Parquin, is the legitimate grandmother of David

Smith, 16 years old, living in Scotland, and James Smith, about 10 years old. Meeting of friends of the minors [in the absence of relations in the parish]: James Hennen, Winfrey Lockett, Evan Bowles, Jeremiah Brashear, and Martin M. Campbell and William Richardson. Mariann Parquin appointed curator of David and tutor of James. William Richardson appointed undertutor of James. Dennis Carlin, Honore Carlin and Alexis Carlin surety for Mariann Parquin.

30 Dec. 1819. Mariann Parquin named as mother of Ann Finch.

Apr. 1827. Ann Smith [decedent] married secondly John M. Watson [Est. #62] and he having died she contracted another marriage with William Finch. She left no children by her last two marriages.

Gen. note. From records pertaining to decedent's second marriage [Marriage Book 1, page 73], we learn that she was born in the City of Nassau, Island of Providence, and that she was the lawful daughter of Jeremiah Tinker and Miriam [Thompson] Tinker. Her mother remarried Louis Parquin(s) 2 Dec. 1818 [Marriage Book 1, page 158]. See her succession, Est. #195, opened in 1830.

#105. MICHAEL GORDY'S PROPERTY [NOT A SUCCESSION]

This is apparently a statement of property brought by Michael Gordy into the marriage he contracted with Sarah A. Robert on 3 Apr. 1816 [Marriage Book 1, page 81]. It is an undated inventory signed by Benjamin Gordy, Peter W. Gordy, Samuel E. Scott, Sarah A. Gordy and Michael Gordy.

*#106. JAMES HENNEN, DEC. 13 OCT. 1820

Mrs. Ann Hennen, widow of the late Dr. James Hennen, deceased, and tutor of Eliza H. Gates, minor child of Thomas Gates, deceased [Est. #41], by his marriage with the late Eliza Hennen, deceased, daughter of the said James Hennen; Alfred Hennen, son and one of the heirs of the

said James Hennen; and Alexander Frere, natural
tutor of Caroline Frere, his daughter by his
marriage with the late Catherine S. Hennen,
deceased, daughter of the said James Hennen
[Est. #59], are petitioners in this succession.
John Towles and Donelson Caffery appointed
appraisers. James Hennen died in New Orleans on
_____ April, 1820.

Fam. meeting for minors: Alexander Frere, father
and natural tutor of Caroline Frere; Levi Foster,
Jared Y. Sanders, Winfrey Lockett, James Campbell,
Robert Trousdale, and Joseph Theall, friends of
said minors, they having no relations in this
parish except the said Alexander Frere and Ann
Hennen, their grandmother.

9 Jan. 1823. Buyers at sale of property of
estate: Samuel Wilkinson, Lloyd Wilcoxon,
Alexander Frere, Joseph Lacy, Rufus Nickelson,
John B. Murphy, Sr., James L. Johnson, Nathan
Kemper, Jones Shaw, M. W. Campbell, James Theall,
Stephen Barabino, John B. Theall, Richard
Fennessy [?], William Desk, Nicolas Verrette,
George Roister [Royster], Agricole Fuselier, James
Campbell, Charles Grevemberg, Reuben Doty, Alfred
Hennen, John Rice, Warren Buford, Dr. B. F. Wells,
W[illiam] Sanders, Daniel P. Sparks, Mrs. Harding,
Donelson Caffery, Winfrey Lockett, Julien LeBlanc,
J. Y. Sanders, Jesse Lacy, John Lees, Leclair
Fuselier, Gabriel Fuselier, Walter Brashear,
Anthony Walker, Mrs. Ann Hennen, Alfred Hennen,
son of Mrs. Ann Hennen. Wit: Ann Davison and Ann
C. Bonney.

7 June 1823. Mrs. Ann Hennen departed this life
in Philadelphia leaving Alfred her only surviving
child and Caroline Frere and Eliza Hennen Gates
her only surviving grandchildren her forced heirs.
Buyers at her sale: Theodore Dumain, Alexander
Frere, Jehu Wilkinson, Walter Brashear, William
G. Sanders, Allen J. Key, Benjamin Lacy, William
Walker, James Dupree, Gabriel L. Fuselier.

#107. LYMAN HARDING, DEC. 11 JULY 1820

Lyman Harding, Esq., attorney and counsellor at law, late of Natchez in the state of Mississippi, departed this life 24 June 1820 intestate, domiciled and residing aforesaid. Left an only son, over 14 years of age, at present in Massachusetts, Winthrop [Sargent] Harding. He had no relations in the state of Louisiana.

12 July 1820. James Sanders and J. Y. Sanders appointed appraisers. Wit: J. Brashear and James Sanders, Jr. (manager of the Harding Louisiana plantation).

29 Dec. 1820. James Sanders appointed curator of the vacant estate of decedent.

June 1827. Donelson Caffery was curator of this estate. Elizabeth Harding has 1/4 interest in the estate as the widow.

5 Dec. 1821. W. S. Harding chooses Samuel Steer [of East Baton Rouge Parish] as his curator ad bona.

This succession does not appear to be complete. Principal succession is probably of record in Natchez.

Gen. note. Lyman Harding was born in Massachusetts, moved to Maryland, thence to Natchez. [Biographical & Historical Memoirs of Mississippi, page 246.] The James Sanders, Jr., manager of Harding Louisiana plantation, was probably the son of William Gunnell Sanders [Est. #181, opened in 1829], and brother of Jared Young Sanders of St. Mary Parish.

*#108. DENIS CARLIN, DEC. 1827

This succession seems to be incomplete. The original petition could not be found, hence the date the succession was opened is not available. The index states the succession was opened in 1825. [Even that date is out of place with the other successions in numerical order]. [No date shown on this petition]. Honore Carlin and Celestin Carlin petition, brothers of decedent. Suzanne [Labaterie] Carlin is the widow of decedent, who left 13 children living at his decease. Decedent died in St. Mary Parish ____ Mar. 1827.

These are the children of Denis Carlin and his wife, Suzanne Labaterie Carlin, gleaned from the records of this succession and the final settlement: 1. Denis, Jr., born 15 Oct. 1796; 2. Ursin or Ursain, born ca. Dec. of 1794; 3. Terrence, born 5 Apr. 1799; 4. Godfroy, born 25 Jan. 1802; 5. Claire, wife of Joseph Allen, born 15 Aug. 1800; 6. Eulalie, wife of Garland Cosby "residing in the state of Kentucky" and represented by Robert Nash Ogden, born 17 May 1803; 7. Dorothy Susanna, wife of R. de la Thule, born 5 Oct. 1806; 8. Urbain, born 21 Feb. 1805; all majors in 1827. 9. Victoire Carmesile, born 29 Dec. 1807, married her cousin, Alphonse Carlin, son of Alexis [they separated]; 10. Theodore, born 20 June 1809; 11. Theolin; these 3 minors above the age of puberty in 1827; and 12. Emma, born 14 May 1816; and 13. Edward, minors under the age of puberty in 1827. In addition to these 13, Dennis Carlin was survived by a granddaughter, Eliza Carlin Muse, daughter of Sampson Muse of East Feliciana Parish by his marriage with Amarant Carlin, daughter of Dennis, deceased in East Feliciana Parish leaving said Eliza as her sole heir. This child must have died in childhood, for she is not mentioned in the final settlement of this succession or in the succession of her grandmother [Est. #213, opened in 1831]. Emertiana, who must have been this child's mother, was baptized 15 Dec. 1799. Other children of this couple who are listed in Bodin but not listed in the succession and therefore must have died are: Susanne, born 20 June 1809, Theodore's twin, and Theotiste, born 9 Jan. 1811. Possibly this could be the child called in the succession Theolin. For additional study of this family, see Bodin I 113 and II 51, as well as other references. Denis, Jr. is "of Rapides Parish, La." There is litigation concern-

ing this succession; it is impossible to glean
details without minute study of the family and each
page of the succession. See also the succession
of decedent's widow, Suzanne Labaterie Carlin,
Est. #213, opened in 1831.

#109. GAINS KIBLE, DEC. 1 OCT. 1821. SEE
ALSO EST. #115; SOME OF THAT ESTATE BELONGS IN
THIS SUCCESSION.

Widow, Nancy Kible, and 12 children are
decedent's legal heirs: 1. Margaret, 2. Gains, 3.
Henry; 4. Lucy; 5. Benjamin _____ ; 6. George [5
May 1823 George was in Lancaster, New Hampshire;
see Est. #115: in 1821 George was merely listed
as being "out of the state"];7. Isaac [married
Sarah Spaulding]; 8. Mary. These first 8
children were by his first marriage, wife unnamed.
9. Charles; 10. Francis; 11. Nancy; and 12.
William, minors, all by his widow.

Ursin Provost and Samuel R. Rice appointed
appraisers. Lewis C. Hutchinson and William
Knight witnessed.

There were no relations to compose a family
meeting so friends made up the meeting.

24 Aug. 1822. Purchasers at sale: Stephen
Barabino, Jeremiah Brashear, Nancy Kible, George
Royster, Nathan Kemper, Charles Kible, Thomas
Wilcoxon, Francis T. Hudson.

22 Mar. 1826. Henry Kible sent affidavit
from Morgan Co., Ala.

* #110. PIERRE ETIE, DEC. 6 DEC. 1821

See also Civil suit #362: Charles Joseph
Antoine of St. Martin Parish vs. Widow and heirs
of Pierre Etie, Sr., deceased, filed 14 June
1822.

Decedent lately died intestate; widow, Victoire
Borel, and 7 children his legal heirs: 1. Pierre
G[uillaume], born 28 Oct. 1797 [Bodin II 94],
married Eulalie Massicot, daughter of Charles
Massicot of St. Charles Parish,[Est. #113, opened
in 1821],[Marriage Book 1, page 190], on 8 Feb.
1820; see his succession, Est. #119, opened in

1822; 2. Constance, wife of Charles Delcambre; 3.
Selesie, these 3 over 21 years of age; 4. Drusin;
5. Joachim; 6. Leocadie; and 7. Marcellite, who
married Salvadore Miguez [Bodin II 94]. Frederic
Pellerin and Nicolas Loisel appointed appraisers.
Fam. meeting for minors: Nicolas Loisel;
Madelaine Borel, the widow Prevost; and Pierre
Borel were relations of minors.
    11 Dec. 1821. Nicolas Loisel appointed under-
tutor to minors.
       Gen. note. Bodin tells us [II 94] that
Pierre Etier, husband of Victoire Borel, was a
son of Pierre Etier and Catherine Baudoin. He
was a native of Bordeaux, France, and a brother
of Antoine Etier, Est. #36.
    #111. JOSEPH GARDEN, DEC. 12 OCT. 1821
  Lately died intestate. Nicolas Loisel and
Joseph Gilbeau appointed appraisers. J. Y.
Sanders and H. Pillenary [?] witnessed. John
Baptiste Bonnemailer [?] appointed curator of the
vacant estate of this decedent. No heirship shown.
    #112. GEORGE W. KING, DEC. 26 MAR. 1821
  Winfrey Lockett petitioned that the decedent
lately died intestate and left a vacant estate.
No heirship shown.
    #113. CHARLES MASICOT, DEC. 30 NOV. 1820
  Augustin Massicot of St. Charles Parish
represents that his brother, Charles Massicot,
departed this life 17 Nov. 1820. Another
petition this date shows that Antoine St. Amand
and Augustin Massicot, both planters residing in
the parish of St. Charles, County of German Coast,
are, respectively, father-in-law and
the brother of the late Charles Massicot. Heirs:
1. Eulelie, wife of Pierre Etier, over 21 years
of age; 2. John Baptist, an adult minor; 3. Marie
Francoise, an adult minor of the parish of St.
Charles [Civil suit #316: Justin Quin of New
Orleans vs. Heirs of Charles Massicot, deceased,
filed 20 Sept. 1821]; and 4. Theophile, a minor
son under the age of puberty. Charles Olivier

and Adrian Dumartrait appointed appraisers. Fam. meeting: Faustin Fortier, Charles Grevemberg, Adrian Dumartrait, and Pierre Etie fils relations of minors.

16 July 1821. Buyers at sale: George Maha---, Nicolas Broussard, Herbert Pellerin, Eugene Borel, Madelaine Borel Prevost, Pierre Etier pere and fils, Nicolas Loisel, Lufroy Provost, Joseph Broussard, John Towles, Charles Olivier, Terence De la Houssaye, Alexander Broussard, Garland Cosby, J. Y. Sanders, John B. Massicot, Adrian/ Andrew Dumartrait, Henry Corney, Dr. Regnoir, Charles Meyers, Mr. Bonmaison, Ursin Darby, Andrew Gauffreau, Daniel P. Sparks, Charles Haraneder [?].

*#114. JESSE E. LACY, DEC. 6 OCT. 1821

Jesse Eagelson Lacy lately died intestate leaving a widow, Mrs. Susan Lacy, and 9 children by his marriage with the said Susan Lacy: 1. William H. Lacy [Bodin lists him as William Eagleson Lacy, born 27 Sept. 1797: II 137]; 2. Joseph; 3. Benjamin; these 3 over 21 years of age; 4. Theodoceous, wife of James Campbell; 5. Susan; 6. Daniel, 7. Jesse; 8. Martha; 9. James [the last 6 being under 21 years of age].

Gen. note. Bodin tells us [II 137] that decedent was from New Jersey, a son of Daniel Lacy and Martha Eagleson, and that he was married to Suzana Andres of South Carolina, daughter of Benjamin Andres of Virginia and Marie Hartgreve [Bodin II 3].

#115. ISAAC KIBLE [KIBBE] & SARAH KIBLE, DEC. 19 NOV. 1821

Rufus Nickelson petitions inasmuch as since the decease of Isaac Kibbe and Sarah Kibbe no person has been legally appointed to represent their minor children, Sarah and Margaret, their only heirs.

1 Dec. 1821. Both recently died intestate. George Royster and William Long appointed appraisers; inventory made at residence of Mrs.

Nancy Kibbe, widow of George Kible (Est. #109). Fam. meeting composed entirely of friends: Mrs. Nancy Kibbe, George Royster, Thomas Makin, William Long, and Patrick Carlin, the minors having no relations in the state.

Sarah and Margaret Kibbe are also the legal heirs of Daniel Spalding, who has lately died, their uncle, brother of Sarah Kibbe [which means Sarah Kibbe's maiden name was also Spa(u)lding, unless Sarah and Daniel were half-brother and -sister, having different fathers].

Rufus Nickelson named tutor; Mrs. Nancy Kibbe named undertutor.

22 Dec. 1821. Buyers at sale: Rufus Nickelson, George Royster, Martin M. Campbell, Dr. John Lees, Jared Y. Sanders, Patrick Carlin, William Armstrong, Samuel E. Scott, Mrs. E. Hudson, Julius Smith, Justus Greaves, John J. Garrett.

#116. WILLIAM BIGGS, DEC. 4 NOV. 1818

Decedent lately died intestate; Nancy Biggs was his surviving widow. James Sanders and Honore Carlin appointed appraisers of the estate; John Richardson and Robert Trousdale witnessed the inventory of the estate.

Minor children "among other children" who survived decedent: Andrew, Susan, Nancy, and Jane Biggs. Fam. meeting for these minors: Catherine Knight, Lemuel H. H. Paris, Nancy Biggs, John Richardson, James Ferguson, Honore Carlin, Luke Bryan [does not specify whether friends or relations; apparently they are friends, the minors having no relations in the vicinity].

James Sanders appointed tutor [apparently to all 4]. Edy Biggs and Charlotte Biggs, adult minor legitimate daughters and heirs of decedent, chose James Sanders as their curator ad bona. James Sanders and John Smith are bondsmen for the estate; J. A. Moore witnessed. William Biggs, adult minor son, chose Luke Bryan for his curator ad bona; Robert Trousdale and Dennis Carlin, Jr., witnessed. Nancy Biggs, the widow, is the natural tutrix of Louisiana Biggs. There are apparently no children surviving decedent who were over the age of 21 years, and Louisiana Biggs must have been the widow's only child.

13 Dec. 1818. Another family meeting: James Sanders, Luke Bryan, Ann Biggs, widow, Winfrey Lockett, Alexis Carlin, Stephen Babarino, James Ferguson, and Adelard Demaret; Robert Trousdale and John Richardson witnessed. John Smith is undertutor of the 4 youngest [to whom James Sanders is tutor, above]; apparently these 4 were "under the age of puberty."

18 Jan. 1819. Buyers at sale: Winfrey Lockett, Michael Hayes, Joseph Guidry, Anthony Walker, David Robbins, Clark Hardy, Stephen Babarino, Luke Bryan, John N. Kershaw, Lloyd Collins, Evan Bowles, Conrad Hartman, Jonathan Smith, Jacob Haifleigh, John Smith, Jones Shaw, John Lees, William Walker, Andrew W. McLean, Joseph Theall, Walter B. Wilcoxon, Joshua Rogers, Purnel J. Reddick, John Richardson, Dennis Carlin, Jr., William Whaley.

29 Dec. 1822. Andrew Biggs, Susan Biggs, and Jane Biggs now adult minors; chose John Smith as their curator ad bona Nancy Biggs, daughter of decedent by first marriage, named above, was either the youngest of the children or she had died by this time. Family meeting: William Biggs, their brother and only relation in the parish [now apparently over 21]; Robert Trousdale; Nancy Biggs [their step-mother]; Evan Bowles; Joseph Legnon; Martin M. Campbell and Samuel Wilkinson witnessed.

Sept. 1826. Nancy Robbins Biggs, widow of decedent and mother of Louisiana Biggs, deceased, a child born during the marriage between her and decedent; Edith Biggs now over 21 and the wife of Ogden A. Langstaff. Nancy Biggs married James Muggah.

No final settlement shown.

Gen. note. Charlotte H. Biggs married James

Dupree 3 Apr. 1837 [Marriage Book 2, page 103].
Decedent married as his second wife Nancy Robbins.
They were the parents of one only surviving child,
Louisiana Biggs, and this child was dead by 1826.
Decedent's first wife's identity is not known by
compiler at this time. Nancy Robbins and William
Biggs were married 19 Oct. 1815 [Marriage Book 1,
page 72]. She remarried James Muggah 3 Sept.
1828 [Marriage Book 1, page 436]. He was formerly
married to Julia Ann Robbins; see her succession
[Est. #163, opened in 1828]. It is very likely
that Julia Ann and Nancy Robbins were sisters
or otherwise closely related. Mrs. Nancy Muggah
died 2 Sept. 1853, aged 66, a native of New
Hampshire. Apparently she and James Muggah had
an only child, Thomas. See Planters' Banner, 15
Sept. 1853, page 3, col. 4. James Muggah's
succession was opened in 1835 [Est. #309].

* #117. PHILIP VERRETT, DEC. 17 APR. 1822
Decedent was of the Parish of Ascension, lately died in that parish. All his children are of age. There is no mention in this succession of his wife. Legal heirs of decedent: 1. Nicolas; 2. Harriet [Henriette], wife of John Baptiste Verrett; 3. Manon, wife of Godefroy Verret; 4. John Baptiste; 5. Eloise, wife of William Moore; 6. Carmelite, wife of Honore Dejean of St. Landry Parish, represented by attorney in fact, Nicolas Verrett.

A Philippe Verete, born in New Orleans, son of deceased Nicolas Verete and Marie Cantrelle, signed a Marriage Contract with Marie Hebert, born in Acadia, widow of Anselme _____, in St. Martinville 7 Dec. 1783. This may be the same man. [St. Martin Parish Original Acts 3, entry no. 89; Marriage Contracts, by Winston DeVille, page 12]. Marie Hebert, wife of Philippe Verette, was daughter of Jean Baptiste Hebert and Claire Robichaud [Bodin I 203]. A Nicholas Verette was married to Marie L. Senitiere; see her succession, Est. #271, opened in 1834. See also his succession, Est. #341, opened in 1837.

#118. NICOLAS HEBERT, DEC. 20 JUNE 1822

Decedent lately died intestate; survived by his 4 children by his marriage with Julie Prevost [daughter of Francois Prevost, Est. # 101]: 1. Modest, wife of Lewis Moore, Jr.; 2. Elizabeth, wife of Zennon Decuir; 3. Alexander; 4. Julie. Only the last named is not of age. Julie Hebert is an adult minor; her curator ad bona is Charles Olivier. Lewis DeBlanc, Jr. and Godefroy Provost are appointed appraisers.

Gen. note. Bodin tells us [I 206] that decedent was a son of Joseph Hebert and Francoise Hebert and that he married Julie Prevost 22 Jan. 1795 at Opelousas. The same source gives the following information: Modiste was born 3 Jan. 1796; Elizabeth, born 3 Aug. 1798; Alexander, born 8 Oct. 1800, married Marie Celine Barras; and Julie, born 28 Oct. 1802, married Louis Eloi DeBlanc.

#119. PIERRE GUILLAUME ETIE, DEC. 31 MAY 1822

Decedent lately died and left a widow, Eulalie Massicot, and 1 child, Pierre, an infant. Eulalie is his mother and natural tutrix. William Desk and Charles Pecot appointed appraisers. See also Civil suit #362, Charles Joseph Antoine of St. Martin Parish vs. Widow and heirs of Pierre Etie, Sr., filed 14 June 1822.

Gen. note. Decedent was a son of Pierre Etier and Victoire Borel, born 28 Oct. 1797. See Est. #110 and Bodin II 94. He married Eulalie Massicot, daughter of Charles Massicot of St. Charles Parish, 8 Feb. 1820 [Marriage Book 1, page 190]. See also Est. #113.

#120. LOUIS LULI DEL BRUNET, DEC. 13 SEPT. 1822

Will (French). Probated on above date. Date signed not apparent to compiler. Alexander Freme and Charles Pecot testify to the will.

Decedent died in this parish. Frederick Pellerin executor.

24 Aug. 1823. Alexander Freme and _____ appointed appraisers. This succession is especially difficult to read.

#121. LUCILE PREVOST, WIFE OF LUFROY PROVOST, DEC. 21 JUNE 1822

Decedent lately died, leaving 2 children by her marriage with Lufroy Provost: Lufroy and Edmond Provost, both minors. Frederick Pellerin and Lewis Moore, Jr., appointed appraisers. See also succession of Lufroy Provost, Est. # 222, opened 23 May 1832.

*#122. ALFRED THRUSTON, DEC. 11 FEB. 1822

Will written in the City of New Orleans. Signed 3 Feb. 1821; probated above date. Testator has no ascendants or descendants. Leaves estate to wife, Elizabeth Thruston, and to her heirs. She to be executrix and Donelson Caffery to be executor. Codicile dated 4 June 1821: "I do agree with my brother Edmund Taylor Thruston to abide by the will of my late father, Charles Minns Thruston, as valid." As of this writing, the will of Charles Mynns Thruston has not been located by the compiler. [See page 175.]

4 Apr. 1822. Lewis Moore, Jr. and John Clark appointed appraisers; George Singleton, Jr., and Isaac L. Baker witness. See Est. #140 for outline of this family.

Alfred Thruston was married to Elizabeth Hudson, daughter of Francis Hudson (Est. #97) and Elizabeth Patterson. The Thrustons were married 13 Dec. 1818 [Marriage Book 1, page 161]. She remarried Thomas H. Thompson, apparently in the late 1820's. See Est. #97.

*#123. MICHAEL HAYES, DEC. 29 AUG. 1823

Petitioner is Rosalie Derouen, widow of decedent, who lately died intestate leaving 10 children, all minors. Apparently petitioner was mother of all the children: 1. Michael, 2. Polly, 3. Agatha, 4. Marcelite, 5. David, 6. John,

7. Marie Caroline, 8. Onezime, 9. Eliza, 10. Delezin. Fam. meeting: Jacques Derouen, John Hays, David Hays (these 3 uncles of minors); Honore Carlin and Celestin Carlin, both friends of the minors. Alexis Carlin named undertutor.

Gen. note. Agatha Hayes married Thomas Bell 7 Jan. 1827 [Marriage Book 1, page 404]. An Elizabeth Hayes married Joseph Ferguson 14 June 1839 [Marriage Book 3, page 28]. Mary Ann Hayes married John N. Kershaw, Jr., 5 Feb. 1829 [Marriage Book 1, page 445]. His succession was opened in 1832, Est. #233.

#124. JOSEPH MARTIN, DEC. 8 MAR. 1823
Will. Sgd. 24 Feb. 1823; probated 17 Mar. 1823. Mentions an only son, Joseph Voltair Martin, aged about 6 months. Mentions also the widow of John Louis Hebert and her children. Witnesses: James L. Johnson, Nicolas Loisel, and Ursin Bourgeois. The widow mentioned was Rosalin Hebert. Charles Olivier named curator of estate, as the will was disallowed.

#125. HILAIRE BOREL, DEC. 19 SEPT. 1823
Petitioner is Hortance Provost, widow of decedent, mother and natural tutrix of the minor children of decedent: 1. Hilaire, 2. Elmore or Elmino, 3. Belliza Borel, decedent's legal heirs. Pierre Borel is undertutor. Nicolas Loisel and Lewis Moore, Jr., appointed appraisers. Fam. meeting: Benjamin Borel, Eugene Borel, "uncles of said minors by the paternal side"; Lufroy Prevost and Philemon Prevost, "uncles of said minors by the maternal side"; and Nicolas Loisel, relation of said minors [does not specify].

2 June 1827. Hortance now wife of Philip Vernice [?].

Gen. note. Hortance Provost was a daughter of Nicolas Provost. See his succession, Est. # 95. This decedent is probably a son of Joseph [Francois] Borel and his wife, Elizabeth Andres. See his succession, Est. #55, opened in 1817, and also the succession of Pierre Borel, probably also a son of Joseph [Francois] Borel, Est. #376, opened in 1838.

Hortense Provost was born 15 May 1798, a daughter of Nicolas Provost and Marie Jeanne Prevost, married Hilaire Borel 12 Apr. 1814 [Bodin II 27, 197].

*#126. LUFOI PROVOST, UNDERTUTOR, VS. HERBERT PELERIN, NATURAL TUTOR [NOT A SUCCESSION]

14 Feb. 1823. Lufoi Provost, undertutor of minor heirs of Herbert Pellerin: 1. Nicolas, 2. Eleonide, 3. Herbert, 4. Julie, 5. Badthazer, 6. Caliste, 7. Octave Pellerin; all of St. Mary Parish and children of the deceased Julie Prevost, wife of Herbert Pellerin.

14 June 1823. Fam. meeting: Madame Veuve [Widow] Marie Prevost, grandmother of said minors; maternal uncles: Godfroy Prevost, Nicolas Philemon Prevost; Lefroi Carlin and Celestin Carlin, friends. Ursant Provost appointed tutor. See also Est. #95 and succession of decedent, Est. #129, Julie Provost, opened 20 Aug. 1821.

*#127. PETER ROBERT, DEC. 18 JUNE 1823

9 Sept. 1820. Mary Ann Robert Scott, wife of Samuel E. Scott, one of the heirs of Elizabeth Robert, deceased late wife of Peter Robert; also Elizabeth J., wife of Peter W. Robert; Sarah A., wife of Michael Gordy; and Martha E., wife of Baynard C. Robert.

18 June 1823. Decedent lately died intestate and left as heirs his widow, Mary Robert, and 6 children: 1. Mary Ann, wife of Samuel E. Scott; 2. Elizabeth J., wife of Peter W. Robert; 3. Sarah A., wife of Michael Gordy; 4. Martha E., wife of Baynard C. Robert; 5. Peter Hickock/Hilkiah Robert [children by decedent's first marriage], and 6. Harriet Robert, by his second marriage. Peter Wilkinson Robert, above, husband of Elizabeth J. Robert,(apparently they were cousins) appointed curator ad bona of Peter Hickock Robert, an adult minor.

24 June 1823. Peter W. Robert and Michael Gordy

surety; Samuel E. Scott and John Rice witnessed. Lloyd Wilcoxon and John Rice appointed appraisers; Thomas J. Makin and Samuel E. Scott witnessed. Mary Robert, Samuel E. Scott, Michael Gordy, P. W. Robert, Baynard C. Robert, John Rice, Peter H. Robert signed division of estate.

25 June 1823. John Rice curator for Peter H. Robert.

Gen. note. Peter Robert was born in 1768 in South Carolina; moved to Beaufort Co., S. C. About 1790 married Elizabeth Jaudon, born 13 Nov. 1774 in South Carolina. Peter Robert, possibly Peter Hickock Robert, married Louise Armstrong 12 July 1824 [Marriage Book 1, page 271]. She was probably a daughter of Margaret Armstrong, Est. #185, opened in 1830.

#128. JULIAN FORTIN, DEC. 26 APR. 1823

Decedent lately died intestate and left no heirs in the state and a small estate. He died at the residence of Nicolas Broussard. Jared Y. Sanders and James Muggah appointed appraisers; Samuel Cochran and N. M. Cochran witnessed. Nicolas Broussard appointed curator of vacant estate of decedent.

17 May 1823. Buyers at sale: Julian LeBlanc, David Robbins, Nicolas Broussard, Lufroy Carlin, James Muggah, Charles Charpantier, Daniel P. Sparks, Mrs. Lewis Moore, John B. Bonvillain [Bonmaison?], Mrs. Conrad Hartman, Peter Hartman, Joseph Clement, Samuel Cochran.

27 May 1825. Jean Julian Fortin had a mother and sisters in New Orleans, but they are not named herein.

*#129. JULIE PROVOST, DEC. 20 AUG. 1821

Julie Provost, wife of Hubert Pellerin, has died intestate and left 7 children by her marriage with Hubert Pellerin, her legal heirs: 1. Nicolas Louis, 2. Eleonide, 3. Hubert, 4. Jules, 5. Baltezer, 6. Calisete, 7. Octave Pellerin. They are all minors under the age of 14 years. Hubert Pellerin, their father, is their natural

tutor. Charles W. Olivier and Louis DeBlanc fils
appointed appraisers. Said children are heirs of
the ancestor, Nicolas Provost [Est. #95, their
grandfather, being the father of their mother, said
decedent]. Fam. meeting: Mary [Marie] Provost,
grandmother; Godefroy Prevost, Lufroy Prevost,
John De Arby, Nicolas Loisel [relationships not
stated]. Francis DeMarc Darby appointed undertutor. All are relations of said minors.
  9 Oct. 1822. Another Fam. meeting: Madam Mary
Provost, Ursin Provost, Philemon Provost, Nicolas
Loisel and Elenor, his wife; Hilaire Borel and
Hortence, his wife; Godfroy Provost.
  Gen. note. Nicolas Louis Pellerin married
Uphumie Dartes 19 Jan. 1832 [Marriage Book 2,
page 23]. See also Est. #126.
  #130. MARIE SAUNIE, ALIAS MADAME CONSTANT,
DEC. 28 APR. 1824
  Mary Saunie, widow of the late Constant
Cavalier, has lately died and left 5 children her
legal heirs: 1. Constance Cavalier, wife of Julian
Durand; 2. Ursin, over 21; 3. Celeste, a minor
above the age of puberty; 4. Marcelin, and 5.
Valsin, the last 2 being minors under the age of
puberty. Fam. meeting: Constance Cavalier, sister
of minors; Ursin Cavalier, brother; Marie Eroin
[?] Saunie, grandmother of said minors; Jean
Baptiste Saunie, uncle; Julian Durand, brother-in-
law of minors. Honore Carlin appointed tutor;
Celestin Carlin undertutor. Celeste, an adult
minor, chooses Honore Carlin for her curator ad
bona and Celestin Carlin for her curator ad litem.
Honore Carlin and Joseph Guedry make bond for the
estate. Celestin Carlin and Charles Trufer [?]
appointed appraisers of the estate.
  #131. HILAIRE BOREL, DEC. 28 NOV. 1823
  Pierre Borel is curator of vacant estate of
Hilaire Borel, deceased, late of St. Mary Parish.
Fam. meeting: Godfroy Prevost, Lufroy Prevost,
Nicolas Loisel, Hubert Pellerin, Philemon Prevost.
No heirship or settlement of this estate is shown.
This may be a segment of Est. #125, above.

No heirship or settlement is shown.

#132. JOSEPH GERHARDSTEIN, DEC. 24 SEPT. 1824

Peter H. Rentrop petitions that decedent died 21 Sept. intestate and left no heirs in the state. This is a vacant estate. Peter H. Rentrop and Henry Rentrop sureties for estate. Lufroy Carlin and Joseph Berwick appointed appraisers.

30 Dec. 1824. Buyers at sale: Lefroi Carlin, David Robins, Henry Renthrop, Amos Merell, Peter H. Renthrop, Henry Knight, Godefroy Prevost; S. Cochran and Nathaniel M. Cochrane witnessed.

#133. JOHN BAPTISTE BERTRAND, JR., DEC. 19 AUG. 1824

Decedent died intestate, leaving a widow, Celeste Miller, and 3 minor children: 1. Hebert, 2. Lastie, 3. Calista Bertrand, by his marriage with the said Celeste Miller, who is their natural tutrix. Inventory taken at the residence of Jacob Miller; Joseph Charpantier and Charles Therio appointed appraisers. Fam. meeting: Jacob Miller, grandfather; Sophia [Offman, or Hoffman, Bodin I 302] Miller, grandmother; Sophia Miller, wife of Jesse Tomblinson, and Margaret Miller, aunts of minors; and John Baptiste Miller, uncle.

2 Oct. 1824. Buyers at sale: Nicolas Broussard, Julian Lablasan, Antoine Bertrand, Celeste Miller, Ursin Prevost, Lufroy Carlin; Lufroy Carlin and William Rochel witnessed. Antoine Bertrand identified as the minors' uncle. Celeste Miller married John Felteman and then after his death married Hypolite Magnian [or Maganow, Magnon].

21 July 1838. Antoine Bertrand appointed tutor, Hypolite Maganow undertutor to Lastie Bertrand and Calista Bertrand. Antoine Bertrand and Hubert Bertrand securities.

Gen. note. Decedent is identified as the son of Jean Baptiste Bertrand and Marguerite Schnexnayder; he married Celeste Miller 17 May 1813 at St. Martinville. Antoine was another son of the above couple. See Bodin I 38.

Celeste Miller was a daughter of Jacob Miller and Sophia Hoffman. She remarried (2) John Louis Felteman 5 Sept. 1824 [Marriage Book 1, page 281] and (3) Hypolite Magnon 1 Feb. 1834 [Marriage Book 2, page 49]. See also her mother's succession, Est. #144, opened in 1826.

Calise Bertrand married Auguste Frederick Rentrop, son of Frederick William Rentrop and Marie Marguerite Liqueur 14 Apr. 1841 [Marriage Book 3, page 40]. See succession of his grandfather, Henry Rentrop [Est. #214], opened in 1832.

#134. JOHN N. KERSHAW, SR., DEC. 15 MAY 1824

Decedent left among other children one minor son, Samuel A. Kershaw, one of the legal heirs. Fam. meeting: Levi Foster, John B. Murphy, Anthony Walker, Solomon Baker, Joseph Allen. Jonathan Smith also signed. All friends of the minor, in default of family. James Dupree appointed tutor of Samuel and curator ad bona of: 1.Thomas B. Kershaw, 2. Elizabeth G. Kershaw, 3. Nedham V. Kershaw, adult minor children and heirs of John N. Kershaw, Sr. They picked Jonathan Smith as their curator ad litem.

1 June 1824. Jonathan Smith represented his wife, Mary Ann Kershaw, and John N. Kershaw, children and legal heirs of decedent, over 21 years of age. They name James Dupree their true and lawful attorney in fact.

31 May 1824. John B. Murphy and George Allen appointed appraisers. Buyers at sale: George Allen, John N. Kershaw, William Walker, Jonathan Smith, Winthrop S. Harding, Hilaire Carlin, Lloyd Collins, Jehu Wilkinson, James Dupree, Francis Lefort [?].

Gen. note. Decedent was in St. Martin Parish records as early as 1806. Nothing further is known of him by compiler at this writing. His wife is not mentioned in the succession and since the minor son, Samuel, had a tutor other than his mother, it may be presumed that she had predeceased her husband. To recapitulate, decedent was survived by 6 children: 1. Mary Ann, wife of Jonathan Smith. For his background, see Est. #44. Mary Ann Kershaw's succession was opened in 1837 [Est. #344];2. John N. Kershaw, Jr., who married Mary Ann Hayes 5 Feb. 1829 [Marriage Book 1, page 445];his succession was opened in 1832, Est. #233; 3. Thomas B. Kershaw, who married Pelagie Borel, probably a daughter of Joseph Borel and Elizabeth Andres [see his succession, Est. #55, opened in 1817]; her succession is Est. #476, opened in 1842. Also see succession of Pierre Borel, Est. #376, 1838; 4. Elizabeth Grace Kershaw, who had a cattle brand registered in her name in 1819 [Vol. II]; Betsy Kershaw married Nathan Bouton [or Banton]17 Aug. 1828 [Marriage Book 1, page 432]; 5. Nedham V. Kershaw; Vardelle N. Kershaw had a cattle brand registered in his name in 1817 [Vol. II]; and 6. Samuel A. Kershaw.

#135A. SARAH MOORE, LATE WIFE OF LOUIS MOORE, SR., DEC. 11 JUNE 1824

Decedent has lately died intestate, leaving 5 children by a former marriage with the late Solomon Andrews, deceased, her legal heirs, all 21 years of age or over: 1. Rachel, wife of James L. Johnson [see Estates #196 and 211, their successions]; 2. James; 3. Ann, wife of Nicholas Edgar; 4. Joseph; 5. Lavinia, wife of John C. Clark. Thomas Wilcoxon and Daniel P. Sparks appointed appraisers.

Gen. note. The surname of decedent's first husband is written in south Louisiana records interchangeably as "Andrews" and "Andrus." Other spellings appear to be "Andres" and "Andress." Solomon Andrews was dead by 14 Feb. 1808, when his succession was opened in St. Martin Parish. This succession contains an inventory only and possibly was opened at the time of the widow's remarriage to Louis Moore, Sr. This is Est. # 17, St. Martin Parish. It is of no help in determining the origin of this surname. There is a strong possibility that Solomon Andrews/Andrus was a brother of Susan Andres/Andrews, a daughter of Benjamin Andres/Andrews of Virginia and Mary Hartgreve [Bodin II 3]. See succession of Jesse E. Lacy, Est. #114. Susan's sons William Lacy and Benjamin Lacy are named as cousins to Solomon's grandchildren, minor children of Rachel Andrews/Andrus and James L. Johnson. [See Est. #196]. Another of Benjamin's daughters, Elizabeth, married Joseph Borel, son of Pierre and Catherine Toupart [Bodin II 3, 27], and their brother, Jean Baptiste Andrus, married Anastasie Savoie at Opelousas [Bodin II 3].

Joseph Andrus/Andrews married Rachel Nicholson 28 Dec. 1820 [Marriage Book 1, page 232] and Lise Borel, 2 May 1825 [Marriage Book 1, page 298], ostensibly the same individual, probably the son of this decedent.

See also succession of decedent's second husband, Lewis Moore, Sr., Est. #202, opened in 1831.

#135B. CELESTE CARLIN, LATE WIFE OF JACOB HAIFLEIGH, DEC. 19 APR. 1825

Jacob Haifleigh states in petition that in 1816 he was married to Celeste Carlin and that in 1822 she died intestate leaving 1 son, William F[rederick] Haifleigh, now about 4 years of age. Evan Bowles appointed undertutor to William Frederick Haifleigh.

27 Sept. 1822. Evan Bowles and Joseph Theall appointed appraisers.

Gen. note. Decedent was a daughter of Celestin Carlin, son of Joseph [Est. #1], and Marie Therese Provost, [Est. #61]. Mrs. Clyde Alpha gives us the information that Jacob Haifleigh was a son of Frederick Haifleigh of Ohio. He remarried Elizabeth Riddle 20 Jan. 1825 [Marriage Book 1, page 287].

See also Est. #242, the succession of Celestin Carlin, opened in 1833.

#135C. CAESAR DOLLY, DEC. 29 JAN. 1825
Inventory taken at the residence of Charles Pecot on 29 Jan. 1825 with Theodore Fay and August Ragney witnessing.

8 Apr. 1825. Buyers at sale: Joseph Allen, Alexander Frere, Sylvain Salles, A. Robin, John M. Andee, Abram Burneur [Bonheur?], Jefferson Caffery, Nicolas Loisel, Levi Foster.
There are some documents in this succession which the compiler could not read. There is no heirship apparent.

*#136. EDMUND TAYLOR THRUSTON, DEC. 17 JULY 1823
Frederick D. Conrad of New Orleans, nephew of decedent, states decedent recently died in St. Martin Parish. There is mention of a will which has been opened and proved in St. Martin Parish, but a copy of it is not included herein. Decedent left one only child, Martha, a female minor under the age of 12 years. David Weeks of St. Martin Parish named executor in the will. Charles M. Norton appointed tutor of the child in the will. He lives in Mississippi and has refused to act as tutor; he recommends Alfred T. Conrad of St. Mary Parish be so appointed.

4 Oct. 1823. David Weeks appointed curator. Lewis Moor[e], David Weeks, A. T. Conrad and Frederick D. Conrad sign St. Mary Parish inventory. Fam. meeting: Frederick D. Conrad, cousin; David Weeks, minor's connection by marriage; Lewis Moore, Nicholas Edgar, Joseph Andrews, Francois Borel, Benjamin Borel, Eugene Borel, the latter friends of said minor.

Alfred T. Conrad, her cousin, appointed tutor; Frederick D. Conrad, also her cousin, appointed her undertutor. Alfred Conrad and David Weeks security.

20 Jan. 1838. Winthrop S. Harding appointed Administrator of estate; states his wife was an heir [indicating Martha Thruston must have died.]

Gen. note. Decedent [of St. Mary Parish]

died in St. Martin Parish [at the residence of David Weeks], where his succession was opened 17 July 1823. This succession [Est. #485] contains only the will. Abstract of this will is below.

Will. Only child, Martha Goodman Thruston, sole and universal heir. Friend [and **nephew?**] Charles M. Norton of Adams Co., Miss., appointed her guardian. Nephew Frederick D. Conrad of New Orleans second choice as guardian. To share in this estate in case Martha Thruston died before marriage or she reaches the age of 21 years: John H. Norton and his brother, Charles M. Norton, sons of "my sister Sarah A. Norton"; Alfred T. Conrad and Frances Elizabeth Conrad, son and daughter of "my sister Frances Conrad, deceased." Friend David Weeks, Esq., executor. Signed 29 Apr. 1823. Probated St. Martin Parish 17 July 1823.

Sidney Norton, Sarah Norton, Louisa Norton, and Courtney Norton are listed in Probate Suit # 12, Nicholas Edgar of St. Landry Parish vs. Heirs of Edmund T. Thruston, filed 12 July 1826, as being heirs of this decedent. Martha Thruston must have been deceased by that time.

Decedent's sister Frances Thruston married Frederick Conrad of East Baton Rouge Parish. See her succession, Est. #80, opened in 1819. Alfred and Frederick Conrad, involved in this succession, were two of their children. Therefore, they were Martha Thruston's first cousins. David Weeks was married to another of their daughters, Mary Clara. Winthrop S. Harding was married to another of their daughters, Frances Elizabeth Conrad, mentioned in the decedent's will.

See also Estates #122, opened in 1822, and 140, opened in 1825, the successions of decedent's brother, Dr. Alfred Thruston, and his mother, Mrs. Ann Thruston.

#137. SOLOMON BAKER, DEC. 4 AUG. 1825
Nancy Baker, widow, petitions. Decedent died

intestate 27 July 1825 leaving no descendants, ascendants, or collateral relatives. Jeremiah Scanlon and John Scanlon appointed appraisers. A Nancy Baker married Thomas French 1 July 1826 [Marriage Book 1, page 338].

#138. ANNE FELICITE ARMAND, LATE WIFE OF AGRICOLE FUSELIER FILS, DEC. 4 JAN 1825

Agricole Fuselier fils natural tutor to his children under puberty: 1. Coralie, 2. Aime, 3. Aspudie [Elizabeth Anne Aspasie] Fuselier. Frederic Pellerin undertutor.
Coralie married St. Marc Darby, of St. Martin. Compiler was unable to read many of the documents included in this succession.

Gen. note. Agricole Fuselier fils was a son of Agricole Fuselier and his wife, Christine Berard, a daughter of Jean Berard and his wife, Anne Broussard. Agricole Fuselier was a son of Gabriel Fuselier de la Claire and his first wife, Jeanne Roman. Agricole Fuselier fils was married to Anne Felicite Armand 19 Aug. 1818 in St. James Parish, a daughter of Jean Baptiste Armand and his wife, Carmelite Cantrelle. They had 3 children, named in the succession. Aimee married John Chastant of St. James Parish; Elizabeth Anne Aspasie married Frederic Adrien Frere of St. Mary Parish. Agricole Fuselier fils married (2) Louise Dumartrait, daughter of Adrien Dumartrait and Louise Pouponne Grevemberg of St. Martin Parish. They had 2 children: Gabriel Agricole Fuselier and Marie Louise Fuselier. [1774 Census.] There is additional information on the background of the Fuselier family in this fine work, p.37-38.

#139. ISAAC REED, DEC. 25 JAN. 1825

Julia Anne Reed, an adult minor daughter, is legal heir of decedent and Leticia Reed, deceased. She chose George Royster as her curator ad bona. Meeting of friends on behalf of the minor, in lieu of relatives, composed of: John J. Garret, Rufus Nickelson, William Kemper, George Cowen and Peyton R. Splane. Lloyd Wilcoxon curator ad litem.

George Royster and Nathan Kemper were security for this estate.

Gen. note. Julia Ann Reed married Benjamin Hudson, son of Francis Hudson [Est. #97] and his wife, Elizabeth Patterson. Benjamin Hudson, ostensibly the same one, married Mary Ann Gordy 14 Mar. 1833 [Marriage Book 1, page 235]; so Julia Ann Reed must have died not long after her marriage, since she was married 6 May 1830 [Marriage Book 2, page 7]. It is not known if she was survived by issue.

*#140. MRS. ANN THRUSTON, DEC. 11 NOV. 1819

Will. Sons: Alfred Thruston and Edmund Taylor Thruston [testator does not call them "my sons" in the will]; mentions land she purchased from Samuel Richardson; husband, Charles Mynn Thruston; 2 granddaughters Sidney Ann Conrad and Elizabeth Frances Conrad. Executors, Alfred Thruston and Edmund Taylor Thruston. Sdg. 28 Apr. 1819. Witnesses: Alfred T. Conrad, George Singleton, Jr., Nicholas Edgar, John C. Clark, James L. Johnson. Submitted for probate 11 Nov. 1819; declared invalid according to the laws of Louisiana because she had other legal descendants who were forced heirs than those named in her will. James L. Johnson and Lewis Moore, Jr., appointed appraisers.

No final settlement shown.

Gen. note. Decedent was the second wife of the Rev. Charles Mynn Thruston, an Episcopal minister of Frederick Co., Va., the eldest of 10 children of Col. John Thruston of Gloucester Co., Va., a third-generation American, being the grandson of Edward Thruston "The Elder," who appears to have been in Virginia as early as 1666. For background of this family, see Early Virginians by Margaret Ann Buckner of Fredericksburg, Va., pages 175-178.

Col. John Thruston was born 24 Oct. 1709, died 20 Feb. 1766, and in 1737 married Sarah Mynn, the Widow Hanes, born in 1717 and died 12 May 1786 [Buckner, page 178]. The eldest of their 10 children was Charles Mynn Thruston, known as "The

Fighting Parson," born 6 Nov. 1738, the Miss. D. A. R. book tells us [page 309] in Gloucester Co., Va., and died in Louisiana in 1812.

The Rev. Thruston served in the Revolution as one of George Washington's original 16 colonels, and lost an arm at Amboy in 1777. He reputedly came to Mississippi in 1808 or 1810. Apparently his family came to Attakapas shortly after his death.

His first wife was Mary Buckner, daughter of Col. Samuel Buckner and his first wife, thought to have been Ann Alexander, probably sister of David Alexander [apparently of York Co., Va.; see Buckner, page 130]. Col. Samuel Buckner was a third-generation American, being grandson of Thomas Buckner [baptized Oxford, England, in 1628], thought to be brother of John and Philip Buckner, all 3 of whom came to Virginia. Thomas Buckner was here by 1669. His wife's identity is not known, but he had at least one son, Samuel. This Samuel's wife's identity is not known either, but he had at least 2 children, Ann and Samuel, the father of Mary Buckner who married Charles Mynn Thruston [see Buckner, page 130].

Mary Buckner was born in 1732, married in 1760 and died in 1765 [Buckner, page 131]. Buckner further tells us [page 179] that they had 3 sons and that her cousin, Ann Alexander, daughter of Col. Alexander of Gloucester Co., Va., took charge of the children and then became their step-mother. The Miss. D. A. R. book gives the date of their marriage [page 309] as 2 Feb. 1766.

The 3 sons of the Rev. Thruston by his first wife were:
1. John Thruston, born 15 Oct. 1761, died 15 Feb. 1802, married 13 Oct. 1782 his cousin, Elizabeth J. Whiting. He served in the Revolution and moved to Louisville, Ky. [Buckner, pages 179-180].
2. Judge Buckner Thruston, born 9 Feb. 1764 in Gloucester Co., Va.; served in the United States Senate from Kentucky beginning in 1805; died in Washington, D. C., 30 Aug. 1845; and is buried in

the Congressional Cemetery there [Biographical Directory of the American Congress, page 1714]. He married Janette January, daughter of Peter January of Kentucky, in 1798 [Buckner, page 180].
3. Charles Mynn Thruston, born 3 Aug. 1765; died 11 Dec. 1800; married 20 Jan. 1796 Frances Eleanor Clark, daughter of John Clark and the widow of Dr. James O'Fallon of Louisville, Ky. She was a sister of Gen. George Rogers Clark, famous western warrior of the Revolution, and William Clark of the Lewis and Clark western exploring team, later governor of Missouri. She was born in 1773, died in 1825 [Miss. D. A. R. book, page 309; and Buckner, page 180].

The 9 children of the Rev. Thruston and his second wife, Ann Alexander, this decedent, were:
1. Sarah Alexander Thruston, born 15 Dec. 1767 [this date is obviously incorrect in the book, where it is shown as 1776; the last 2 digits are obviously transposed]; married 17 Dec. 1784 George Flowarden/Flowerdew Norton of Winchester, Va. The Miss. D. A. R. book tells us he died in Marion Co., Miss. [page 309]. It is not known where or when Sarah died. The Miss. D. A. R. book gives 3 children for this couple [page 309]: 1. John Hatley Norton, who apparently died unmarried; 2. Charles Mynn Norton, who married Mary Poiner Terrell, younger sister of the wife of Edmund Taylor Thruston; and 3. an unnamed daughter who died unmarried in Louisiana. See succession of Edmund Taylor Thruston, Est. #136. Also see notes following will of the Rev. Thruston, page 178.
2. Frederick Thruston [see Est. #80], born 15 Mar. 1770; died unmarried in Louisiana before 1848.
3. Mary Buckner Thruston, born 31 July 1772; was living in 1848; married Col. Charles Magill of Winchester, Va.
4. Frances Thruston [see Est. #80], born 3 Feb. 1774; died 1813; married 25 Apr. 1793 Frederick Conrad of Winchester, Va.

5. Elizabeth Mynn Thruston, born 6 Apr. 1775; married 10 Aug. 1794 [William] Henry Daingerfield of Winchester, Va.

6. Alfred Thruston, born 14 May 1778. He married Elizabeth Hudson in St. Mary Parish 13 Dec. 1818 [Marriage Book 1, page 161]. She was a daughter of Francis Hudson [Est. #97] and Elizabeth Patterson. After his death she remarried Thomas H. Thompson. Alfred Thruston was a doctor and served a while in the U. S. Army. He died in the early part of 1822 in St. Mary Parish. His succession is Est. #122, opened 11 Feb. 1822.

7. Louisa Thruston, born 23 Mar. 1782; married in 1797 Capt. Edmund H. Taylor of Louisville, Ky., possibly a relative. This is probably the family after whom Edmund Taylor Thruston was named.

8. Sydney Ann Thruston, born 2 May 1783; died 12 Sept. 1803; married Alfred Powell of Winchester, Va.

9. Edmund Taylor Thruston, born 24 Oct. 1785; married in September of 1812 Sarah Terrell, daughter of Micajah Terrell [Miss. D. A. R. book, pages 302-304]. See page 173 herein. Edmund Taylor Thruston died in the early summer of 1823 in St. Martin Parish. His succession is Est. #136 of St. Mary Parish. He and his wife were survived by one daughter, Martha Goodman Thruston, but not for very long. See his succession.

Because the families of the Rev. Thruston have been confused and because of the prominence of these people and their descendants, I am giving herein the will of the Rev. Thruston, which mentions exactly one-half of his children. I am indebted to Mr. Sidney L. Villere of New Orleans for this copy of the will.

[Unless otherwise specified, the above information on the children of the Rev. Thruston is from the Buckner book, pages 179-182.]

[Continued on page 175]

#141. BLANK

#142. JAMES THOMAS, DEC. 2 OCT. 1820
Will. Mentions 4 children: 1. Mary, 2. Owen, 3. Sophia, and 4. Peyton Thomas. Brother, Alexander Thomas, "at present in the State of Georgia" appointed administrator and executor. Allen J. Key "to remain on the Island of Cote Blanche until my brother Alexander shall arrive from the State of Georgia." Executed and signed at the Island of Cote Blanche 15 Sept. 1820. Witnesses: George W. King, Henry Lockett, Joseph Theall, Allen J. Key. Pvd. 2 Oct. 1820.

5 Dec. 1820. Alexander Thomas sworn as Executor.

15 Jan. 1821. Jared Y. Sanders and Garland Cosby appointed appraisers; Winfrey Lockett and _____ witnessed.

17 Mar. 1821. Alexander Thomas, Winfrey Lockett, Joseph Theall, William Sterling, and Isaac L. Baker secutities. Alexander Thomas named curator of all 4 children.

Meeting of friends, the minors having no relations in this state: Dennis Carlin, Martin M. Campbell, Hilaire Carlin, Sempson Cox, James Ferguson.

17 Nov. 1824. Oglethorpe Co., Ga. Alexander Thomas recognized as minors' guardian [minors not named].

22 Nov. 1824. Micajah W. Thweatt and wife, Mary J., formerly Mary Jane Thomas, daughter of James Thomas, deceased, now of Baldwin Co., Ga., formerly of Hancock Co., Ga.

Peyton Thomas died in 1831 unmarried. See his succession, Est. #200, opened in 1831.

#143. WILLIAM BOYCE, DEC. 8 NOV. 1825
Will. No legal heirs. Buckingham F. Wells executor. Undated. Witnesses: Robert Nash Ogden,

Winfrey Lockett, Winthrop S. Harding, James Wall
[?], John Hartman. Pvd. 8 Nov. 1825. Dr.
Buckingham F. Wells appointed executor.

21 Nov. 1825. Levi Foster and James Sanders
appointed administrators. Witnesses: James Foster,
Jr., and J. B. Murphy.

3 Dec. 1825. Buyers at sale: Winthrop S. Harding, Charles D. Brashear, Henry Nimmo, Hilaire
Carlin, Col. Foster. Witnesses: Joseph Theall and
Winfrey Lockett.

#144. SOPHIA MILLER, WIFE OF JACOB MILLER,
DEC. 28 SEPT. 1826

Decedent left 7 children, over 21 years of age:
1. John B.; 2. Sophia, wife of Jesse Tomblinson;
3. Margaret, wife of John B. Copel; 4. Celeste,
wife of John Louis Felteman; 5. Marie; 6. Madelin,
wife of Pierre Carrantine; and 7. Catherine, wife
of John B. Felteman. James Muggah, Charles M.
Charpantier, and Charles Farie [?] appointed
appraisers; witnesses: Julien LeBlanc and Lufroy
Carlin.

Gen. note. Decedent's maiden name was
Hoffman [Bodin I 302]. Jean Baptiste Miller was
married to Mary Rosalie Henry, widow of Joseph
Ring; see his succession, Est. #266, opened in
1834. Sophia Miller was married to Jesse
Tomlinson/Tompkins 23 Nov. 1815 [Marriage Book 1,
page 78]. His second wife was Adelle Julie
Broussard, married 13 Apr. 1830 [Marriage Book 2,
page 5]. See his succession with his first wife,
Est. #225, opened in 1832. Marguerite [Margaret]
Miller was born 4 May 1798 [Bodin II 172].

#145. JOHN W. BAKER, DEC. 1 MAR. 1826

Decedent died at the plantation of Isaac L.
Baker 22 Feb. 1826 intestate leaving no
descendants; 3 sisters and 1 brother "live in
Kentucky". They are not named herein.

13 Mar. 1826. John Towles and John B. Murphy
appointed appraisers. Isaac L. Baker and John
Towles are sureties. Isaac L. Baker appointed
curator.

17 May 1826. Buyers at sale: William Shaw, Joseph Allen, John Towles, Edmund Reeves, Joshua Gibson, Lewis Baker.

Gen. note. See the succession of Joshua G. Baker, Sr., Est. #15, for details about decedent.

#146. JOHN MURPHY, DEC. 25 SEPT. 1826

Decedent lately died intestate; his legal heirs are 3 children and 1 grandchild: 1. Thomas, who has left the state and present whereabouts are not now known; 2. Alexander Porter, grandson and heir in right of his deceased mother, Sarah Ann Murphy, deceased daughter of decedent and late wife of James A. Porter, residing in the state of Tennessee; which 2 absent heirs are represented by Robert Nash Ogden; 3. John B. Murphy; 4. Lydia Murphy, wife of Donelson Caffery. Agricole Fuselier and Evan Bowles appointed appraisers; witnesses: Winfrey Lockett and John J. Taylor.

Gen. note. Decedent's tombstone in the Franklin cemetery gives the information that he was born in Ireland in June of 1752 and died in August of 1824. His wife's identity is not known to compiler at this time. Est. #191 in St. Martin Parish is also that of a John Murphy. It is mostly in French. This decedent died 27 Mar. 1815 and his widow was Levinia Murphy. No heirship was apparent. Any connection between these 2 individuals is not known.

John Barrett Murphy, decedent's third child listed above, is also buried in the Franklin cemetery. His tomb states that he was born in North Carolina 9 Oct. 1800 and he died in Feb. of 1862. His first wife was Emma L. Taylor; her succession was opened in 1833, Est. #244. He remarried Mrs. Lucy Brown 10 May 1833. This date is taken from her tombstone, also in the Franklin cemetery, which gives her full name as Lucy Cross Brashier Murphy, born Long's Lick, Kentucky, 24 Nov. 1802, died 10 May 1886, married (1) Daniel W. Brown on 30 May 1825, (2) John B. Murphy.

Sarah Ann Murphy, wife of James A. Porter and

mother of Alexander Porter, "residing in the state of Tennessee," was probably buried in Tennessee. They may have resided in Nashville, and James A. Porter may have been a son of Alexander Porter, uncle of Alexander Porter, owner of Oaklawn Manor, who lived in Nashville. See <u>Oaklawn Manor</u> by Lucile Barbour Holmes (Franklin, La., 1968), page 1; and also <u>Alexander Porter, Whig Planter of Old Louisiana</u> by Wendell Holmes Stephenson for further information on this interesting family.

#147. <u>HENRIETTA BORREL. SALE OF PROPERTY BELONGING TO 1 MAR. 1826 [NOT A SUCCESSION]</u>

Auction of slaves belonging to Henrietta Borel, widow of Joseph Prevost, deceased. There are no further details. 2 slaves were bought by Madame Henrietta Borel and William Sterling. Witnesses: Lloyd Wilcoxon and _____. This is not a succession.

#148. <u>SUSAN LACY SPLANE, DEC. 8 MAY 1826</u>

Will. Decedent is the wife of Payton R. Splane. Father was Jesse E. Lacey. Husband to be executor. Witnesses: B. F. Wells, Levi Foster, and Alva Wright. Signed 4 Feb. 1826; probated 8 May 1826. She apparently left no descendants. See her father's succession, Est. #114, opened in 1821.

#149. <u>SAMUEL HENDLEY, DEC. 12 JAN. 1826</u>

Decedent lately died leaving no relatives in this parish or state.

26 Apr. 1826. Levi Foster and Jacob Haifleigh appointed appraisers. James Foster appointed curator.

#150. <u>SQUIRE POWEL, DEC. 26 FEB. 1826</u>

Decedent departed this life 22 Feb. 1826 at the residence of Frederick Pellerin. He died intestate. James L. Johnson, justice of the peace, made an inventory.

13 Apr. 1826. Frederick Pellerin and Gabriel L. Fuselier appointed appraisers. Isaac L. Baker and John B. Murphy were sureties. Isaac L. Baker appointed curator.

15 May 1826. Buyers at sale: Agricole Fuselier, Gabriel L. Fuselier, Joseph A. Lacy, William Green Powell, Solange Sorrel.

3 Apr. 1827. Martha Gibson, late Powell, of County of Scott, State of Kentucky, appoints her son Walker Powell, also of County of Scott, State of Kentucky, to recover estate of her deceased son, Squire Powell, deceased.

2 June 1827. Elizabeth Powell, wife of William Myers of Decatur Co., Ind., apparently sister of Walker and decedent. Walker is appointed attorney, but decedent's name is not mentioned in this document.

May Court, 1827, Scott Co., Ky. Rachel Powell, infant of Martha Powell and over 14 years of age; Walker Powell appointed guardian; also appointed guardian of John Powell, infant of Martha Powell under the age of 14 years. Squire Powell stipulated brother of these minors, Rachel and John Powell.

#151. WILLIAM STONE, DEC. 30 SEPT. 1826

Euphemie Craig, widow of decedent, natural tutrix of Davis A. Craig Stone; father of this minor was decedent; under the age of puberty.

12 Oct. 1826. Isaac Randolph appointed undertutor.

13 Oct. 1826. Fam. meeting for this minor: Antoine LeBlanc, Edward LeBlanc, Norbert LeBlanc, Clite LeBlanc, and Milledge McCale, all friends, apparently in lieu of relatives.

12 Oct. 1826. Decedent had 2 sons by a former marriage: 1. Samuel, a minor over the age of puberty; 2. William Stone, a minor under the age of puberty - both residing in the state of New York represented by John Brownson.

Plantation of decedent located on the Island of Petit Ance.

John Hayes and David Hayes appointed appraisers.

10 July 1827. John C. Marsh appointed curator to the other 2 sons.

Gen. note. Euphemie Craig married (2) John C. Marsh; see his succession, Est. #320, opened in 1836.

#152. PIERRE BOUTTE, F. M. C., DEC. 14 NOV. 1826

Will in French. Brothers Louis Hylaire Boutte and Phillepot Boutte, Executors. Charles Olivier and Maximilian Decuir appointed appraisers. No legal heirs mentioned, other than in the will.

#153. EMELIE PELERIN, LATE WIFE OF FRANCOIS PIERRE SIGUR, DEC. 11 SEPT. 1826

Parish of Iberville. Decedent lately died intestate in said parish of Iberville, leaving 9 children by her marriage with Francois Pierre Sigur: 1. Laurent; 2. Felicite, wife of Charles Pecot; 3. Elagie [?], wife of Theodore Fay, residing in St. Mary Parish; 4. Edward; 5. Alexander; 6. Treville [?]; 7. Numa; 8. Amemaide; 9. Adelaide, wife of Ambrose Colerin Dubriel, residing in the Parish of Iberville. Agricole Fuselier and Nicolas Loisel appointed appraisers.

Petition and inventory only in this succession.

Gen. note. Decedent married Francois Pierre Sigur 13 Nov. 1788; he was son of Laurent Sigur and his wife, Anne Roche. Decedent was a daughter of Gregoire Pellerin and his wife, Cecelia Prejean. [1774 Census, pages 41-2; for additional information on these families, see these pages]. Also see Est. #17, the succession of Marie-Joseph Pellerin, sister of this decedent. Charles Pecot's succession [Est. #574] was opened in 1845. Aminaide Sigur's succession [Est. #582] was opened in 1846.

#154. JACOB NOPPER, DEC. 29 APR. 1826

Decedent lately died intestate. His widow, Margaret Ring, requests inventory. Decedent left no heirs ascending or descending. Brother John Nopper, deceased, left 3 children: 1. Augustine, 2. Adelaide, 3. Marcelin Nopper, heirs of Jacob Nopper by representing their father. James Muggah and Nicolas Broussard appointed appraisers.

Celeste Saunie is the widow of John Nopper.
10 July 1826. She is natural tutrix to her minor children, 1. Adelaide and 2. Marcelin Nopper, children and heirs of her said husband, John Nopper, deceased. Augustine Nopper, one of the said heirs, is over 21 years of age.

Gen. note. Adelaide Nopper married Jacob Charite. [See Est. #50, opened in the name of J. Charel in 1816.] They were married 15 Oct. 1827 [Marriage Book 1, page 385].

7 Sept. 1826. Fam. meeting for 2 minors: Peter H. Rentrop, Thomas Wilcoxon, Lufroy Carlin, David Robbins, Peter Hartman, friends, ostensibly in lieu of any relatives in the area.

Buyers at sale: Peter Hartman, Jacob Jarret [Charite, Charel, etc.], William Collins, George Haydel, James McMurtry, Louis Daigle, Anthony Hartman, David Robins, Placide Palaski, Margaret Ring, Charles Farie [?], Jean Baptiste Broussard, Jacob Miller, Hypolite Magnon, William Rochel, Lufroy Carlin, Jean Loulon [?], Tarance [?] Burris [?], Daniel P. Sparks, James Andrews/Andrus, Augustine Nopper, Martin Lanore [?], John Martin, Samuel Cochran, Thomas Wilcoxon.

#155. ANN EDGAR'S PROPERTY; SALE AT AUCTION 2 JUNE 1827 [NOT A SUCCESSION]

Property of Ann Andrus, wife of Nicholas Edgar, now of the Parish of St. Landry. Buyers at sale: Benjamin Borel, Jean Baptiste Boulerice [?], James L. Johnson, Joseph Andrus, Charles St. Pierre, Charles Hebert, John C. Clark, Louis E. DeBlanc, Lewis Moore, Jr.

#156. JOSEPH ALLAIN [ALLEN]; SALE OF PROPERTY BELONGING TO ESTATE OF 16 JUNE 1827 [NOT A SUCCESSION]

[States so done at his request]. Buyers at sale: Henry Foote, Evan Bowles, James _____, Celestin Carlin, Joseph Alain, Honore Carlin, Stephen Babarino, Winfrey Lockett, Philip Vernice, Ursin Carlin, Jefferson Caffery, Jehu Wilkinson, Francis Lufert.

#157. JOHN LEES, DEC. 2 FEB. 1827

Widow is Hester [Esther, Easter] Lees; 4 children by his marriage with said Hester, his legal heirs: 1. Rosanne, wife of William Branner, over 21 years of age; 2. James, a minor over the age of puberty; 3. John and 4. Maria, both minors under the age of puberty, represented by their mother, the said Hester Lees, their tutrix. Decedent died intestate. James Sanders, Sr., and Matthew Nimmo appointed appraisers.
This succession appears to be incomplete. There is no legal proof apparent to the compiler that Hester Lees is the mother of the 2 older children. [They married in 1806. Civil Suit #351]

Gen. note. Mrs. Esther Lees, a native of Maryland, died 28 Nov. 1853, aged "about 80." [Planters 'Banner, 1 Dec. 1853, page 3, col. 3.]

#158. FRANCOIS CEZAR [CASSAR] BOUTTE, PERE, DEC. 8 OCT. 1827

Decedent "of the Parish of Iberville" died in said parish and succession opened there. Frederic Pellerin and Charles Olivier are curators named in will, filed in Iberville Parish and not included herein. Inventory in Parish of St. Mary made at the residence of Baron Bayard. Louis DeBlanc and Claude Frilot appointed appraisers.

5 Dec. 1827. Buyers at sale: Nicolas Loisel, Baron Bayard, Francois C. Boutte, Francois Legnon.

One document in French.

See also Estates #48 and 69.

Gen. note. Decedent was a son of Andre Claude Boutte and Francoise Bodin dit Miragrouin. For details of this family, see page 44 of the 1774 Census. Decedent married Marie Therese De Gruys 12 July 1778. They were the parents of at least 3 children: 1. Francois Cezar Boutte fils, who was born 18 May 1780. On 5 Jan. 1803 he signed a marriage contract with Marie Louise Celeste Gonsoulin, native of Attakapas, born 9

Sept. 1780, a daughter of Jean Francois Gonsoulin (who died in St. Martin Parish in 1819) and Marie Louise Celeste de la Gautrais [DeVille, page 30, and Family Tree - see below for full title]. Marie Louise Celeste Gonsoulin was the first of 13 children born to this couple. For further details of this family, see <u>Family Tree of Heirs in Suit 29,145 of St. Mary Parish: Louisiana State Mineral Board vs. Marie B. Abadie et als</u> in the Office of the Clerk of Court of that parish, in Franklin. The marriage of Francois Cezar Boutte fils and Marie Louise Celeste Gonsoulin appears to be the same marriage recorded in French 10 Sept. 1807 as the first marriage in St. Mary Parish, Marriage Book 1, page 1.

#2. Marie Hortense Boutte, who married (1) Achile Berard [see his succession, Est. #48] and (2) Benoist Baron Bayard.

[Continued on page 184]

#159. MARIE THERESE DEGRUY, LATE WIFE OF ABOVE DECEDENT, DEC.

This succession is entitled "late wife of Pierre Boutte." The compiler feels this is an error and the estate, probably filed at the same time as the one immediately above, is the succession of the wife of Francois Cezar Boutte, <u>pere</u>, probably misread as Pierre Boutte. It is entirely in French. For a complete record of these successions, please refer to the Office of the Clerk of Court, Iberville Parish, Plaquemine, La. They should be of record there, though they may not be in good condition.

#160. WILLIAM LYON, DEC. 25 SEPT. 1828

Joseph Theall petitions. Decedent lately died intestate leaving no heirs in the state. Estate consists of personal property. Joseph Theall appointed curator of vacant estate. Joseph Theall, Isaac L. Baker, Robert Trousdale, and Winfrey Lockett appointed appraisers at the house of Mason Harper in Franklin, where decedent died.

No heirship is shown.

#161. GEORGE SINGLETON, SR., DEC. 15 NOV. 1828

Decedent lately died in St. Mary Parish. One of his legal heirs, Owen Singleton, resides in the State of Kentucky. John W. Singleton, another of his heirs "attended at plantation where said deceased resided at time of his death." Witnesses: James L. Johnson and Benjamin Lacy. John W. Singleton appointed curator.

2 Nov. 1829. James L. Johnson and Lewis Moore, Jr., appointed appraisers; witnesses: William Hutchings and Joseph E. Johnson.

3 Nov. 1819. Petition of Owen Singleton of Wayne Co., Ky., gives major heirs of decedent: 1. John W. Singleton, 2. George Singleton, 3. Sidney Singleton, 4. Washington Singleton, 5. Jefferson Singleton. The 6th heir, minor brother of the above 5, is Wesley Singleton, all now of St. Mary Parish. Real estate is included in this succession. John W. Singleton appointed curator ad bona of minor, George Singleton appointed his curator ad litem.

24 Dec. 1833. Owen Singleton now of Randolph Co., Mo.

#162. JOSEPH HEMPHILL, DEC. 29 AUG. 1828

Decedent late of the City of Philadelphia, Penna., has lately died in St. Mary Parish and has no heirs resident in the State of Louisiana; died at the plantation of Mr. Washington Jackson. Seals affixed to personal belongings of decedent in the presence of John B. Theall and John E. Carson, Jr. Donelson Caffery appointed curator of sealed items.

6 Jan. 1829. Seals removed in the presence of Donelson Caffery and John Smith. John Brownson appointed curator of said estate and Alexander R. Splane attorney of absent heirs. Donelson Caffery and John B. Theall appointed apprasiers. John Brownson and Donelson Caffery sureties for estate.

Jane Hemphill, widow, is mother of the

decedent; Matthew Hemphill, brother of decedent. Both are of Galway, County of Londonderry in Ireland. Samuel Hemphill of Denymore, also of the County of Londonderry, Ireland, is another brother. James Willson of Philadelphia is an uncle of decedent.

#163. JULIE ANN ROBBINS, LATE WIFE OF JAMES MUGGAH, DEC. 3 SEPT. 1828

Decedent lately died intestate leaving 7 children by her marriage with James Muggah her legal heirs: 1. John, 2. James, 3. Henry, 4. David, 5, Charles, 6. Samuel, 7. Julie Ann Muggah, all minors. Joseph Charpantier and Peter H. Rentrop appointed appraisers. James Muggah tutor to minors, David Robbins undertutor. There is no record of a family meeting, and the relationship of David Robbins to the minors is not specified.

Gen. note. James Muggah married as a later wife Nancy Biggs, born Robbins, widow of William Biggs. See his successsion, Est. #116, opened in 1818. Perhaps Nancy and Julie Ann were sisters. Apparently James Muggah and Nancy Robbins had an only son, Thomas. See Planters Banner, 15 Sept. 1853, page 3, col. 4. John Muggah's succession was opened in 1856, Est. #932; that of Henry J.'s in 1856 also, Est. #933. Charles R. Muggah married Sarah _____ ; Planters' Banner, 6 Oct. 1853, page 3, col. 2. Julia Ann Muggah married the Rev. Stephen J. Davis of New Orleans in that city 12 June 1847; Planters' Banner, 24 June 1847, page 2, col. 4. A Stephen Davis had married Mary Jane Scudder in St. Mary Parish 21 Oct. 1845 [Marriage Book 3, page 100].

#164. CECILE ROSALIE SELENIE PELLERIN, LATE WIFE OF ANTOINE FRANCIS SELANGE SORREL, DEC. 18 OCT. 1828

Decedent died intestate leaving no children; Frederic Pellerin and Marie Ann Pecot, her father and mother, are still living; one sister, Coralie Pellerin, and one brother, Charles Frederic

Pellerin; these are her legal heirs. Gabriel L. Fuselier and Laurent Legnon appointed appraisers.

*#165. PIERRE DARTEST, DEC. 24 SEPT. 1828
Decedent recently died intestate; his widow is Julia Ann Legnon; 5 children of this marriage are his legal heirs: 1. Lovesgen [?], 2. Euphemie, 3. Nevell, 4. Ernestine, 5. Adrian Dartest, all minors. Real estate is included in this estate. Frederic Pellerin and Alexander Sigur appointed appraisers. Julia Ann, the widow, is natural tutrix of the minors; Joseph Legnon is undertutor of the 5 minors and the unborn infant with which the widow is now pregnant.

2 Feb. 1829. Fam. meeting: Louis Legnon and Eugene Legnon, uncles of minors; Eugenie Dartest, aunt of minors; Laurent Segur and John Armelin fils [?], friends of said minors.

19 Aug. 1833. Fam. meeting: Joseph Legnon, maternal uncle and undertutor; Louis and Eugene Legnon, maternal uncles; Nicolas Louis Pellerin [the minors' brother-in-law]; Jean Armelin [?]; and Laurent Sigur, friends. Julia Ann Legnon remarried to John Hawkins of St. Mary Parish. Lovesgen [?] is to be emancipated. Louis Legnon is tutor to Neville. Nicolas Louis Pellerin is tutor to Ernestine. Eugene Legnon, tutor to Adrian. Joseph Legnon remains undertutor. Julia Ann removed as tutrix because John Hawkins has not sufficient property to secure the minors' estate. Nicolas Louis Pellerin was married to Euphemie Dartest 19 Jan. 1832.

17 Sept. 1836. Neville, Celestine Ernestine, and Pierre Adrien are still minors. [Note: the unborn child at the time of decedent's death must have miscarried or died; it is not mentioned anymore in the succession after the initial statement as to its impending birth.]

Gen. note. Nicolas Louis Pellerin was a son of Hubert Pellerin and Julie Provost. See her succession, Est. #129, opened in 1821.

#166. MARIE THERESE BOUTTE, LATE WIFE OF

SAMUEL CHARLES MAYER, DEC. 27 MAY 1828

Order from Iberville Parish judge to proceed with an inventory of her estate in St. Mary Parish. Francis Duplessis of the Parish of Iberville appointed undertutor to the minor, Charles Christian Mayer, son of Samuel Charles Mayer and the decedent; his father is his tutor. Euphemie Ida Mayer, wife of Francis Mestayer, and Emelie Mayer, wife of Ursin Gonsolin, also children of the decedent and her legal heirs.

3 June 1828. Honore Carlin and Martin Demarest appointed appraisers.

For a complete record of this succession, see records of the Clerk of Court of Iberville Parish, Plaquemine, La.

Decedent was a daughter of Francois Cezar Boutte, Sr., and his wife, Marie Therese Degruy, Estates #158 and 159, above. See page 184.

*#167. JULIE PREVOST, LATE WIFE OF NICOLAS HEBERT, DEC. 9 OCT. 1828

Decedent is the widow of the late Nicolas Hebert, deceased; she lately died leaving 4 children of her marriage with Nicolas Hebert: 1. Modest, wife of Louis Moore, Jr.; 2. Elizabeth, wife of Zenon Decuir; 3. Alexander; 4. Julie, wife of Louis Eloi DeBlanc; her legal heirs. All are 21 years of age or over. Godfroy Provost and _____ appointed appraisers.

Gen. note. Decedent was a daughter of Francois Prevost and his first wife, Genevieve Bonin. See his succession, Est. #101. Nicolas Hebert was a son of Joseph Hebert and Francoise Hebert. See his succession, Est. #118. Louis Moore, Jr. was a son of Lewis Moore, Sr. See the succession of the father, Est. #202, opened in 1831. Alexander N. Hebert was born 8 Oct. 1800; married Marie Celine Barras [Bodin I 188].

#168. LOUIS BAKER, DEC. 18 AUG. 1828

Decedent died 27 July 1828. Mrs. Lucy L. Baker is the widow of the decedent; he resided on the plantation of Isaac L. Baker. John Towles and

Nathan Kemper appointed appraisers. Decedent left 2 minor children under the age of puberty: 1. Joshua and 2. Elizabeth Baker, his only legitimate heirs. Lucy Baker is their natural tutrix. Isaac L. Baker, their paternal uncle, is appointed undertutor.

18 Oct. 1832. Joshua Baker states he is the only uncle and nearest relative of the minor children of his brother, Lewis Baker, deceased. Says their mother, Lucy Baker, has left the state. Isaac L. Baker died. See his succession, Est. #207, opened in 1831.

16 Nov. 1833. Fam. meeting. Alexander Porter, Jr., paternal uncle by marriage of minors, and the following friends: James Sanders, Donelson Caffery, John Hartman, Alexander R. Splane.

8 July 1833. James Plaisted appointed curator ad hoc; Joshua Baker appointed tutor. Minors are still under puberty.

Gen. note. Decedent was a son of Joshua G. Baker, Sr. See his succession, Est. #15.

#169. ALEXANDER S. SOUTHERLAND, DEC. 24 JAN. 1828

Decedent, formerly of New Orleans but last of the City of New York, died intestate lately in the last named city leaving no heirs residing in the State of Louisiana. Real estate is included in this succession.

11 Feb. 1828. Isaac L. Baker of St. Martin Parish appointed curator of vacant estate.

18 Apr. 1828. Nathan Kemper and John Towles appointed appraisers.

7 Oct. 1828. Jane Webb of Grunge Walk, Bermondsey, County of Surrey in England, spinster, lawful aunt and curatrix or guardian of Jane Sutherland, spinster, Ann Sutherland, spinster, William Sutherland and Mary Sutherland, minors, the natural and lawful and only children of Alexander Smith Sutherland, formerly of New Orleans but late of the City of New York in the United States of America, widower, deceased.

#170. PETER REGNIER, DEC. 3 SEPT. 1828

Edward Simon, attorney, petitions. Decedent formerly of St. Mary Parish, but for many years resided in the Kingdom of France; departed this life toward the month of September, 1827, in the City of Lyon in the Kingdom of France. Heirs absent from the State of Louisiana. Edward Simon appointed curator. Most of this succession in French; heirship not apparent to compiler.

*#171. BENJAMIN GORDY, DEC. 13 MAR. 1829

Petitioner is Mrs. Phoebe Gordy, wife of decedent and natural tutrix to 3 minor children of decedent by his marriage with Phoebe Gordy: 1. Samuel E., 2. Elender [Nelly], 3. Benjamin H. Gordy. Samuel E. Scott and Benjamin C. Robert appointed appraisers; witnesses: John W. Dough and Peter H. Robert.

30 Mar. 1829. Fam. meeting: Michael Gordy, Peter W. Gordy, Jules Smith, Elijah Smith, and John Armstrong; all relations of the minors, but relationships not given. Peter H. Robert is appointed undertutor.

30 Apr. 1829. Buyers at sale: Peter W. Gordy, Bayard C. Robert, John C. Cook, Samuel E. Scott, Mrs. Phoebe Gordy, Michael Gordy, John D. Gwinball [?], Elijah Smith.

8 June 1836. Phoebe Gordy has remarried Nathan Wooster; witnesses: Henry Thompson and Edwin Cockle. John J. Garrett appointed tutor to the minors. Fam. meeting: Michael Gordy, paternal uncle; Alfred Smith, maternal uncle; John J. Garrett, maternal uncle by marriage; John C. Gordy and John Garrett, cousins; Bennet A. Curtis, cousin by marriage.

13 Mar. 1837. Phoebe and Nathan Wooster appointed natural tutrix and co-tutor.

Gen. note. Decedent was married to Phoebe Smith 26 Dec. 1820 [Marriage Book 1, page 212]. She was a daughter of Julius Smith and Sarah Armstrong. See his succession, Est. #227, opened in 1832; also the succession of her grandmother,

Margaret Armstrong, Est. #185, opened in 1831. John J. Garrett was apparently the minors' great uncle by marriage; he married Phoebe Armstrong in 1812. Phoebe Armstrong was the aunt of the minors' mother.

Eleanor Gordy married Joshua B. Carey 24 Jan. 1839 [Marriage Book 3, page 23]. His succession was opened in 1860 [Est. #1057].

#172. JOHN STEIN, SR., DEC. 25 JUNE 1829

St. Martin Parish. Petitioners: John Stein, Jr.; William Stein; Mary Stein and her husband, Josiah French; Elizabeth Clark, widow of John Stein, Sr., natural tutrix of: Philip, James, and Edmond Stein. All are of the Parish of St. Martin and the legal heirs and representatives of John Stein, Sr., late of the Parish of St. Martin, deceased. This succession includes real estate in St. Mary Parish.

Gen. note. Est. #623, St. Martin Parish, was opened for this decedent 23 June 1829. All the heirs were named in the foregoing St. Mary petition. There is a final settlement of this succession dated 20 June 1833. The widow was deceased at that time, as was William Stein. Though the statement was never made in either succession, the way the final settlement reads, the older children as well as the minors at the time of the father's death, were the children of Elizabeth Clark.

John Stein, Jr. and Sally Garrett were married 24 July 1825 [Marriage Book 1, page 311]. She was a daughter of William Garrett [see Est. #12] and Agatha DeRouen. Sarah Ann Garrett and Ethan Allen were married 23 June 1836 [Marriage Book 2, page 90]. Mary Stine and Josiah French were married 1 Apr. 1810 [St. Martin OA 25, page 54].

#173. REUBEN PICKET, DEC. 27 MAR. 1829

Alexander R. Splane, attorney, petitions. Decedent was late of the County of _____ in the State of South Carolina; lately died. Heirs are absent from the State of Louisiana.

Alexander R. Splane appointed curator.

16 Apr. 1829. Raymond Bernard and Frederick Pellerin appointed appraisers. William W. Bowen is attorney for the absent heirs, which are not named herein. William B. Bowers indicated as attorney for absent heirs and then as attorney for James B. Pickett of Fairfield District, S. C., and Robert Nash Ogden of West Feliciana Parish. No final settlement shown and heirs not specified.

*#174. JULIEN LESSASSIER, DEC. 6 OCT. 1829

Lewis Moore, Jr., petitions, brother of Louisa Moore, widow of Julien Lessassier. Lewis Moore, Sr. and Peter H. Rentrop appointed appraisers. Decedent was in partnership with James Owens. Louisa Rebecca Lesassier was his only child and heir; Louisa Moore, the widow, is her natural tutrix.

15 Oct. 1829. Fam. meeting: Lewis Moore, Sr., grandfather of the minor; Levi Foster, Winfrey Lockett, William Sterling and Seth Lewis, Jr., friends. Lewis Moore, Jr. is undertutor.

Gen. note. Louisa Moore was a daughter of Louis Moore, Sr., Est. #202, opened in 1831. She remarried Mishaux H. Carroll 29 Dec. 1830 [Marriage Book 2, page 10]. Her succession is Est. #730, opened in 1851.

Rebecca L. Lessassier married Joseph Davis 3 Sept. 1839 [Marriage Book 3, page 31].

#175. DAVID SMITH, DEC. 18 FEB. 1829

Matilda Smith is decedent's widow. Marion Parquins, grandmother and curator of James Smith, minor brother and heir of decedent.

14 Dec. 1829. Fam. meeting for James: Louis Parquins, husband of his grandmother; and the following friends, no other relations being in the State except his grandmother: Col. Winfrey Lockett, Hilaire Carlin, Joseph Theall, and Matthew Nimmo. Honore Carlin and Martin Demaret appointed appraisers.

Gen. note. David Smith married Matilda J. Bailes 20 Jan. 1827 [Marriage Book 1, page 356].

See her succession, Est. #257, opened in 1833; also decedent's parents successions and that of his grandmother's: Est. #19, 104, and 195, respectively.

*#176. SULLY BOULLIET, DEC. 14 JAN. 1830

Marie Rose Cecile Bouellet, daughter of Gabriel Bouellet and Marie Antoinette Pecot, his wife, their only child, a minor about the age of puberty, is heir of her brother, decedent. Gabriel Bouellet is her natural tutor. Dr. John Armelin [?], her cousin, is her curator ad bona.

20 Jan. 1830. Fam. meeting: Dr. Solange Sorel and Laurant Segur, cousins; Gabriel Bouellet, father; Jean Armelin, uncle; and Raymond Bernard, friend, in default of other relatives in the parish.

25 Jan. 1830. Dr. Solange Sorrel and Raymond Bernard appointed appraisers. Inventory conducted at the plantation of Frederick Peter.

#177. FRANCIS TURNER HUDSON, DEC. 17 DEC. 1829.

Isabella Kemper is the widow of decedent. Nathan Kemper is her father. George Royster and John J. Garrett appointed appraisers. Isabella Kemper Hudson is the natural tutrix of the minor children: 1. William Francis and 2. Thomas Thompson Hudson, both under the age of puberty. Fam. meeting: Benjamin Hudson and John M. Kemper, uncles of the minors; George Royster, John J. Garrett, and Julius Smith, friends. Nathan Kemper, their grandfather, is undertutor.

2 Sept. 1834. Daniel S. Norton of the town of Mount Vernon, County of Knox, State of Ohio, is mortgage creditor of the succession.

Gen. note. Decedent was a son of Francis Hudson and Elizabeth Patterson. See his father's succession, Est. #97, opened in 1817. Isabella Hudson married Hatton R. Fleetwood 4 Feb. 1841 [Marriage Book 3, page 36]. This may have been the widow of this decedent.

William Francis Hudson married Claire Elodie

Fay, daughter of Theodore Fay, 22 Feb. 1848
[Planters' Banner, 24 Feb. 1848, page 3, col. 2].

#178. LEON BOUTTE, DEC. 21 JULY 1829

Parish of St. Landry. Lise Chachere is the widow of decedent and natural tutrix of Magdelene, Francois, and Louis Leopold Boutte; Leontine Boutte and her husband, George Bengrurel [?], all of St. Landry Parish; and Marguerite Boutte and her husband, William Gil, of West Baton Rouge Parish; all legal heirs and representatives of decedent, formerly of St. Landry Parish, are petitioners in this succession.

Fam. meeting for minors: Antoine Boutte, paternal uncle; Julien Lile Chachere and Constant Chachere, maternal uncles; Dominique C. Sittig [?], uncle by marriage; and George Benguerel, brother-in-law of minors. Louis Chachere fils is undertutor.

5 Oct. 1829. Isaac L. Baker and Zenon Decuir appointed appraisers.

Some documents in this succession are in French.

Gen. note. An Antoine Boutte is identified as a son of Andre Claude Boutte [see Est. #158]. There is no proof herein that this is the same individual.

*#179. ELIZA ANN MARSH, DEC. 29 JULY 1829

St. Martin Parish. Petitioner is John C. Marsh of St. Martin Parish, her husband. He states she died in August of 1826 in New York City. Five children were the issue of this marriage: 1. George, 2. Sarah Craig, 3. Margaret H., 4. Eliza Ann, and 5. Helen McKay Marsh, all minors; Helen McKay Marsh has died since the death of her mother. John C. Marsh is the natural tutor to the remaining 4. Ranson Eastin is undertutor.

29 July 1829. Fam. meeting: David Weeks, Charles Olivier, Lewis Moore, Jr., and John W. Jeanerette, friends, and Samuel Stone of Lafayette Parish, their cousin and only relative in the state.

Gen. note. Since one of her children was named Craig, decedent may have been Eliza Ann Craig, sister of Euphemie Craig, 2nd wife and widow of William Stone [Est. #151]. The husbands of these 2 women, William Stone and John C. Marsh, were in business; the firm of Stone & Marsh is listed in the 1820 St. Mary Parish Federal Census. After the deaths of their spouses, Euphemie Craig and John C. Marsh were married. See their succession, Est. #320, opened in 1836. Samuel Stone, son of William Stone by his first marriage, is referred to as the Marsh minors' "cousin and only relative in the state." William Stone may have been related by blood to one of the minors' parents; or this may have been a "cousin-by-marriage" reference.

#180. JEFFERSON CAFFERY, DEC. 20 AUG. 1829

Alix Demaret is the widow of decedent and natural tutrix of: 1. Ralph Earl, 2. Mary Clarissa, and 3. Jefferson Caffery, minor children of the decedent. Fam. meeting: Martin Demaret, Adelard Demaret, Ursin Demaret, maternal uncles, and Levi Foster and James Ferguson, husbands of maternal aunts of the minors. Donelson Caffery is undertutor. Decedent was in partnership with Herbert Eastin in Lafayette Parish.

* #181. WILLIAM G[UNNELL] SANDERS, SR., DEC. 15 SEPT. 1829

Jared Y. Sanders is petitioner, for himself and representing Eleanor Y[oung] Sanders, a minor heir of decedent; Nancy Sanders, wife of William G[eorge] Dixon [of East Feliciana Parish, La.]; James Sanders, Jr., petitioner for himself and representing Thomas Y[oung] Sanders and Davis H. Sanders, 2 minor heirs; William G[unnell] Sanders, Jr.; and Mary Sanders, wife of John Watkins [of Wilkinson County, Miss.], petitioners, all legal heirs of William G[unnell] Sanders, Sr., and Mary [Young] Sanders, his wife, both deceased, late of Wilkinson Co., Miss.

Fam. meeting: Jared Y. Sanders, brother; and

Robert Trousdale, Edmund M. Sale, Levi Foster, and Joseph Theall, friends of the minors [in lieu of other relatives in the parish].

Gen. note. William Gunnell Sanders, Sr., was born 16 Feb. 1769 in Loudon Co., Va. About 1790 he married Mary Young in Chester Co., S. C., eldest daughter of Revolutionary War soldier William Young, also of Chester Co., S. C., and Elender McClerkin. Elender McClerkin was the eldest child of James McClerkin, who with his children [it is assumed the wife died and was buried in Northern Ireland prior to this journey] arrived at Charleston, S. C. from Northern Ireland in January of 1773 on the ship "Lord Dunluce;" James McClerkin was born about 1725 and died in 1795 in Chester Co., S. C. His will is extant.

In 1804 and 1805 William G. Sanders sold his Chester County property and in 1807 he owned land in Adams Co., Miss. [from the Adams Co. Tax Roll, Mississippi State Department of Archives and History, Jackson, Miss.].In 1815, as a "resident of Adams Co., Miss." he purchased land in Wilkinson Co., Miss. In 1813 he purchased land in St. Mary Parish, La., but apparently he and his wife never lived in Louisiana. Their older sons apparently took care of the St. Mary Parish property. William died in Wilkinson County in 1825 and Mary in either 1827 or 1828.

William Gunnell Sanders, Sr., and James Sanders, Sr., of St. Mary Parish, La., were brothers. They may have been sons of James Sanders who was in the Natchez District [Adams County] by 1787. If this James was their father, their mother and 2 sisters were in South Carolina in 1797, when the elder James' will was probated in the Natchez District; but they have not been identified at this writing.

James, Sr., appears to have been in the Attakapas District about 1800. The James Sanders, Jr., who appears in the early records of St. Mary Parish, was the son of William G. Sanders, Sr.

James Sanders, Sr., had a son James, but he was too young to have participated in the early affairs of the parish.

William and Mary Sanders had 8 children: 1. Jared Young Sanders, born 8 Mar. 1791 in Chester Co., S. C. He apparently came to St. Mary Parish in 1813 when his father purchased land here. On 29 Apr. 1818 he married Rachel Nixon Hulick, eldest daughter of Barnet Hulick [see Est. #96, opened in 1816]. This first J. Y. Sanders became St. Mary Parish's 4th sheriff, serving from 1818-1821. He died in November of 1862 at his plantation near Brashear City [now Morgan City], "Inglewood." 2. Nancy Sanders, born in 1793 in Chester Co., S. C., married William George Dixon in Adams Co., Miss., 28 Dec. 1811. They lived in what is now East Feliciana Parish, La., and had 9 children. Nancy died 12 Aug. 1851. The graves of her husband and herself at this writing are still marked and are located on what is now known as the Carruth plantation in that parish. 3. James Sanders [the James Sanders, Jr. of early St. Mary Parish records], was born ca. 1796 in Chester Co., S. C. He married Lucretia Swayze 11 Mar. 1826 in Wilkinson Co., Miss., and died there apparently about the time his uncle, James Sanders, Sr., of St. Mary Parish died [1839]. He apparently left no issue. 4. William Gunnell Sanders, Jr., born 11 Mar. 1801, in Cheraw Co. [?], S. C.; married Rebecca Hall, daughter of James Hall and Catherine _____, who were married in Berkeley Co., Virginia [now West Va.], in 1798, in St. Martin or St. Mary Parish ca. 1824. He died in one of those parishes in 1835 or 1836. His succession was opened in both parishes. He and his wife had 5 children. 5. Mary Sanders, born about 1804 in Chester Co., S. C., and married John Watkins in Wilkinson Co., Miss., 13 Dec. 1820. She and her husband had several children. He died in 1850 and shortly thereafter this family left

Wilkinson County for parts unknown to the
compiler. This is the only child of this couple
to have children that I have not been able to
trace and establish contact with a descendant.
6. Eleanor Young Sanders, born ca. 1810 in Adams
Co., Miss.; married Rankin Rogers ca. 1830 in St.
Mary Parish [?]; had 6 children and died in St.
Mary Parish 30 Nov. 1842. Her succession is Est.
#542, opened in 1844. 7. Thomas Young Sanders,
born ca. 1813, Adams Co., Miss., died Wilkinson
Co., Miss.,ca. 1841, sofaras is known to
compiler, unmarried; 8. Davis H. Sanders, born
ca. 1816 in Wilkinson Co., Miss.; married
Elizabeth _____, apparently in Wilkinson
Co., Miss. He died sometime in December of 1853,
apparently, in Wilkinson County, Miss., without
issue.

#182. JEAN BAPTISTE MILLER, DEC. 1 FEB. 1830

Mary Henry is the surviving wife of decedent.
Louis Moore, Sr., and Charles Theriot appointed
appraisers. John Martin and _____ Clemens
witness. The widow renounces interest in the
succession. Minor children of hers by the
decedent are mentioned, but not named.
This is the same decedent as that for Est. #266;
see that estate for details.

Gen. note. Decedent is a son of Jacob Miller
and Sophie Hoffman, and married Marie Henry
[Bodin I 302]. See also Est. #28, & Est. #144.

#183. ANTHONY W. BAKER, DEC. 20 JAN. 1830

Inventory shows "in account with Isaac L.
Baker." Notation in 1828 reads "Joshua Baker
expenses of disinterring body and burying remains in Episcopal church yard at Norfolk."
A notation in 1826 reads "Amt. paid for Kitty &
child bought at sale of John W. Baker's Estate
for children of Lewis Baker." Note at end of
inventory: "The above account is correct and is
filed by me for the approbation of the Heirs of
A. W. Baker, deceased, the balance to be paid

over by me as they may direct -- St. Mary's, 20 Jany. 1830. /S/ Isaac L. Baker."
    Gen. note. This decedent is one of the heirs and sons of Joshua G. Baker, Sr. See Est. #15.

* #184. JOHN REEVES, DEC. 9 NOV. 1830
    Parish of Lafayette. Decedent late of the Parish of Lafayette. Singleton W. Wilson and David Bell appointed appraisers.
    31 Jan. 1831. Joseph Reeves purchased at auction the real estate involved in this succession. No heirship shown.

* #185. MARGARET ARMSTRONG, DEC. 31 JAN. 1831
    Peter H. Robert petitions. Albert Buford is a minor child under the age of puberty of Elizabeth Armstrong and James Buford, her husband, both of St. Mary Parish, deceased. Albert is one of the legal heirs to the estate of Margaret Armstrong, his grandmother, late of this parish, deceased.
    3 Feb. 1831. Peter H. Robert appointed tutor to Albert Buford; John Armstrong, tutor to James A. Buford. James Buford, minor son of Elizabeth Armstrong and James Buford, petitions that he is grandson of Margaret Armstrong; John Armstrong is his uncle. James Armstrong Buford is this minor's full name.
    1 Feb. 1831. George Royster and Robert B. Royster appointed appraisers. Phoebe Armstrong, John Armstrong, and John J. Garrett signed inventory.
    5 Feb. 1831. Fam. meeting for the 2 minors: John J. Garrett, Peter H. Robert, Sarah Smith, and John Armstrong, near relations of minors [specific relationships not given]; George Royster, friend. John J. Garrett appointed administrator of estate. Robert B. Royster and Seth Lewis, Jr., witness.
    14 Mar. 1831. Buyers at sale: John J. Garrett, William Smith, Robert B. Royster, Peter H. Robert, Julia Smith. No settlement shown.
    Gen. note. James Buford, husband of Elizabeth

Armstrong, was probably the son of Warren and Mary Buford, Ests. #16 and 22. Decedent was married to John Armstrong, perhaps the 1813 St. Mary taxpayer. The marriage of Phoebe Armstrong and John Joshua Garrett, 13 Mar. 1812 [Marriage Book 1, page 8], gives the name of her father as John Armstrong.

John Armstrong's succession, Est. #238, opened in 1833, states that John Joshua Garrett was his brother-in-law, indicating that Phoebe and John Armstrong were brother and sister. John Joshua Garrett was a son of Joshua Garrett [Ests. 12 & 20]. Phoebe Armstrong Garrett's succession [Est. #592] was opened in 1846. Her husband died 25 Aug. 1849 at the age of 66. His birthdate was 3 Sept. 1783, and he was born in Opelousas. See Planters' Banner, 30 Aug. 1849, page 3, col. 2.

Sarah Smith, who signed the inventory, was undoubtedly another daughter of decedent. See Benjamin Gordy's succession, Est. #171, opened in 1829. John Joshua Garrett is referred to in that succession as the decedent's minor children's "maternal uncle by marriage." Actually, he was their great-uncle. Sarah Armstrong was married to Julius Smith [Est. #227, opened in 1832]; their daughter Phoebe married Benjamin Gordy.

Peter H. Robert, tutor of one of the Buford minors, was probably the Peter Robert who married Louise Armstrong [probably another of decedent's daughters] 12 July 1824 [Marriage Book 1, page 227]. This is probably Peter Hickock Robert, son of Peter Robert [Est. #127, opened 1823] and his first wife, Elizabeth Jaudon.

William Armstrong was listed in the 1820 St. Mary Parish Federal census. He married Polly Hardy 19 May 1825 [Marriage Book 1, page 301]. He could have been another of decedent's sons.

To recapitulate, John and Margaret Armstrong, this decedent, are known to have had 4 children: 1. **Elizabeth**, who married James Buford; 2. John, identified as uncle of Elizabeth's children; 3.

Phoebe, married John Joshua Garrett, identified as John Armstrong's brother-in-law; 4. Sarah, married Julius Smith; her grandchildren identified John Joshua Garrett as their "uncle by marriage; and 2 probable children: 5. Louisa, married Peter H. Robert, appointed tutor to one of the Buford minors; and 6. William Armstrong.

#186. PETER W. GORDY, DEC. 6 MAR. 1830

Michael Gordy is appointed tutor to his nephews, William, Archibald, and Peter Gordy, minor sons of Peter W. Gordy, deceased. Alexander R. Splane is undertutor. Seth Lewis, Jr., and Joshua Baker witness. Seth Lewis, Jr., and Alexander R. Splane appointed appraisers; Edmund N. Sale and Ephriam P. Forest witness.

26 Nov. 1831. Fam. meeting composed of family friends in default of near relatives to be found in the parish or within 30 miles of it: Seth Lewis, Jr., Levi Foster, John Carson, John J. Garrett, and Winfrey Lockett.

1 July 1834. Fam. meeting: Benjamin Hudson, cousin by marriage; in default of other relations: James Sanders, John J. Garrett, John Hartman and William B. Lewis.

Gen. note. Peter W. Gordy, Benjamin Gordy [Est. #171, opened in 1829], and Michael Gordy were brothers. Michael Gordy was identified as uncle of Benjamin Gordy's minor children, as he is of Peter W. Gordy's minors in this succession.

Decedent married Harriet Smith 28 July 1815 [Marriage Book 1, page 68]. She was a daughter of Archibald Smith and his wife, Elizabeth Smith. She apparently predeceased her husband, since she is not mentioned in this succession, and another was named tutor to her children.

William Smith Gordy, who was probably this decedent's son since the wife was a Smith, married Caroline E[lizabeth] Gordy on 2 Jan. 1839 [Marriage Book 3, page 22], his first cousin, she being a daughter of Michael Gordy. She died 26 Jan. 1847, aged 22 [?]. Her succes-

sion was opened in that year, Est. #605. See
Planters' Banner, 18 Feb. 1847, page 2, col. 4.
  Decedent was a son of Thomas Gordy. See the
succession of Benjamin Gordy, Est. #171.

#187. BAZELIE TENNANT, WIFE OF GERARD
       CHRITIEN, DEC. 15 MAY 1830

Decedent was the widow in first marriage of
Gabriel Fuselier, lately wife of Gerard Chretien
and lately of St. Martin Parish.

  18 May 1830. Agricole Fuselier pere and Charles
Grevemberg appointed appraisers. Seth Lewis, Jr.,
and David Anderson witness. There is another
inventory in this succession, but no heirship is
shown.

*#188. HENRIETTE VERETT, DEC. 15 MAR. 1830

Minor children of the decedent and Jean
Baptiste Verrett, their natural tutor: 1. Jean
Baptiste, 2. Carmelite, 3. Arcissi, 4. Josephine,
5. Francoise, and 6. Henriette Verett; some of
these names are not clearly spelled and written
in the petition, and they are not renamed in any
other document in the sucession.

  Fam. meeting: Godfroi Verett; Nicholas Verett;
and Jean Baptiste Verrett, uncles of the minors;
Joseph Provost, cousin of the minors; and Ursin
Carlin, friend. Ursin Carlin and Francois
Sinequer appointed appraisers.

  Gen. note. Decedent was a daughter of
Philippe Verrett and Marie Hebert, daughter of
Jean Baptiste Hebert and Claire Robichaud [Bodin
I 203]. Jean Baptiste Verrett, decedent's husband,
was a son of Auguste Verret and Marie Bujol.
Henriette Verrett and Jean Baptiste Verrett were
married 17 Feb. 1810 [Bodin I 390]. Some of
their children were born: 1. Francoise, 1 Mar.
1820; 2. Henriette, 14 Mar. 1821; 3. Josephine
Domitille, 30 Dec. 1815; and 4. Marie Celeste,
10 Nov. 1817. This fourth child is not listed
in her mother's succession, or else the name was
unclear therein or she was called by another
name, as sometimes happened. She may have pre-

deceased her mother. These dates are from Bodin I 390.

#189. SAMUEL B. RANDALL, DEC. 29 NOV. 1830
Frederick N. Ogden was petitioner. Decedent died on _____ day of Nov., 1830, leaving no heirs known to petitioner; petitioner named curator of estate.

2 Feb. 1831. David Bell and Jesse E. Lacey appointed appraisers. Alexander R. Splane is attorney for absent heirs, who are not listed. Buyers at sale: Owen Thomas, William Jarvis, Terrence Hughes, John Lockett, Samuel E. Bell, William B. McNamara, Thomas Wilson.

No settlement shown.

#190. VICTOR EDWARD VARNIER, DEC. 6 FEB. 1830
Will in French. Agricole Fuselier pere and Joseph O. Devezin appointed appraisers. Theodore Fay, sole executor. David Anderson and Seth Lewis, Jr. witness. No heirs given [other than in will] and no settlement is shown.

*#191. HYACINTH DUMINEL, DEC. 5 MAR. 1830
Theodore Duminil appointed tutor to Joseph Duminil, only child and legal heir of decedent. Joseph Duminil is referred to as nephew of Theodore Duminil.

12 Mar. 1830. John Smith and James Smith appointed appraisers. Fam. meeting: Franoois Duminel, grandfather; Henry Foote, husband of aunt of minor; and in default of other relatives: John B. Murphy, John Smith, and James Campbell, friends.

19 Apr. 1830. Buyers at sale: Theodore Duminel, Henry Foote, Ursin Carlin, Francois Siniqure, John Ditch, Joseph Hobby.

Many of the documents in this succession are in French.

7 Feb. 1838. John B. Murphy gives affidavit that decedent died and was buried "sometime in the year 1830." Deponent further states that he attended the funeral of this decedent.

31 Jan. 1838. Theodore Duminel is tutor to Joseph Duminil; a minor, the only child and legal heir of Hyacinth Duminil by his wife, Caroline Stanholt, both deceased, and as such is the grandchild and one of the heirs of Mrs. Catherine Odille, deceased, wife of Francois Duminil, also now deceased, minor's grandmother and grandfather, and is also one of the legal heirs of Nicolas Theodore Odille, deceased, late of Falaise, Department of Calvados, Kingdom of France, a brother to his grandmother. Joseph Guedry is appointed undertutor.

5 Feb. 1838. Francois Sineture gave affidavit that Catherine Odille died and was buried "some time in the year 1820." Fam. meeting: Francois Sineture, great uncle by marriage; Rosamond Sineture, maternal cousin; Henry Foote, paternal uncle by marriage; in default of other relations: Adelard Carlin, Euphrasy Carlin and Henderson Crawford, friends.

No date. James Sanders, Sr., and Hilaire Carlin, "Planters," gave affidavit that they both knew Francis Duminil and Catherine Odille, his wife; that they first knew them in 1807 and 1808; knew that they had but 3 children and legal heirs: 1. Hyacinth Duminil; 2. Adelaide Duminil, now the wife of Henry Foote; and 3. Theodore Duminil. Adelaide and Theodore are living and that Hyacinth died some years since.

Gen. note. Jean Baptiste Hiacinthe Dumesnil m. Caroline Tenhol; their son, Joseph Hiacinthe Dumesnil, was born 27 Nov. 1826 [Bodin I 152]. Carolina Tenhold (t), daughter of Frederick and Marguerite Adelaide Guidry, was born 8 Feb. 1799 [Bodin II 221]. Frederick Tenhold, native of Holland, a son of Jean Henry Tenhold and Jeanne Garetzen, married Marguerite Adelaide Guidry on 18 June 1797 in St. Martinville [Bodin II 221]. Theodore Dumesnil, another son of Francois Dumesnil and Catherine Odille, married Claire Adelaide Tenhold, probably a sister of Caroline.

Joseph Hiacinthe Dumesnil married Herene Madeline Gidry [Bodin II 88]. Henry Foote married Adelaide Dumesnil 31 July 1822 [Marriage Book 1, page 240].

#192. JOHN DOWN, DEC. 20 OCT. 1830

Harry Bradley petitions. Decedent died at the home of Daniel P. Sparks on 13 Oct. 1830, and he left no relations in this state or heirs in the state. Petitioner is acquainted with the heirs.

1 Nov. 1830. Henry Bradley appointed curator of the estate.

2 Dec. 1830. Daniel P. Sparks and Numa Cornay appointed appraisers. William Jarvis and Seth Lewis, Jr. witness.

1 Feb. 1831. Buyers at sale: Henry Bradley, Dwight & Hartman, E. P. Faust, Robert Trimble, A. R. Splane; James Steele and William A. Seay witness.

No dates. Affidavits by the following: Calvin Down of New Haven, Conn.; Lymen Prindle and Abigail D. Prindle, his wife, of Orange, Conn.; Enoch Summers and Sarah W. Semmes, his wife, also of Orange, Conn.; and Andrew Down and Eliza L. Down, minors under the age of 21 years, also of Orange, Conn., by their mother and guardian, their father being dead, Sarah Down of Orange, Conn. Calvin, Abigail D. Pringle, Sarah W. Semmes or Summers, Andrew, and Eliza L. Down being the brothers and sisters of John Down[s]. Sarah Down is decedent's mother. Her husband is not named.

#193. WESLEY FENISTER, DEC. 26 FEB. 1830

Ephriam P. Forest petitions. Belongings are sealed at the residence of Joel Coe and Joel Coe appointed guardian of same. Decedent lately died intestate leaving no legal heirs known to petitioner.

13 Nov. 1830. Winfrey Lockett and John W. Dough appointed appraisers.

No settlement or heirship shown.

#194. LOUIS CHACHERE, DEC. 6 APR. 1830

Parish of St. Landry. Decedent late of St.

Landry Parish.
    18 Aug. 1836. Benjamin Hudson and Nicolas Louis Pellerin appointed appraisers. No heirship shown.
        * #195. MARIAN PARQUIN, DEC. 23 OCT. 1830
    Decedent is the late wife of Louis Parquin. Honore Carlin and Martin Demaret appointed appraisers. Seth Lewis, Jr.,and Levi Foster witness. There is no heirship indicated in this succession; but see Ests. #19, David Smith, opened in 1813; #62, John M. Watson, opened in 1818; #82, Charlotte Thwaites, 1820; and #104, Ann Finch, 1819.
        Gen. note. Mirian, Miriam Thompson, this decedent, was first married to Jeremiah Tinker. This family apparently lived in Nassau, Island of Providence [see Marriage Book 1, page 73, marriage of Ann Tinker Smith to John M. Watson]. Jeremiah Tinker's death date is not known; his widow remarried Louis Parquin 2 Dec. 1818 [Marriage Book 1, page 158]. The Tinkers had at least 2 children: 1. Ann [see her succession, Est. #104, opened in 1819]; and 2. Charlotte [Est. #82, opened in 1820]. Est. #393 is the succession of Charlotte's daughter, Charlotte Frederica Thwaites, wife of William Garcegain [?] Caulfield [of the County of Middlesex, Great Britain],opened in 1839. A land conveyance in 1833 [Book D-7, folio 92, Entry # 759], identifies her and James Smith, surviving son of Ann Tinker Finch, as grandchildren and the only heirs of this decedent. Charlotte Thwaites Caulfield's children were: 1. Emma Stratford Caulfield, 2. Eliza Frederica Caulfield, 3. William Austin Caulfield, 4. Ada Caulfield, and 5. Madeleine Caulfield.
    Mrs. Clyde Alpha of Franklin shared most of the above genealogical information about this family with the compiler.
        #196. JAMES L. JOHNSON, DEC. 8 MAY 1830
    Petitioners are: Rachel Andrus, widow of the decedent and natural tutrix of: 1. Solomon, 2. Sarah, 3. Margaret, 4. Rachel, 5. Eliza, 6.

Catherine, and 7. Henry Johnson, minor heirs of decedent. [Note: Rachel Andrus Johnson's succession, Est. #211, opened in 1831, names another minor, Mary, omitted from this list. Mary Johnson might have been born after her father's death, but this is not indicated. According to her father's succession, Mary Johnson, died as a child.]; Joseph Johnson; and Nancy Johnson, wife of Joseph Hobby, all of St. Mary Parish, La.

11 May 1830. Evan Bowles and John W. Jeanerette appointed appraisers; Reuben Doty and Isaac L. Baker witness.

12 May 1830. Fam. meeting: Joseph Johnson, son of decedent; Joseph Hobby, son-in-law of decedent; Joseph Andrus, uncle of the minors; Benjamin Borel, cousin of the minors; and Reuben Doty, husband of one of their cousins [Reuben Doty was married to Mary Eurasie Borel, sister of Benjamin; both were children of Joseph Borel and his wife, Elizabeth Andres, probably a sister of Rachel Andrus' father, Solomon Andrus; see the succession of Joseph Andrus, Est. #55, opened in 1817]. Evan Bowles was appointed curator ad litem of the adult minor heirs and undertutor to those under the age of puberty. Isaac L. Baker and R. McCarty witness.

14 June 1830. Buyers at sale: Peyton Lynch, Peter H. Rentrop, Mrs. Rachel Andrus, the widow Johnson, Eugene Borel pere, Joseph Hobby, Evan Bowles, Joseph Johnson, Joseph Andrus, Robert C. Trimble, James Campbell, Reuben Doty.

13 Apr. 1833. Solomon Johnson is tutor to Margaret Johnson and Henry Johnson.

24 Apr. 1833. William Sharp is curator ad bona to Sarah Johnson, minor above the age of puberty. Fam. meeting for Sarah: James and Joseph Andrus, maternal uncles; Benjamin Borel, Benjamin Lacy and William Lacy [see Est. #135A for the Lacy connection], cousins. James Andrus did not appear, so the minor's brother, Solomon Johnson, of St. Martin Parish, took his place. Benjamin

Hudson named curator ad bona instead of William
Sharp. James Plaisted undertutor to the minors
yet under puberty.
   9 June 1835. Joseph E. Johnson is tutor to
Eliza and Caroline Johnson [Catherine, above?];
Fam. meeting: Joseph E. Johnson, brother; Joseph
and James Andrus, maternal uncles; William Lacy
and Benjamin Lacy, maternal cousins.
   31 Mar. 1835. Mary Johnson [not listed above],
one of the minors, is mentioned as having died.
William E. Lacy, Joseph A. Lacy, and Daniel Lacy
are included in a family meeting. Benjamin Hudson
is tutor to Sarah Johnson; Joseph E. Johnson, is
tutor to Caroline and Eliza Johnson; Jesse E.
Lacy, tutor to Rachel Johnson.
   2 Mar. 1835. Solomon Johnson was of Rapides
Parish, La.
   4 Apr. 1843. Joseph Johnson tutor to Caroline
and Henry Johnson.
   23 Jan. 1852. Baldwin Co., Ga. John L. Thomas
is guardian of the minors, Mary Elizabeth Thomas
and James L. Thomas, minor heirs of Martin Thomas
and his wife, Margaret Johnson, deceased.
   No final settlement apparent.
      Gen. note. Margaret A. Johnson married
Martin Thomas 7 July 1836 [Marriage Book 2, page
93]. Her succession was opened in 1844, Est. #
525; the succession of Martin Thomas was opened
in 1845, Est. #555.
      * #197. PETER ROBINET, DEC. 7 JAN. 1832
   Marie Zelwin Theriot, is widow of the decedent
and natural tutrix of their minor son, Nicolas
Robinet. Charles Theriot, the minor's grandfather,
is undertutor. Fam. meeting: Julien LeBlanc,
grand uncle of the minor, and Marcellien Theriot,
his uncle, being the only relatives in the parish;
John Joshua Garrett, William H. Barker [or
Basker], and Charles M. Charpantier, friends.
   19 Jan. 1832. Julien LeBlanc and Lufroi Carlin
appointed appraisers.
   30 May 1832. Marie Zelwin Theriot appointed

natural tutrix and Charles Theriot undertutor of Peter Robinet, posthumous son of Peter Robinet, decedent.

11 Apr. 1835. Peter Robinet, decedent, was the lawful son of Nicolas Robinet and Marie Verdeen, his wife, both deceased, on Bayou Sale. Jean Baptiste Verdeen and Pierre Verdeen, both full brothers of Marie and residents of St. Mary Parish, are deceased, the first in New Orleans and the second on Bayou Sale. Alexander Verdeen, another full brother of Marie, has died in the Parish of Terrebonne, where he was a resident. Jean Baptiste, Pierre, and Alexander Verdeen left no lawful heirs.

20 Apr. 1835. Fam. meeting: Zephrine Theriot, maternal uncle of the minors; Julien LeBlanc, maternal great uncle; Michael Hartman, maternal uncle by marriage; and Charles Charpantier and Jean Lanlon [?], friends.

7 Feb. 1839. Marie Zelwin is about to contract a second marriage; does not say to whom. [See also Ests. #259 & 260.]

#198. JOHN T. TOWLES: FAMILY MEETING 6 APR. 1831 [Pertains to the son of Dr. John T. Towles by his first marriage. No heirship information is included. See Est. #232 & 236.]

#199. ANN BOWES, DEC. 13 JULY 1831

George Royster represents that his deceased wife, Anna Bowes, left at her decease 4 children: 1. Robert B.; 2. Thomas J.; 3. Elizabeth Virginia; and 4. Nancy Poindexter Royster, the last 2 minors and the first 2 majors. George Royster confirmed as natural tutor to the girls. Doesn't state when decedent died; she died in the Parish of St. Mary. Martin Demaret appointed undertutor.

14 July 1831. James Sanders, Sr., and Jared Y. Sanders appointed appraisers.

2 Feb. 1832. Fam. meeting: Dr. John Towles, James Sanders, Jared Y. Sanders, Benjamin Hudson, and William Seay composed this meeting for the minors. [It is not so stated, but these must have

been friends of the minors in lieu of relatives in the parish.]

Gen. note. Robert B. Royster married Sarah Kemper 20 Jan. 1830 [Marriage Book 2, page 1]; she was a daughter of Nathan Kemper [Est. #221, opened in 1832] and Ann Whitaker. Sarah Kemper Royster's succession was opened in 1856, Est. #945. Robert M. [?] Royster's succession was Est. #993, opened in 1858. This is probably the same person.

Thomas J. Royster was an army officer and died unmarried 5 Sept. 1832 of cholera at an army camp near Rock Island; see his succession, Est. #258, opened in 1833.

Elizabeth Virginia Royster had a cattle brand registered in her name in 1824; she married Jesse Eagleson Lacy 18 Sept. 1832 [Marriage Book 2, page 31]; he was a son of Jesse Eagleson Lacy and Susan Andrus/Andrews. See Est. #114.

Ann [Nancy] Poindexter Royster had a cattle brand registered in her name also, in 1825; she married Robert B. Brashear 3 June 1835 [Marriage Book 2, page 222]; he was a nephew of William S. Barr [Est. #223, 1832]. See Robert B[arr?] Brashear's succession, Est. #947, opened in 1857.

* #200. PEYTON THOMAS, DEC.   5 MAR. 1831

Owen Thomas petitions; also Sowel Woolfolk of Muscogee County, Ga., husband of Sophia W. Thomas, on behalf of his wife and as agent and attorney-in-fact for Mary J. Thomas, wife of Micajah W. Theweatt of the same county and state. They are the legal heirs and representatives of decedent. [Relationships are not specified herein; but see Est. #142, succession of James Thomas, opened in 1820, father of this decedent. Owen Thomas is identified therein as Peyton Thomas' brother and Sophia and Mary J. as his sisters.]

Levi Foster and James Sanders appointed appraisers.

16 July 1835. On 2 Dec. 1826 Owen Thomas was appointed curator ad bona of Peyton Thomas, this decedent, then a minor above the age of puberty. Now the said Peyton Thomas has died and Owen

Thomas prays for cancellation of the bond.
[The succession of Sowel Woolfolk is Est. #219, opened in 1832.]

#201. CHARLOTTE CAULFIELD'S PROPERTY   26 JULY 1831   [NOT A SUCCESSION]

James Smith represents that Mrs. Charlotte Caulfield is an absent person living in the County of Middlesex near London in the Kingdom of Great Britain; he represents himself as her nearest relation "in this country"; their relationship is not specified. James Smith is appointed curator of her estate. Honore Carlin and Martin Demaret are appointed appraisers.

[James Smith and Charlotte Caulfield were first cousins. See Ests. #82 and 195.]

* #202. LEWIS MOORE, SR., DEC.   6 MAY 1831

Petitioners: I. Lewis Moore [Jr.]; II. Louisa Moore, wife of Meshoux Carroll, all of St. Mary Parish; and III. John Moore of St. Landry Parish. They, together with IV. William Moore of St. Landry Parish and V. Joseph A[ndrew] Moore of St. Martin Parish, are the lawful children and only legal heirs of decedent, late of St. Mary Parish.

George Heydel and Joseph Clement appointed appraisers.

Gen. note. Perrin tells us [page 63, Biographical section] that Judge Lewis Moore of Berkeley Co., Va. [now West Virginia], served as a major in the Revolution. Bodin tells us [II 176] that Lewis Moore of Berkeley Co., Va., married Rebecca Henshaw. They had 4 sons, according to Perrin, and Lewis Moore settled near Berwick's Bay and there became a wealthy planter and property owner; and J[oseph] Andrew Moore was a son who married [wife's name not given] and reared 12 children. Bodin further tells us [ibid.] that another son, Lewis, born in Berkeley Co., Va., married Modest Hebert, daughter of Nicolas [Est. #118], at St. Martinville 12 Feb. 1811.

The Congressional Biographical Directory tells us [page 1350] that John Moore (who served in

Congress from Franklin and New Iberia) was born in Berkeley Co., Va., in 1788. He was married twice: (1) to Adelaide Demaret, daughter of Louis Demaret [Est. #94]; (2) in 1841, to Mary Clara Conrad, a daughter of Frederick Conrad and Frances Thruston [Est. #80], widow of David Weeks. John Moore died in Franklin 17 June 1867 and is buried on his estate, "The Shadows," in New Iberia, his wife's plantation from her first husband, David Weeks.

William Moore, decedent's fourth son, was prominent in early St. Mary Parish records. A William Moore married Eloise Verret, daughter of Philippe Verret [see Est. #117]. This is probably the same man.

It is not known whether Rebecca Henshaw accompanied her family to Louisiana. A Mrs. Lewis Moore was an 1813 St. Mary taxpayer. This may have been Mrs. Lewis Moore, Jr. Est. #135A, opened in 1824, is the succession of Sarah Moore, late wife of Lewis Moore, Sr. She was the former wife of Solomon Andrews/Andrus and was survived by their 5 children.

In addition to his 4 sons, this decedent was survived by a daughter. Louise Camille Moore had a cattle brand registered in her name in 1818. Louisa Moore's first husband was Julien Lessassier, whose succession [Est. #174] was opened in 1829. She remarried Mishaux [Meshoux] H. Carroll 29 Dec. 1830 [Marriage Book 2, page 10]. Her succession is Est. #730, opened in 1851.

Est. #21, in the name of L. Moore, is listed as a petition only. It is almost assuredly a petition in connection with this family.

#203. EDWARD A. BROUSSARD, DEC. 6 JAN. 1831

St. Martin Parish. Inventory authorized of property in St. Mary Parish belonging to the community "heretofore existing between Edward A. Broussard and Anne Thibodeaux, his wife."

27 Jan. 1831. Charles Olivier and Charles Hebert appointed appraisers. Philip A. Jolly and Louis Dugas witness. The inventory was also

signed by the following with no explanation as to why: Leon Broussard; Belisaire Broussard; Anne Thibodeaux; Drousin Broussard; Aurelin Dugas; Desire Dugas.

This estate was probably settled in St. Martin Parish, and persons interested in this family should seek full information there.

#204. DR. BUCKINGHAM F. WELLS, DEC. 15 DEC. 1830

Will. Mother, Percis Wells of the State of New York, County of Warren. Brothers and sisters: Thaylor, Samuel, and Lydia Wells; Judith, married to Doctor Laurence, and Sarah, married to Joshua Tanner; all of the State of New York. Alexander Jackson of St. Mary's [Parish] and William W. Bowen, attorney at law of Opelousas, to be executors. Sgd. 25 May 1830; proved 15 Dec. 1830. There are no witnesses to the will. William H. Flagg testifies that the signature is genuine. Winfrey S. Lockett and O. D. Langstaff witness.

20 Jan. 1831. Alexander Jackson requests inventory. Boyd Smith and William H. Flagg appointed appraisers. David Weeks and Angelo Borgia witness.

2 Feb. 1831. Buyers at sale: Alexander R. Splane, Edwin Cockle, James Steele, A. Vincent, Samuel E. Bell, E. H. Burns, Jesse E. Lacy, Dr. Lyman, David Bell, Dr. Fields, F. N. Ogden, Seth Lewis, W. A. Seay, Mr. Wilson, F. Austin, J. Saunders; James Steele & Seth Lewis, Jr. witness.

3 Oct. 1833. State of New York, Washington Co. William A. Wells of the town of Jackson in the County of Washington, State of New York, and Edmund Wells of the town of Smithville in the County of Chenango [?] in the same state represent that Samuel Wells was their brother; that Persis Wells was his wife; that Samuel has been dead more than 15 years; that he died leaving his wife, Persis, and Buckingham F. Wells, Judith Wells, Sarah Wells, Thayler Wells, Lydia Wells, and Samuel Wells, his children; that Persis Wells is now living; that Judith Wells is

now married to Dr. James Lawrence and Sarah Wells is now married to Joshua Tanner; and that Samuel Wells and Lydia Wells, for whom Nathan A. Wells is named guardian, are minors under the age of 21 years.

7 July 1832. Nathan A. Wells of Luzerne in the County of Warren, State of New York, gives affidavit that he was also a brother of Samuel Wells.

#205. URIAH SANDY, DEC. 26 FEB. 1831

John W. Gibson petitions. Decedent lately died and has no heirs in the state known to petitioner.

11 Mar. 1831. John Gibson appointed curator of this estate.

23 Mar. 1831. Jacob W. King and P. R. Splane appointed appraisers. Sandy lived at the residence of J. W. King in the town of Franklin. William Davis and James Steele witnessed.

7 Apr. 1831. Buyers at sale: Levi Foster, ___ Bendy, King, James Richards, J. Perl, Captain Powell, Coleman, John W. Dough, Louis Moore, John Hoovy [?], Dr. Gibson, Captain Dough, John M. Kemper, John Huffy [Hoovy?], Francis Austin.

No heirs shown. No final settlement.

#206. DUNCAN MC CLOED, DEC. 20 NOV. 1830

Levi Foster represents that decedent died recently leaving no will or heirs or relations.

14 Dec. 1830. Levi Foster appointed curator of estate.

[Decedent apparently was a butcher. This list of "Butcher Accounts" was included in the estate.]
George Allen, Joseph Alin, John M. Bateman, M. Birdsall, John Bell, Constance, O. Cornay, L. Collins, M. M. Campbell, Alexis Carlin, Joel Coe, Captain J. W. Dough, H. Ely, B. Elliot, J. N. Sale, J. N. Field, McFerren, Levi Foster, B. Godfrey, Mrs. Hall, N. Holbert, Mason Harper, B. Hudson, T. Hughes, W. S. Harding, D. S. McIntosh, J. W. Ring [King?], B. Lockett, F. Lefort, O. D. Longstaff, James & Mrs. Lees, W. Lockett, John O. Lacy, Seth Lewis, Jr., Isam Lewis, C. Latour,

Mestayer, James Newman, M. Nimmo, Perry, John Parkerson, Corp. of Franklin for balance due, Estate of Eads, Richard Faulk, Celestin Geoge, Joseph Robert, William Collins, Jacob Hays, Marin Mouton, Jr., Albert Stansbury, Charles Tranghan, Ambroise Toups, William Hargrave, William Stephens, Olesime Mouton, John Lamar, Edward Dublaugh, Thelender Campbell, John Crawford, John B. Theall, Edward Merriman, John Merriman, Jr., Mr. Merriman's bill, Able Lyons. "Notes": James H. Hargrave, Luke Bryan, Jr., John Merriman, Joseph White, William Stephens, Charles B. _____, Joseph Mills, John Fowler, Mason Harper, Notley Young, James Foster, Jr., W. Lockett, Jacob W. King, E. N. Sale, W. Lockett, Mason Harper, Seth Lewis, Jr., Samuel E. Scott. [Accounts continued]: Ursin Perret, J. B. Perret, P. W. Robert, William Richardson, John Smith, William Sharp, G. Serra, William Sterling, Twiley, Joseph Theall, James F. Theall, Mrs. John Theall, P. Veeder, Thomas Wallace, James Younger, J. Y. Sanders.

No heirship shown.

*#207. ISAAC L. BAKER, DEC. 5 JULY 1831

James W. Byrne of the City of New Orleans represents he is a creditor of the decedent, "who died 4 months since in the parish of St. Martin."

9 Aug. 1831. Agricole Fuselier pere and Donelson Caffery appointed appraisers. James Steele and Archibald B. Bein witness. Joshua Baker was an heir of Isaac L. Baker; they were in partnership. Apparently they owned a plantation jointly and ran it together.

3 Jan. 1832. Buyers at sale: Joshua Baker, Alexander Porter, Jr., Mrs. Elizabeth Rogers, Michael Knight, Jr., Nathan Kemper, A. Fuselier pere, John N. Kershaw, John J. Garrett, G. L. Fuselier, Louisa R. Baker, Peter H. Renthrop, Julien LeBlanc, Numa Cornay, James Steele, Pierre Goyneau, George Haydel, G. B. Thomas, J. Casson, Clarke Nettleton, Dr. Kilgore, Joseph Bryan, Edward N. Sale, Lufroy Carlin, Dr. Solange, Joseph

Andrus, William W. Walker, T. C. Verno [?],
Joseph Berwick, Tom Sorrel, Coleman Triplot [?],
Samuel Wilkinson, John Hudson, S. Carlin, Dr.
Thomas Youngblood, Benjamin Lacey, Captain Powell,
Thomas Kershaw, Joseph Bryan, W. Bendy, Colo.
Dancey, John Smith, John O. Lacey, Dr. John Towles;
John Towles & Edwin L. Cockle witness.

No other heirs mentioned than Joshua Baker.

Gen. Note. Decedent was a son of Joshua G. Baker. See Est. #15.

#208. MERCELITE MAXENT, WIFE OF LOUIS DE FERIET, DEC. 15 APR. 1831

Probate judge in New Orleans grants authority to take inventory of the property belonging to the community which existed between Louis de Feriet and his deceased wife, this decedent.

1 June 1831. Agricole Fuselier pere and Charles Grevemberg appointed appraisers. James Steele and Seth Lewis, Jr. witness.

No heirship or settlement shown.

#209. JULIE DECOUX, WIDOW OF LOUIS PELLERIN, DEC. 4 DEC. 1830

Parish of St. Martin. Authority granted to take an inventory of a tract of land belonging to the estate of decedent.

20 Dec. 1830. Frederick B. Pellerin and Joseph O. Devezin appointed appraisers. Seth Lewis, Jr., and James Steele witness.

No heirship shown.

Gen. note. Louis Pelerin was a son of Louis Gerard Pelerin and Marie Marthe Hubert Belair. Louis Gerard Pelerin was born in France. Louis Pelerin and decedent were married in St. Martinville 26 Oct. 1786. Born of this marriage were:
1. Alexandre, born 20 Apr. 1788; 2. Bartholome Valsin, born 8 Sept. 1801; 3. Don Martin, who married Marie Zoe St. Julien at Lafayette in 1825; 4. Edmond, born 12 May 1792; 5. Eugene, born 10 Apr. 1790, married Cleonide St. Julien in 1826 at Lafayette; 6. George, born 7 May 1794; 7. Jacques Louis, born 26 Mar. 1797; 8. Louis

Alexandre, born 12 Jan. 1800; and 9. Marie, born 7 Feb. 1796. [Bodin I 313-14]

#210. SILAS RAWLS, DEC. 2 FEB. 1831

Daniel Rawls petitions. He is brother of decedent.

Co. of Lafayette, Territory of Arkansas. Daniel Rawls, guardian of Job B. Rawls, minor orphan and heir of Silas Rawls, deceased, tutor of said minor, prays to be released from bond; minor is now in St. Mary Parish and within the jurisdiction of the Parish court.

Philip A. Rawls is also decedent's minor son and nephew of Daniel Rawls. P. Davis, Jolly [?], and Philip Vignaud appointed appraisers.

30 Jan. 1832. Fam. meeting: [composed of friends]: John D. Wilkins, Philip Vignaud, Simon Patout, Francois Vincent and Olduf LaBauve.

Gen. note. Job B. Rawls registered cattle brands in 1845 and 1846. The succession of Philip Alston Rawls was opened in St. Mary Parish in 1848, Est. #632.

#211. RACHEL N. ANDRUS [ANDREWS], WIDOW OF JAMES L. JOHNSON, DEC. 16 MAR. 1831

Petitioners: I. Solomon Johnson and II. Joseph E. Johnson, children and heirs of decedent, represent that she died on the ____ day of February, 1831, leaving 7 minor children: 1. Margaret, 2. Rachel, 3. Sally, 4. Eliza, 5. Caroline, 6. Henry, and 7. Mary Johnson [Mary was not named in the initial petition of her father's estate; she may have been a posthumus baby.]

29 Mar. 1831. Fam. meeting: Solomon Johnson and Joseph E. Johnson, brothers of the minors; Joseph Hobby, husband of their sister, Nancy; Joseph Andrus and Benjamin Borel, their cousins. Evan Bowles appointed tutor to Sally Johnson, a minor over the age of puberty; and to Eliza, Caroline, and Henry, minors under the age of puberty. John W. Jeanerette appointed tutor to Margaret, a minor over the age of puberty. Jesse

E. Lacey appointed tutor to Rachel, a minor over the age of puberty. Joseph Andrus appointed tutor to Mary, an infant child.

30 Mar. 1831. John W. Jeanerette and Joseph Andrus appointed appraisers. James Steele and Reuben Doty witnessed.

Buyers at sale: Nicolas Loisel, Solomon Johnson, Joseph E. Johnson, Benjamin Nichols, W. Hudson, John G. Richardson, Thomas H. Thompson, Daniel Rawls, Henry Penn, John W. Singleton, R. Doty, John B. Bulrice, Joseph Andrus, Ursin Provost, J. Stine, Sidney Singleton, R. C. Trimble, Solie [?] Dubrauel [?], G. Singleton, Col. Richardson, Joseph Hobby, Charles Hebert, Parris, Fifi Bulrice, Oleuf Labauve, Louis Moore. James Steele and J. W. Jeanerette witnessed.

6 July 1832. James Plaisted, undertutor to Sally, Eliza, Caroline, Henry, and Mary, represents that Evan Bowles is deceased.

20 July 1832. Fam. meeting: Joseph and Solomon Johnson, Benjamin Lacy, John W. Jeanerette, and Joseph Andrus [no relationships specified].

Robert B. Royster appointed tutor to Caroline and Eliza; John W. Jeanerette, to Henry; William Sharp, to Sally. P. P. Briant and Seth Lewis, Jr., witnessed [no date indicated].

[See Est. #196, opened in 1830, the succession of decedent's husband, James L. Johnson.]

Gen. note. Decedent was a daughter of Solomon Andrus/Andrews and his wife, Sarah _____, who married as his second wife Lewis Moore, Sr. See her succession, Est. #135A, opened in 1824.

#212. THOMAS SPENCER, INVENTORY AND CONVEYANCE OF PROPERTY OF 18 JULY 1831
[NOT A SUCCESSION]

Thomas Spencer vs. His Creditors. By virtue of an order from the Parish Court of the Parish and City of New Orleans.

8 Oct. 1831. Sale of property to Charles Luale [?]. See Book F of Conveyances, page 262.

#213. SUSAN LABATRE CARLIN, WIDOW OF DENIS CARLIN, DEC.   31 DEC. 1830

4 Jan. 1831. John B. Murphy and Adelarde Carlin are appointed appraisers. Pelletier De la Houssaye and Drozel [?] Judice witness.

Theolin, Edouard, and Emma Carlin are minor children of the decedent.

Fam. meeting for the minors, composed of: Honore Carlin, uncle of the minors; Ursin, Godfroy, and Terrence Carlin, brothers of the minors; and Joseph Allen, husband of one of the heirs.

19 Feb. 1831. Buyers and sureties at sale: [I could not make out all of the names on this list] George Heydel, Urbain Carlin, Ursin Carlin, Dorothea Carlin, wife of Robert H. De la Thule, Jared Y. Sanders, Hilaire Carlin, Sylvin Salles, Claire Carlin, wife of Joseph Allen, Godfroy Carlin, Terrence Carlin, Octave Cornay, John M. Bateman, James Campbell, Henry R. Nursen, John Long, Carmesele Carlin, Theodore Carlin, Honore Carlin, N. Verret. Signed by Terrence Carlin, Ursin Carlin, Emma Carlin, Theolin Carlin, Claire Alin, Theodore Carlin, Godefroy Carlin, Dorothea de la Thule, Joseph Alin, Carmesile Carlin, Honore Carlin for self and Garland Cosby and wife, Urbain Carlin. Witnessed by John Brownson and _____ Simon.

There was another auction in St. Martin Parish in 1837 and another in St. Mary Parish in 1832.

1 May 1834. Emma Carlin now the wife of Jean Baptiste Verret fils. [This is the only thing approaching a listing in this succession of all the heirs]: Terrence Carlin; Dennis Carlin, Jr.; Claire Carlin and her husband, Joseph Alin; Godefroy Carlin for himself and as curator ad bona of Theolin Carlin; Urbain Carlin; Carmesile Carlin; Dorothea Carlin, wife of Robert F. G. de la Thule; Honore Carlin, curator of Emma Carlin and agent for Eulalie Carlin, and her husband, Garland Cosby [of Kentucky]; Theodore Carlin; and Ursin Carlin [mentioned as a brother of the minors at a Family meeting on 19 Feb. 1831].

[There is no mention in the settlement of the

Muse child, grandchild of the decedent, or of the son Edouard, mentioned as a minor in this succession.]

See also Est. #108, succession of decedent's husband, Denis Carlin, Sr.

Gen. note. This decedent, Suzanne Labaterie, was a daughter of Jean Labaterie and Marthe Dizlande [Bodin I 217].

#214. HENRY RENTROP, DEC. 10 MAY 1832

Will. Heirs were grandchildren, children of decedent's 3 children: 1. Caroline Rentrop, Madam Maxil Bourg, 2. Peter H. Rentrop, 3. Frederick William Rentrop. Mentioned specifically were grandson Valsin H. Rentrop, son of Peter H. Rentrop; 3 grandchildren: Rosaly, Honorine, and Edmond, the children of Maxil Bourg. No executor was named, and there were no witnesses. Mentions real estate in Assumption Parish. Sgd. 1 May 1828. Filed 10 May 1832. Henry Knight, Nathaniel M. Cochran, and Mathew Rogers witnessed genuineness of decedent's signature on the will.

10 May 1832. Nathaniel M. Cochran and Henry Knight appointed appraisers.

7 July 1832. Peter Henry Rentrop petitions. Decedent lately died at his [petitioner's] residence. Inventory made there.

26 Aug. 1828. Assumption Parish. Peter H. Rentrop appointed undertutor to minor children of Marguerite Licaire and Frederick Rentrop, her late husband [a true copy of document taken from the succession of Frederick Rentrop]: Auguste, Eliza, Tarqile [Terzile], Celeste [Sarah], and Henry M. Rentrop.

1 Feb. 1834. Fam. meeting at the residence of the widow of Frederick Rentrop for her minor children: Auguste Rentrop, their brother; Henry Knight, Jr., cousin; Nathaniel M. Cochran and Anthony Hartman, cousins by marriage; and in default of other relations [Henry Knight, Sr., being sick and unable to attend said meeting] Mischaux H. Carroll, friend. Witnesses: Julien

LeBlanc and Homer Hines.

21 Jan. 1833. Rosalie Bourg is the wife of Marcellin Verret of Assumption Parish.

29 June 1835. Sarah and Henry Rentrop are still minors.

8 July 1835. [There is litigation in connection with this succession.] Caroline Rentrop is a resident of Mobile, Ala., the wife of Maxil Bourg of Assumption Parish. They separated 25 May 1822. [Sarah Rentrop is also known as Celeste.]

Terzile Rentrop is now the wife of Zepherin Theriot of St. Mary Parish. Elizabeth Rentrop is now the wife of Benjamin Malbrook of Lafourche Parish.

8 June 1835. Fam. meeting for Sarah and Henry Rentrop: Auguste Rentrop, their brother; Zepherin Theriot, their brother-in-law; Henry Knight, Sr., uncle by marriage [he married Marguerite Liqueur's sister, Mary Madeleine Liqueur]; Henry Knight, Jr., cousin; Nathaniel M. Cochran, cousin by marriage; Charles Theriot and Julien LeBlanc, friends.

Gen. note. Decedent was married to Anne Catherine Elizabeth Trappe. He was a native of Prussia. They had 3 children, mentioned in the foregoing succession.

1. Peter Henry Rentrop, born in Westphalia, married Marguerite Bertrand at St. Martinville 19 Oct. 1812. Her succession was opened in St. Mary Parish in 1855, Est. #880.

2. Sarah Charlotte Juanita Caroline Rentrop married Maximilien Bourque [Bourg].

3. Frederick William Rentrop, born in Prussia, married Marie Marguerite Liqueur, daughter of Jean Liqueur and Marie Anne Malbrou. She was a sister of Mary Madelaine Liqueur, who married Henry Knight, son of Jacob Knight and Christine Enfile [see Est. #102]. Frederick Rentrop predeceased his father. Marguerite Liqueur Rentrop's succession was opened in 1842, Est. #488.

Peter Henry Rentrop and Marguerite Bertrand had:

4. Valsin Rentrop - Had a cattle brand registered in his name in 1816 and married Harriet or Henrietta C. Knight 24 Mar. 1836 [Marriage Book 2, page 82].

5. Caroline Rentrop - Married P. J. Pavy [see <u>Planter's Banner</u> 31 July 1852, page 3, col. 3].

6. Octave Rentrop.

7. Tarquile Rentrop.

8. Dorsino L. Rentrop - Married Modeste Guidry [Est. #929, opened in 1856]; he died 25 Oct. 1853 [<u>Planter's Banner</u>, 17 Nov. 1853, page 3, col. 3]. His succession was opened the next year, Est. #852.

9. Pamela Rentrop.

10. Detour Rentrop.

Caroline Rentrop and Maxile Bourg [of Assumption Parish] had:

11. Rosalie Bourg - Married Marcellin Verret of Assumption Parish. He may have been a son of Marcellin Verret who was a St. Mary Parish 1813 taxpayer and included in the 1820 St. Mary Parish federal census.

12. Honorine Bourg.

13. Edmond Bourg.

Frederick William Rentrop and Marie Marguerite Liqueur were married 18 Nov. 1805 at Plattenville. Their children were:

14. Auguste Frederick Rentrop - Married Calice Bertrand 14 Apr. 1841 [Marriage Book 3, page 40]. She was a daughter of Jean Baptiste Bertrand, Jr., and Celeste Miller [see Est. #133].

15. Elizabeth Rentrop - Married Benjamin Malbrook 15 Sept. 1834 [Marriage Book 2, page 61].

16. Teville Marguerite Rentrop - Married Zepherin Theriot 29 May 1834 [Marriage Book 2, page 56]. He was a son of Charles Theriot. [See Est. #197.]

17. Celeste Sarah Rentrop or Sarah Celeste Rentrop.

18. Henry Maurice Rentrop.

The above information is a resume of data summarized from this confused and confusing succession. Details are drawn from the Marriage records of St. Mary Parish and from Bodin I 325 and II 159, 199.

#215. MALAIN AILLIAN, WIFE OF NICOLAS MULLIAN, DEC. 31 MAY 1832

Lafourche Parish, La. Nicolas Mullian confirmed as natural tutor to his children: Francoise, Marie Louise, Nicolas, Palmice, Auguste, and Teups [?] Mullian by decedent, his late wife. Joseph Aillian of Lafourche Parish is appointed undertutor. No relationship given. Probably he was the minors' uncle, the decedent's brother.

2 June 1832. Decedent died in 1825 at the residence of Joshua Baker in St. Mary Parish. John J. Garrett and Walter B. Wilcoxon are appointed appraisers. Peter H. Rentrop and _____ witness.

#216. ELIZA PREVOST, A MINOR   2 MAY 1832
[NOT A SUCCESSION]

Eliza Prevost, minor daughter of Madelaine Prevost, deceased, has been under the tutorship of Madelaine Borel, her grandmother, who now wishes to be relieved. Eliza, being over the age of puberty, chooses Robert McCarty to replace her. Ursin Provost is appointed undertutor. No relationship is given; he is probably her uncle.

1 June 1832. Godefroy Prevost and Nicolas Phileman Prevost appointed appraisers. The inventory was made at the late residence of Lufroy Prevost, deceased, of all the property belonging to the succession of Madelaine Prevost, deceased. Lufroy Provost and Jacques Judice witness.

Gen. note. Magdeleine Provost, or Madelaine, was a daughter of Madelein [Magdalen] Borel and Francis Provost. See his succession, Est. #101. Madelaine Provost married Joseph Prevost [Bodin II 197]. Eliza was their child. Joseph Prevost was a son of Jean Baptiste Prevost and Augustine Armand. He and Madeleine Provost were married at St. Martinville 13 Oct. 1812 [Bodin ibid.]

#217. YOUNGBLOOD HEIRS. 17 APR. 1832

William Youngblood petitions. He is natural tutor to Mary Rebecca, Joseph Alston Moore, and Eliza Youngblood, his minor children. He is confirmed therein. Dr. Thomas Youngblood is confirmed as undertutor to his neices and nephew. There is no mention of the minors' mother. The father's full name appears to be General C. William Youngblood. [Note: this does not imply a military rank. It was not unusual for "General" to be a given name at that time.]

#218. GREENBURY B. THOMAS, DEC. 20 MAR. 1832

At the late residence of decedent, seals were affixed to his personal belongings. John J. Garrett and Dr. Clark Nettelton witnessed. Thomas Edwards appointed guardian of the belongings.

25 Apr. 1832. Seals were broken in the presence of Dr. Nettelton and William Smith.

26 Apr. 1832. John L. Thomas of Baldwin Co., Ga., brother of the decedent, appointed curator of the vacant estate. He represents that the decedent lately died. James Plaisted is attorney for the absent heirs.

4 May 1832. Michael Gordy and John J. Garrett are appointed appraisers.

22 Jan. 1833. Baldwin Co., Ga. William Sanford and Elizabeth, his wife, sister to decedent, appoint John L. Thomas their attorney; Joseph W. Denson and Martha, his wife; Martha Thomas, widow and relict [widow] of James Thomas, deceased, mother of the decedent, listed as heirs. James Thomas is a witness, but no relationship is given.

12 Feb. 1833. Buyers at sale: John L. Thomas, Honore Carlin, Winfrey Lockett, Joseph Berwick, Barthelot Lockett, John M. Bateman, Edwin Cockle, Bryce Elliot, Martin Thomas, Walter Wilcoxon, Thomas Edwards, James Sanders, William Sanders, Hilaire Carlin, G. & P. Bryan, Robert B. Brashear, Mason Harper, William Cook, John Garrett, Dr. James Smith, William J. Nash, Baynard

C. Robert, E. N. Sale, P. Wilkinson, J. Baker, M. Gordy, Dr. Youngblood, Thomas Wilcoxon, Jessey Hulick. Alexander R. Splane and John S. Rutland witnessed.

#219. SOWELL WOOLFOLK, DEC. 19 MAR. 1832

Sophia W. Thomas, widow of decedent, who lately died in Muskogee [?] Co., Ga., of which place petitioner is resident. Decedent was in partnership with Owen Thomas of St. Mary Parish. James Thomas was petitioner's deceased father; Peyton Thomas, deceased, her brother. Decedent left a minor daughter by petitioner, Mary Sowell Woolfolk. Sophia is confirmed as natural tutrix to the minor. Thomas' Island and other real estate are included in this succession.

23 Mar. 1832. Winfrey Lockett and Jared Y. Sanders appointed appraisers. John M. Bateman and Joseph G. Wilson witnessed.

27 Mar. 1832. Sophia W. Thomas appointed administrator of the estate.

17 May 1832. Owen Thomas, Sophia's brother, appointed undertutor to the minor.

4 Mar. 1837. Sophia W. Thomas now married to William D. Hargrove of Muskogee Co., Ga.

24 May 1837. Muskogee Co., Ga. Mary Jane Thomas, wife of Micajah W. Thweatt, sells to Sophia Wardlaw Thomas, wife of William D. Hargrave, the undivided fourth part of a tract of land in St. Mary Parish called "Cote Blanche or Bell's Island," being the same acquired by this vendor by inheritance from James Thomas, her deceased father.

Gen. note. See Ests. #142, 196, and 200.

*#220. ROBERT BELL, DEC. 16 APR. 1832

Melanie Materne, widow of the decedent, petitions. Decedent leaves 2 minor children by petitioner: 1. John Adams and 2. Elvina Bell. Petitioner confirmed as natural tutrix to the minors. Nicolas Verret appointed undertutor [no relation stated.]

26 Apr. 1832. Fam. meeting for the minors: Robert Bell fils of Lafayette Parish, their

brother; Nicolas Materne, Gustin [?] Materne, and Jean Baptiste Materne, their uncles; and Charles Primot, their brother-in-law.

Ursin Carlin and Joseph Castagenier [?] appointed appraisers. Joseph A. Lacy and A. Fuselier fils witnessed.

9 Mar. 1836. Partition: decedent's 5 children and heirs: 1. Robert Bell; 2. Melite Bell, widow of Irillon Broussard; 3. Claire Bell, wife of Charles Primot, these children of decedent by his first marriage [wife's identity not stated; see below]; 4. Adam [John Adams]; and 5. Elvina Bell, both minors, by the second marriage, with petitioner. Adam Bell [John Adams] has died since the father's death.

19 Apr. 1838. Lucien Verret appointed under-tutor to Elvina, succeeding Nicolas Verret, deceased.

Gen. note. Decedent was a son of Samuel Bell, a Revolutionary soldier, probably the Samuel Bell who was listed in the 1792 Militia Census of Attakapas. Samuel Bell had at least 5 sons: Robert (this decedent), John, Thomas, David, and Samuel. David Bell married Emily Sophia Nixon [see page 39]. Samuel Bell died in December of 1834 [Est. #288]. His wife at that time was Agathe. In 1830 his age was 70, hers 80. It is not known if she was the mother of his children. [Files of Mrs. Clyde Alpha, Franklin, La.]

Melanie Materne was a daughter of Adam Materne/Matherne and Marguerite Martin [Bodin I 290]. Decedent's first wife was Angelica Julie Broussard, daughter of Simon Broussard and Marguerite Blanchard;

[Continued in Addenda Section, on page 182]

*#221. NATHAN KEMPER, DEC. 1 FEB. 1832

Decedent died 29 Jan. 1832. Petitioner is Nancy [Whitaker] Kemper, his widow. Decedent's heirs are: 1. John M. Kemper, over 21 years of age; 2. Isabella, daughter and widow of Francis T. Hudson, over 21; 3. Sarah, daughter and wife of Robert B. Royster; 4. Jane, wife of Alexander R. Splane; 5. Samuel, minor son over the age of puberty; 6.

Nancy, minor daughter under the age of puberty; 7. Elizabeth F., minor daughter under the age of puberty; 8. Thomas Jefferson, minor son under the age of puberty; 9. William P. Kemper, minor under the age of puberty, grandson of decedent, represented by Eliza J. Kemper, his mother and natural tutrix.[Eliza J. Kemper was Eliza Hulick, widow of William Peter Kemper, deceased son of this decedent.]

Nancy Kemper confirmed as natural tutrix of Samuel, Nancy, Elizabeth F., and Thomas Jefferson Kemper, minor children of said tutrix by Col. Nathan Kemper. Alexander R. Splane is appointed their undertutor.

9 Feb. 1832. George Royster and Martin Demaret appointed appraisers; Walter B. Wilcoxon and Bennet A. Curtis witnessed.

4 June 1832. Jared Y. Sanders appointed undertutor to William P. Kemper.[Note: he was uncle by marriage to the minor, being married to Rachel Nixon Hulick, sister to minor's mother, Eliza Hulick.]

Fam. meeting for the Kemper minors [apparently all of them]: Samuel Kemper, Robert B. Royster, James Sanders, Sr., James Sanders, Jr., and Martin Demaret, relations and friends [does not specify which are which].

Gen. note. Decedent was one of 3 brothers: Nathan, Reuben and Samuel, settled first in Feliciana and there fomented the unsuccessful "Kemper Rebellion" of the West Floridas in 1804, right after the Louisiana Purchase, against Spain. They were sons of Peter Kemper of Essex Co., Va., who was a captain in the American Revolution. Nathan Kemper, the above decedent, was born in September of 1775 in Fauquier Co., Va., and was married in East Baton Rouge Parish 24 July 1801 to Nancy Whitaker, who was born 23 Dec. 1785 and died 25 Aug. 1838 [see Est. #380, opened in St. Mary Parish in 1838]. William Peter Kemper, their first child, was possibly named for both grand-

fathers; he was born in St. Mary Parish in November
of 1802; 27 April 1825 in St. Mary Parish he married Eliza Hulick and very shortly thereafter he died.
His exact death date is not known. His son, William
Peter Kemper, Jr., was born in 1826 after his father's
death. Eliza Hulick, widow of William P. Kemper, did
not remarry and died in St. Mary Parish in May of
1862. She was born in July of 1801 in Elizabeth, N.
J. See her father's succession, Est. #96. William
P. Kemper, Jr.,married twice: (1) Mary Jane Coe of
Rapides Parish, 6 July 1848. She died 30 Jan. 1849
without issue; (2) Mary Monica Reynolds Rogers,
born in Boston, Mass., in 1838. They were the
parents of 8 children. [This information on the
Kemper family has been graciously supplied by my
cousin, Mrs. M. A. Sublette, of New Orleans.]

*#222. LUFROY PROVOST, DEC. 23 MAY 1832

Marie Doralise Judice, widow, petitions. Decedent left 6 children: 1. Lufroy and 2. Edouard
Provost, by his first wife, Lucile Provost, deceased, both under 21 years of age, Lufroy being
emancipated by marriage; 3. Celestine, 4. Marie
Louisa, 5. Alexander Luke, and 6. Claire Emma
Provost, minor children under the age of puberty,
petitioner being natural tutrix to her 4 children.
Nicolas Philemon Provost, their uncle, is appointed undertutor to the 4 younger children, and tutor
to Edouard, above the age of puberty. Robert
McCarty is appointed undertutor to Edouard.

31 May 1832. Frederick Pellerin and Louis E.
DeBlanc appointed appraisers.

1 June 1832. Fam. meeting for the minors:
Lufroy Provost, their brother; Godfroy and Ursin
Provost, their uncles; Jacques Judice, grandfather
of Doralise's 4 children; and Alexander Judice,
their uncle.

17 Feb. 1834. Fam. meeting. Godfroy Provost
and Ursin Provost, paternal uncles; Jacques Judice,
grandfather; and Alexander and Francois Doleze
Judice, maternal uncles of Doralise's children.

Gen. note. Decedent married his first wife

1 Oct. 1812 [Marriage Book 1, page 13]. She died ca. 1822, as her succession [Est. #121] was opened in that year. See Bodin II 133.

*#223. WILLIAM S. BARR, DEC. 23 FEB. 1832

At the request of Robert B. Brashear, the store and personal effects of decedent were sealed. F. G. Birdsall was appointed guardian until the seals were removed. Edwin L. Cockle and William Sharp witnessed.

19 Mar. 1832. Robert B. Brashear represents that the known heirs have refused administration of the estate [they are not named]. Furman G. Birdsall and Archibald B. Bien appointed appraisers; Franklin Wharton is attorney for the absent heirs.

Notes and accounts due decedent: Notes: James Campbell, Levi Foster, John B. Lockett, Jacob W. King, James Ferguson, W. B. McNamara, W. B. Wilcoxon, Samuel K. Kershaw, Matt Birdsall, John P. McMillen, James Heron, Joshua Baker, Winfrey Lockett, James Smith, O. Cornay, B. A. Curtis, George Mitchettesee [?], on order of E. Bowles, Mr. Gordy's note in favor of R. Hungerford, James F. Theall, Romain Verdin, Robert S. Carson, John Parkins, John W. Dough, John C. Cook, G. B. Thomas, E. N. Sale, M. Knight, W. A. Seay's order in favor of Hubbert, O. D. Langstaff, Louis Sterling, James Sanders, John O. Lacy, Sol. Johnson, Jacob Haifleigh, D. S. McIntosh, Gregoire Boden, Thomas Kershaw, Terence Carlin, Thomas Bell, Thomas A. Adams, Rice & Seay, Benjamin Hornsby, P. Y. [?] Robert, W. C. Thayer, Elijah Smith, Campbell note, L. Fuselier note, George Schwing, Mrs. Matilda Smith, Lenore Boden, Madam Dartice, Robert Trousdale, W. B. Wilcoxon, Jesse E. Lacy, James Lynch, George Royster, Anthony Walker, John Wesson, Elijah Boyce, Mrs. Carmozel, George Archer, Adelard Demaret, John Senett, Placide Carlin, Michael Gordy, John E. Carson, J. & R. P. Allisson, George Senet, James Smith, D. W. & S. A. Wilson, William Sharp, Mrs. Lees, Seth Lewis, Jr., Smith

Plantation, William A. Seay, C. C. Tyson, Henry
Bradley, Mrs. Younger, Capt. Brown (Schr. Scumbio),
Mrs. Carson, Joseph Yo Ya, Mrs. Abby Sanders (Mrs.
James Sanders, Sr.), Paul Debarr, Thomas Fvets [?],
Mrs. Elliot, John Barrabino, Terence Hughes, Randel
Dad [?], Mrs. Smith, Wm. M. McCarty, James Riley,
Lloyd Collins, Elijah Smith, Mrs. Hall, Duncan
McLeod, Gaytavae Serra [?], Mrs. King, Henry R.
Nursen judgment, S. E. Scott judgment, Oream [?]
Carlin, Joshua Baker, Thomas Wilcoxen, William W.
Hatfield, Benjamin Hornsby, Jeremiah Brashear,
William H. Flagg, Adam Crow, E. N. Sale, Francis
Austin, John M. Cook, William Richardson, John
Rice, Robert Royster, A. R. Splane, Daniel Morison,
Alexis Carlin, Amos Surril, Richard Hungerford, Rev.
Spencer Wall, Celestin Carlin, John B. Murphy,
Joseph Johnson, Dr. B. F. Wells, deceased, Hilaire
Carlin, E. Coffin "ran away" owing $4.55, John O.
Lacy, James Hays, Cornay & Haydell, James Walker,
G. B. Thomas, deceased, W. Brashear, I. L. & J.
Baker, Owen Thomas, L. Key, Mrs. Hayes, R. B.
Brashear, Octave Cornay, Capt. John S. Havens,
Miss E. Sanders [Eliza?], James F. Theall, P. H.
Robert, Edgar Demaret, Eugene Sennet, Benjamin
Root, Joseph Prevost, Mrs. Susan Lacy, Thomas H.
Adams, E. H. Walton, Theolin Carlin, Mrs. Susan
Carlin, deceased, Charles M. Charpantier, Peter
Dejournatt, John B. Theall, George Mahe, Bryce
Elliot, Grigured Bodin, Thomas Johnson, B.
Sojourner, John Kershaw, Francis Dancey, Mrs.
Joseph Allin, Louis Sterling, John C. Cook,
Samuel E. Scott, Euphrasey Carlin, Stephen
Barrabino, George Russell, Joshua Garrett, Louis
Parquin, P. W. Robert, Robb R. Barr, Moses Walker,
G. Whiting & Co., John Rogers "ran away" owing
$3.50, Robert S. Carson, Thomas Buford, Joseph
Andrus, James Campbell, Capt. William H. Bassett,
Dejournatt & McKerral, Miss Nancy Biggs, Thomas
Wallace, E. Bowles, James Muggah, David Robbins,
Gilliam & Gibson, D. S. McIntosh, Matthew Nimmo,
Jr., Rice & Seay, Peter Jupiter [?], Jacob Knight,

Mrs. Hannah Theall, J. W. Gibson, Benjamin Hudson, John Ditch, Prior Bryan, Mrs. E. Kemper, Robert Cook, James Clark "ran away" owing $29.75, Winfrey Lockett, Romain Verdine, Joseph, Solomon Johnson, B. Rush Garrett, Luke Bryan, Jr., S. W. Wilson, David Hays, Hall & Bein, Lloyd Wilcoxen, William Jarvis, George Westrem [?], Mrs. Caffrey, Dr. J. W. Lyman, Cypriar, William B. McNaman, Joseph Bryan, Samuel Anderson, James Ferguson, Raniels [?] Kilgore, Joseph Tarkington, John Parkinson, John Hays, Mr. Gilbert, William G. Sanders, John Rumal, Peter Veeder "ran away" owing $9.62-1/2, Martin Demaret, Milton Johnson, Robert C. Trimble, Miss Caroline Nixon, Mrs. Bell, John Hartman, Dexter Watson, William Walker, William A. Armstrong "ran away" owing $34.02, James Lacy, J. P. Gilliam, John A. Waddle, John Armstrong, Brashear & Barr, F. G. Birdsall, Henry Foote, Mrs. Ann Birdsall.

Accounts: Bartlett Lockett, John Smith, William P. Cook, Sr., Miss Sally Johnson, Herbert Arceneaux "ran away" owing $120, Julius A. Johnson, John W. Field, James Sanders, Jr., David Bell, William Garrett, Hippolite Braud, Israel Moore, Michael Knight, Urbain Carlin, Joseph Theall, Legure Hays, O. D. Longstaff, Burton Perry, John Pattie, Gilliam & Atkinson, Miss Fannie Theall, William Allirie [?], Thomas Kershaw, William Rochelle, Doct. Atkinson, Maximillian Barbino, Theodore Carlin, Lufroy Carlin, Dwight & Hartman, Jonathan Lacomb, Capt. J. Smith, Ursin Demaret, Donelson Caffery, Watson Mc Kerral, Godfroy Carlin, John White, Thomas Wilson "ran away" owing $8, John B. Pennel "ran away" owing $25.50, Samuel Wilkinson, Jonathan Smith, William H. Cook, Jr.,R. P. Rogers, Joseph Greaves, Joseph Dugat "ran away" owing $433.37-1/2, John Johnson, John M. Bateman, Joel Vamoix [?], John B. Benriss [?], F. Wharton, Desire Carlin, Mrs. Rogers, Capt. E. Patterson, Jesse Hulick, W. Bendy, Jared Y. Sanders, Henderson Crawford.

Witnesses: William Sharp and Edwin L. Cockle. Inventory completed 24 Mar. 1832. R. B. Brashear and Franklin Wharton, attorney for the absent heirs, signed.

2 Apr. 1832. Petitioner appointed curator of the vacant estate. Robert B. Brashear and Walter Brashear sureties. W. B. Wilcoxen and F. Wharton witnessed.

30 Apr. 1832. Buyers at sale: Henry Foote, J. B. Perret, Bartley Lockett, John Johnson, Hall & Bien, Thomas Bell, Levi Foster, Whiting & Co., J. W. Bigson, A. Fuselier fils, Stephen Barbarino, J. B. Murphy, G. L. Fuselier, Alex Frere, L. E. Cockle, A. R. Splane, Michael Knight, Joshua Baker, John Rice, John Carson, H. I. Carlin, Anthony Walker, F. C. Cook, Hilaire Carlin, Silvin Sales, John McFarrow [?], John Hudson, J. B. McNamar, J. E. Carson, Devina [?] Theodum [?], Louis Parquin, McKerral & Dejarnatt, Joel Coe, John DeHart, William Wofford, Joshua Baker, J. M. Cook, H. Atkinson, Watson McKerral, Israel Moor, Dexter Watson, J. N. Kershaw, W. Lockett, Julien LeBlanc, E. Boyce, W. A. Seay, J. F. Theall, J. W. Lyman, Col. Nettelton, B. A. Curtis, Alfred Smith, James Ferguson, James Lacy, A. J. Key, Adelard Carlin, F. B. Birdsall, J. A. Dwight, Michael Gordy, J. B. Bullock, Don Caffery, S. Barbarino, R. Hungerford, Theodore [?] Dineina [?], A. Mountaine [?], W. G. Sanders, Daniel Lacy, Patten Miller, Henry Bradley, J. W. Dough, Adelard Carlin, F. Wharton, H. Atkinson, J. N. Frilo [?],

1 July 1833. Robert Barr Brashear is still curator of the estate.

28 June 1837. Firman G. Birdsall is curator of the estate.

8 June 1852. Edmund P. Dwight is curator of the estate.

9 July 1853. James Y. Smith vs. R. B. Brashear civil suit is involved in this succession. Robert B. Brashear departed this life in 1856 leaving his wife, Nancy P. Brashear, as the

testamentary executrix of his estate [Est. #947, opened in 1857].

There is no final settlement of this estate apparent. It continues up until the Civil War. 10 Apr. 1860 is the last date I found. It seems to continue into the succession of Robert B. Brashear.

Gen. note. Decedent was apparently a brother of Margaret Barr, wife of Dr. Walter Brashear. Robert Barr Brashear was their son. See the succession of Margaret Brashear, Est. #306, opened in St. Mary Parish in 1835.

Robert Barr of the County of Fayette, State of Kentucky, a brother of Margaret Barr Brashear, died 20 Feb. 1836, without issue. His heirs were Maria Barr, wife of Elisha Warfield; Nancy Barr of Fayette Co., Ky.; Eliza Barr, wife of David Todd of Missouri; and the surviving children of Dr. Walter Brashear. These were apparently sisters of Margaret Brashear and this decedent.

I am indebted to Mrs. Clyde Alpha of Franklin for this information.

#224. WILLIAM BIGGS, DEC. 3 MAR. 1832

Alexander R. Splane petitions that decedent lately died leaving no heirs or will. His estate consisted of property being "an undivided portion of the Estate of his deceased father" [Est. #116]. This is declared to be a vacant estate.

21 Mar. 1832. Alexander R. Splane appointed curator of the estate.

16 July 1832. Winfrey Lockett and Jared Y. Sanders appointed appraisers.

17 July 1832. Decedent is entitled to 1/8 share of the estate of his father.

No settlement is shown. His brothers and sisters must have been his heirs. See their father's succession, Est. #116.

#225. SOPHIA MILLER, WIFE OF JESSE TOMLINSON, DEC. 23 JULY 1832

Jacob Miller petitions. He is grandfather of Catherine and James Tomlinson, minor children of his daughter, Sophia, by Jesse Tomlinson, both deceased.

Fam. meeting: John Louis Felleman and Jean Baptiste Copel, their only connections, and Julien LeBlanc, Charles Theriot, and George Heydell, friends. Jean Baptiste Felleman appointed tutor of Catherine and Jean Laulon, tutor of James; Alexander R. Splane, undertutor to both. Witnesses: Constance Comeaux and M. W. Carroll. Julien LeBlanc and Charles Theriot appointed appraisers.

28 June 1833. Fam. meeting [minors still under the age of puberty]: Jacob Miller, grandfather; Jean Baptiste Felterman and Pierre Carrantine, uncles by marriage, being the only relations in the male line and capable of attending this meeting except Baptiste Copel, who is sick and cannot attend [relationship not given]; Julien LeBlanc and Joseph Clement, friends. Mischaux W. Carroll and Alexis Hebert witnessed.

29 June 1833. Buyers at sale [& sureties]: Andrew Brien, Henry W. Farley, Jean Baptiste Felterman, Jean Loulon, Charles Theriot, Jacob Miller, A. W. Dismukes, A. R. Splane, M. W. Carroll. John Martin and David Robbins witnessed.

[See also Ests. #144 & 225.]

#226. WILLIAM COCHRAN, DEC. 14 AUG. 1832

Jared Y. Sanders petitions that decedent, of the State of Mississippi, has lately deceased; that he was decedent's agent and attended to his business before his death; that he has no known heirs in Louisiana or persons qualified by affinity or relationship to claim the administration of said estate; therefore, petitioner requests that he be appointed curator.

23 Aug. 1832. Jared Y. Sanders and James Sanders make bond. P. P. Briant and Edwin N. Sale witnessed.

27 Aug. 1832. Jared Y. Sanders appointed curator of this vacant estate. Seth Lewis, Jr., and William A. Seay appointed appraisers. John B. Bimus [?], Esq., and P. P. Briant witnessed.

16 June 1833. Samuel Templeton and Jane Cochran, both of Warren Co., Miss., are administrator and administratrix of this estate. [No relationship to decedent given.] No settlement of this estate shown.

#227. JULIUS SMITH, DEC. 3 AUG. 1832

Sarah Smith, widow of decedent, is petitioner. Decedent was "lost at sea some time last summer." There are 9 children, the issue of the marriage between her and decedent: 1. Phoebe, now the widow Gordy [see Est. #171, opened in 1829]; 2. Margaret, now the wife of Thomas Edwards; 3. Elijah; 4. Alfred, these 4 being majors, over the age of 21 years; 5. Julian and 6. William, both minors over the age of puberty; 7. Ralph, 8. Joshua, and 9. Julius, minors under the age of puberty.

Sarah Smith is confirmed as natural tutrix to the minors and Joshua Garrett, undertutor. George Royster and John O. Lacy appointed appraisers. John P. Hudson and James Ferguson witnessed. Sarah Smith appointed administratrix of the estate.

Gen. note. Decedent was married to Sarah Armstrong, daughter of Margaret Armstrong. See the latter's succession, Est. #185, opened in 1830. Phoebe Smith was married (1) to Benjamin Gordy 26 Dec. 1820 [Marriage Book 1, page 212] (2) Nathan Wooster 2 July 1835 [Marriage Book 2, page 73], who also predeceased her [his succession was opened in St. Mary Parish in 1843].

Margaret Smith married Thomas Edwards 21 Jan. 1833 [Marriage Book 2, page 13]. Her succession was opened in 1846 [Est. #584]. Thomas Edwards died 20 Oct. 1833. See his succession, Est. #261.

Alfred Smith married Martha Cook 21 Mar. 1838 [Marriage Book 3, page 5]. Ralph D. Smith married Abigail E. Spears 28 Dec. 1848 [Planters' Banner, 4 Jan. 1849, page 2, col. 4.]

#228. EVAN BOWLES, DEC. 28 AUG. 1832

The regular originating petition is apparently missing from this succession. Dorothea Carlin is decedent's widow. Thomas E. Bowles and Matilda Bowles are both legal heirs and children of the decedent, both over 21 years of age. Alexander Field is the husband of Louisa Bowles, another legal heir of said marriage; James Plaisted is the counsel representing the absent heirs, Eleanor and Susan Bowles, minors, absent from the state. Celestin Carlin is curator pro tem; Honore Carlin, curator ad hoc.

Martin Demaret and Octave Cornay appointed appraisers. Edwin L. Cockle and Benjamin R. Garrett witnessed.

Included in the succession file is a letter dated 20 Aug. 1818 from John Bowles to his brother Evan from Washington Co., Md. Their sister Polly is dead.

2 Sept. 1832. Fam. meeting for the minors Eleanor and Susan Bowles: Thomas E. Bowles, Matilda Bowles, Alexander L. Fields, Celestin Carlin and Honore Carlin, the last 2 named being brothers of Dorothea Carlin, their mother.

27 Aug. 1832. Honore Carlin appointed under-tutor to minors.

28 Aug. 1832. Celestin Carlin, their oldest uncle, is appointed the minors' tutor. [Note: their mother was not deceased.]

21 Dec. 1833. Eleanor Bowles, a minor above the age of puberty, represents that her uncle Celestin has died, leaving her without a tutor. Susan Bowles is now the wife of Franklin Shield of the State of Kentucky and is now an absent heir. Alexander L. Fields is undertutor to Eleanor.

9 Jan. 1834. Jehu Wilkinson is tutor to Eleanor.

7 Jan. 1834. Benjamin Franklin Shields and Susan Bowles, his wife, of Hopkinsville, Co. of Christian, State of Kentucky, appoint James Allison of St. Mary Parish to represent them.

13 Mar. 1837. Final partition. Dorothea Carlin, decedent's widow; heirs: 1. Thomas E. Bowles; 2.

Matilda Bowles, widow of Henry Goodrich, deceased; 3. Miss Eleanor Bowles; 4. Eliza Bowles, wife of Alexander L. Fields; 5. Susan A. Bowles, wife of Benjamin F. Shields; Edwin L. Cockle and Henry Thompson witnessed.

 Gen. note. Alexander L. Fields, husband of Louisa/Eliza Bowles, married (2) Catherine F. Kimberly of New Haven, Conn., 26 Aug. 1847 [Planters' Banner, 26 Aug. 1847, page 2, col. 5]. Eleanor Bowles married Capt. Simon C. Mathison; see her succession, Est. #587, opened in 1846. He married (2) Jane Pooley 26 Dec. 1847 [Planters' Banner, 6 Jan. 1848, page 2, col. 4]. He died 28 May 1851, aged 42 years, a native of Scotland [ibid., 31 May 1851, page 3, col. 2]. His succession, Est. #741, was opened that same year.

 Dorothea Carlin, this decedent's widow, was a daughter of Joseph Carlin. See his succession, Est. #1. Dorothea's succession was opened in 1855, Est. #885.

 #229. SAMUEL W. WING, DEC. 4 SEPT. 1832

 J. W. Lyman petitions. Decedent, formerly of Massachusetts, has lately died here. Decedent has no relations here. Petitioner was physician to decedent in his last illness. Benjamin R. Gant, Esq., appointed to represent the absent heirs. No real estate is involved in this succession. Decedent died at the residence of Levi Foster. Petitioner is appointed curator of this vacant estate. Archibald Bein and John Hartman are appointed appraisers.

 6 Oct. 1835. Buyers at sale: John G. Richardson, Thomas Kirkham, Henry Foote, J. W. Gibson.

 No heirship is shown.

 *#230. JOSEPH THEALL, DEC. 2 JULY 1832

 Will. Legatees: Joseph Lyman, Jr.; Susan Reaves, widow of John Reaves; mother [unnamed]; brother James F. Theall; wife, Nancy; brothers' children, James F. Theall's daughter, Nancy, and

John B. Theall's children. Executors: Judge [Jehu] Wilkinson, Frederick Pellerin, and A. Fuselier, Sr. Sgd. 9 Feb. 1832. Probate date not given.

2 July 1832. Jared Y. Sanders, justice of the peace, retired to the home of the decedent, lately deceased, and placed seals on the personal effects. Mrs. Nancy Theall is the widow. John P. McMillen and Thomas Maskie [or Maskell] witnessed.

2 Oct. 1832. Seals raised. Jehu Wilkinson and Honore Carlin witnessed. Nancy Theall, widow, and James F. Theall, brother, petition. The 3 testamentary executors [named in will] declined; request that John Brownson be so appointed. Hannah Theall, mother of decedent, and John B. Theall, the only remaining brother, concur. John Brownson is so appointed. Jehu Wilkinson and Honore Carlin appointed appraisers. Edwin L. Cockle and Spencer Wall witnessed.

12 Oct. 1832. John B. Theall's children are named: Ruffin and Henry Mixter Theall.

23 Jan. 1833. Nancy Wilcoxon of Lafayette Parish appointed curator ad hoc to the children of John B. Theall of Lafayette Parish, La.

28 Jan. 1833. In default of relatives, friends composed a meeting for these minors: Levi Foster, Notley Young, Charles Kibbe, Alfred P. Moss, and James Dougherty, all of Lafayette Parish.

6 Feb. 1833. Fam. meeting for Nancy Theall: James Campbell, Joseph A. Lacy, William H. Lacy, Benjamin Lacy, relations [not specified]. Daniel Lacy signed but he is not named in the document; he must be the 5th member of the Family Meeting, the usual number attending. William Sharp, who also signed, must be her undertutor; it is stated in the document that the undertutor is present, but he is not identified. Seth Lewis, Jr., and Joseph S. Tarkington witnessed.

19 Aug. 1837. Nancy Theall, decedent's widow, is married to Joseph S. Tarkington. [They were married 11 Aug. 1833: Marriage Book 2, page 42.]

15 Aug. 1839. Hannah Theall is deceased. [See

her succession, Est. #425, opened in 1840.]

1 Aug. 1845. Nancy Theall, daughter of James F. Theall, is the wife of Malcolm A. Fraser.

#231. NICOLAS VEEDER, DEC. 8 NOV. 1832

A. R. Splane petitions, representing that the decedent lately died intestate, leaving no heirs in the state known to petitioner. Real estate is involved in the estate.

29 Nov. 1832. James Allison and Bennett A. Curtis appointed appraisers. James L. Norris is curator of this vacant estate. Benjamin R. Gant, Esq., represents the absent heirs. Edwin L. Cockle and Seth Lewis, Jr., witnessed.

14 Jan. 1833. Buyers at sale: James S. Norris, John Long, M. Campbell, A. G. Vincent, Seth Lewis, N. Verret, Benjamin Nichols, Michael Night [sic], Alfred Campbell, John Johnson, Castagne, Joseph A. Lacy, Jared Y. Sanders, Joseph Andrus, Jesse Hulick, David Bell, Joseph Andrus, J. W. Dough, Doct. Gibson, John Ditch, Jarvis, James Campbell, W. A. Seay.

No heirship shown

* #232. DR. JOHN [THOMAS] TOWLES, DEC. 31 OCT. 1832

Anne A. Conrad, widow. Decedent departed this life 26 Oct. 1832. She is natural tutrix of her minor children: 1. Thomas, 2. Charles Mynn, 3. Mary Elizabeth, 4. Ann Frances, 5. Gertrude Elizabeth, and 6. Philip Slaughter Towles. Winthrop S. Harding, Frederick D. Conrad of East Baton Rouge Parish, and David Weeks are sureties.

2 Nov. 1832. John Turnbull Towles, minor son of decedent's first marriage with Susan Turnbull, is now absent from the state.

1 Nov. 1832. Seals affixed. Robert P. Rogers and Edwin L. Cockle witnessed. Winthrop S. Harding is guardian of John [above], and Edmund N. Sale is appointed his counsel.

11 Nov. 1833. Fam. meeting for the minors of decedent's second marriage: David Weeks and

William T. Palfrey, uncles by marriage; in default of other relatives: George Royster, Donelson Caffery, John B. Murphy, Jehu Wilkinson, and Agricole Fuselier, Jr. Winthrop S. Harding is their undertutor.

29 Oct. 1834. West Feliciana Parish, La. Daniel Turnbull is tutor to John Turnbull Towles. [See Est. #236, below.]

24 Feb. 1834. Buyers & sureties at sale: Theodore Fay, G. L. Fuselier, John T. Towles, Daniel Turnbull, Joshua Baker, P. H. Rentrop, Eli Riggs, David Weeks, Elisha Embrie [?], Benjamin Hudson, Charles Grevemberg, James Muggah, Honore Carlin, William J. Nash, John G. Richardson, Martin Demaret, Charles Conrad, Reubin Doty, Henderson Crawford, Donelson Caffery, O. D. Longstaff, John B. Murphy, Daniel P. Sparks, Frederick D. Conrad, Joseph Gerbeau, Agricole Fuselier, LaClaire Fuselier, Washington Jackson, E. L. Cockle, Nathan Wooster, John Brownson, William Pumphrey, Richard Lynch, George Heydel, Lewis Sterling, Zenon Decuir, W. T. Palfrey, Lufroy Carlin, C. M. Conrad, Joel Coe, John Carson, John Linton, Julien LeBlanc, John P. Hudson, James Smith, Dr. C. Nettelton, R[ankin?] Rogers, Joseph Bryant, Celestin T. Carlin, Charles M. Charpantier, Peter H. Rentrop, John Lay, John Smith. [Note: some names I could not identify.]

Gen. note. Decedent was born 8 May 1779 in Spotsylvania Co., Va., and came to St. Mary Parish in 1804. His first wife was Susan Turnbull, born 16 May 1793, at Baton Rouge and died in St. Mary Parish 19 Apr. 1817, a daughter of John Turnbull and Catherine Rucker, a Virginian. John Turnbull was a native of Dumphrieshire, Scotland. He died in 1799, his wife in 1832. She is buried on "Inheritance" Plantation in West Feliciana Parish. They had 6 children: 1. Susan, wife of this decedent; 2. Isabella, wife of Robert Semple; 3. Sarah, wife of Lewis Sterling [see Est. #100]; 4. Walter; 5. Daniel, married Martha Barrow; this couple built beautiful "Rosedown" Plantation, still extant in West Feliciana Parish; and 6. John Turnbull.

After his first wife's death, Dr. Towles married Ann Alexander Conrad,* probably in St. Mary Parish, 24 Oct. 1818. She was a daughter of Frederick Conrad and Frances Thruston. See Ests. #80 and 140. [*See page 184A]

Susan Turnbull Towles' only surviving child was John Turnbull Towles. He was a sugar planter in West Feliciana Parish. On 15 May 1835 he married Frances Peyton Eskridge. They had a large family. He died 28 Oct. 1878. He and his wife are buried at "Weyanoke" Plantation in West Feliciana Parish, La. [The foregoing information on this family is from "Susan's Tombstone" by Morris Raphael in the Sunday Iberian of New Iberia, La., 12 Sept. 1971, page 25. I also wish to thank Mrs. Sarah Towles Reed of New Orleans, a descendant of John Turnbull Towles, for information.]

The Mississippi D. A. R. book tells us [pages 259-60] that Catherine Rucker was a daughter of Peter Rucker of Orange or Prince Edward County, Va. He was married twice: (1) Sarah Cowherd and (2) a Miss Davis. He served in the Revolutionary War and also furnished supplies, and had also served in the French and Indian War under Col. Robert Slaughter. He came early to Mississippi and settled south of Natchez on the river. Peter Rucker had at least 5 children [by which wife is not stated.]

#233. JOHN N. KERSHAW, DEC. 5 OCT. 1832

Mary Hays, widow of decedent, who lately died intestate leaving no children born at the time of his death, "but from the natural course of human events, your petitioner supposes that a child will be born in a very short time who will be entitled to inherit the estate of decedent." Alexander R. Splane was appointed curator of the estate.

6 Dec. 1832. Mary Ann Kershaw is the infant daughter of decedent. Mary Ann Hays confirmed as natural tutrix. Jonathan Smith is appointed administrator of the estate. John O. Lacy and Henderson Crawford appointed appraisers. Lufroy Carlin and Thomas Edwards witnessed.

7 Aug. 1833. Fam. meeting: Thomas B. Kershaw, paternal uncle; Jonathan Smith, paternal uncle by marriage; James Hays, maternal grandfather; John F. Jackson, maternal uncle [by marriage?]; Levi Foster, distant relation; and James Ferguson, friend. Alexander R. Splane is undertutor.

17 Aug. 1836. Mary Hays is now the wife of John W. Richardson.

17 Sept. 1836. Fam. meeting: Jonathan Smith, uncle by marriage; Thomas B. Kershaw is sick and unable to attend; Clark Nettelton, James Ferguson, Nathan Wooster, and Jacob W. King, friends. Nathan Wooster appointed tutor.

15 June 1842. Fam. meeting: Jonathan Smith; Andrew Smith, first cousin; Thomas Kershaw, uncle; Sam Kershaw, uncle; and James Ferguson. They are described as "the nearest relations."

11 July 1842. Fam. meeting: Jonathan Smith; Andrew Smith; and William Pumphrey, Anthony Walker, and Samuel Kemper, friends. Mary Hays, minor's mother, is deceased.

15 Nov. 1843. Daniel Dennett is tutor.

3 Feb. 1846. Fam. meeting: Jonathan Smith, uncle; Andrew Smith, cousin; John Smith cited but does not appear [relationship not given]; Robert W. McMillan, John M. Foote, and Robert Johnson, friends. John J. Jackson of Iberville Parish, an uncle appointed tutor. [Note. Mary Hays' mother may have been married to a Mr. Jackson before she married James Hays.]

Gen. note. Decedent was a son of John N. Kershaw, Sr. His succession was Est. #134, opened in 1824. Decedent was married to Mary Ann Hays, daughter of James Hays, 5 Feb. 1829 [Marriage Book 1, page 445]. A cattle brand was registered in Attakapas in 1802 in the name of Jacques Haze. Mary Ann Hays remarried John W. Richardson 14 Aug. 1833 [Marriage Book 2, page 43].

John F. Jackson married Phrosine Collins 11 Mar. 1830 [Marriage Book 2, page 4]. Andrew C. Smith married Elizabeth Judd Rose 4 Jan. 1844 [Marriage Book 3, page 67].

#234. W. H. FRERE - MISSING

#235. BARTHELEMY MC CARTY, DEC. 15 OCT. 1832

Parish of Orleans, City of New Orleans. Armand Petot testamentary executor and universal legatee of decedent. Refers to original petition and inventory; neither, or copy of neither, is included in this succession. St. Mary Parish inventory is shown. Lewis Moor [Moore] and Robert C. Trousdale are appointed appraisers.

Gen. note. Jean Baptiste McCarty is listed in *American State Papers* in connection with land claims [Vol. III, page 120]. One of his land claims went to a son, Bartholomew; another, to a son, Edmund.

#236. JOHN T[URNBULL] TOWLES - NOT A SUCCESSION [SEE EST. #232, ABOVE]

4 Feb. 1833. Walter Turnbull is the only other individual who stands in the same degree of relationship to minor and he also resides in West Feliciana Parish, as Daniel Turnbull.

17 June 1833. Petitioner is himself, a minor over the age of puberty. Requests that his maternal uncle, Daniel Turnbull, of West Feliciana Parish, be appointed his tutor.

15 Nov. 1833. Samuel Wilkinson and John Smith are appointed appraisers of the minor's property. Jacob Anselen and Jeremiah H. Allen witnessed.

20 Aug. 1833. Joshua Baker is undertutor.

#237. CORNELIA S. EVANS, WIFE OF JOHN DE HART, DEC. 16 FEB. 1833

John DeHart petitions; Cornelia Evans, his wife, lately died leaving 4 children, all under the age of puberty: 1. John Evans, 2. Margaret E.,

3. Sarah Ann, and 4. Cornelia S. DeHart. John DeHart confirmed as natural tutor. John M. Evans, uncle, appointed undertutor. Family friends composed council for minors: Alexander R. Splane, Franklin Wharton, James Al------, John W. Gibson, and Ogden D. Longstaff. John DeHart and John Evans are the minors' only relations.

21 Feb. 1833. Inventory made at the residence of Capt. John DeHart. Agricole Fuselier, Sr., and Alexander Jackson appointed appraisers; H. B. Hutcheson and John N. Parkerson witnessed.

Decedent is also called "Louisa Cornelia."

Gen. note. Estate No. 27, opened in 1812, one of the missing successions, is listed in the name of "J. Evans." A John Evans is listed in the 1810 Attakapas Federal Census. This may have been the father of John and Cornelia Evans.

#238. JOHN ARMSTRONG, DEC. 14 FEB. 1833

Joshua Garrett is the petitioner, a brother-in-law of decedent. Seals were affixed to the personal belongings of the decedent at the house of Mrs. Gordy. John J. Garrett appointed Administrator of this estate.

18 Feb. 1833. Alexis Carlin and Jonathan Smith are appointed appraisers.

14 Mar. 1833. Buyers at sale: James Hayes, Alfred Smith, John C. Cook, Thomas Edwards, John Garrett, Dr. Clark Nettelton, A. Bridgefore [?].

No heirship is indicated.

Gen. note. Decedent was a son of Margaret Armstrong, Est. #185, opened in 1831. See that succession for details of this family.

#239. BENJAMIN B. WITHINGTON, DEC. 25 FEB. 1833

William L. Withington [Worthington] of New Orleans, brother of this decedent, petitions. Decedent died intestate. Petitioner is his only heir residing in the state. Petitioner appointed curator of estate. W. T. Palfrey and Winfrey Lockett appointed appraisers. John B. Lockett and John Caffery witnessed.

#240. LOUISA ARMSTRONG, WIFE OF PETER H[ICKOCK] ROBERT, DEC. 2 MAR. 1833

Peter H. Robert petitions; requests an inventory of the estate of his wife, decedent. John C. Cook and John Rice are appointed appraisers. Michael Gordy and John J. Garrett witnessed.

9 Mar. 1833. Petitioner is confirmed as natural tutor of: 1. Jo Ann, 2. Diana, 3. Solathost [?], and 4. Louisa Robert, his minor children all under the age of puberty, legal heirs of Louisa Robert, his deceased wife, and petitioner.

13 Mar. 1833. Peter William Robert is undertutor to the minors. Fam. meeting: Baynard C. Robert, uncle-in-law to the minors; Michael Gordy, uncle-in-law; John J. Garrett, uncle-in-law; John Coe [Joel?] and Bennett A. Curtis, friends.

3 June 1841. Peter H. Robert is dead and the daughter Louisa Robert is also dead. Alfred Smith is tutor to the remaining minors.

Gen. note. Decedent was probably a daughter of Margaret Armstrong [see Est. #185, opened in 1831]. Peter Hickock Robert was a son of Peter Robert and his first wife, Elizabeth Jaudon. See his succession, Est. #127, opened in 1823.

Dianna Robert married Henry L. Bouta or Bonta 25 Apr. 1844 [Marriage Book 3, page 74].

Bayard C. Robert was married to Martha E. Robert, minors' paternal aunt; Michael Gordy was married to Sarah A. Robert, another paternal aunt. John J. Garrett was married to Phoebe Armstrong, a maternal aunt.

#241. WILLIAM MARDEN, DEC. 25 FEB. 1833

Henry A. Thomas petitions. Decedent lately died indebted to petitioner. Edwin L. Cockle and Thomas Youngblood are appointed appraisers. Seth Lewis and Henry J. Gibbons [?] witnessed. Petitioner appointed curator of estate.

22 July 1833. Buyers at sale: A. Youngblood, Hilaire Carlin, William B. McNamar, William

Whitney or Whiting, James A. Anderson. H. Lefort,
Franklin Wharton, Seth Lewis, Thomas Youngblood.
22 Sept. 1834. H. C. Dwight appointed curator.
No heirship shown.

#242.CELESTIN CARLIN, DEC. 10 APR. 1833

Lufroy Carlin petitions; decedent lately died intestate leaving several heirs, among them petitioner and 1 minor child. [Note: the minor was William Frederick Haifleigh, son of Jacob Haifleigh and decedent's daughter, Celeste Carlin, whose succession, Est. #135B, was opened in 1822.]

12 Apr. 1833. John J. Garrett and Martin Demaret appointed appraisers. Honore Carlin and Sylvain Salles witnessed.

8 June 1833. Fam. meeting for William Frederick Haifleigh, grandson of decedent. Jacob Haifleigh confirmed as natural tutor and Adelard Carlin, uncle of minor, appointed undertutor to said minor. Lufroy and Celestin Theodule Carlin, maternal uncles; Miss Aimee Carlin, maternal aunt; Hilaire Carlin and Octave Cornay, maternal uncles by marriage; and Alexis Carlin, another maternal uncle, compose family meeting for the minor. [Note: an Alexis Carlin is not listed as an heir of this decedent, living or deceased, in the partition order. This must be a reference to the minor's great-uncle, brother of decedent. See Est. #1.] Hilaire Carlin is the husband of Josephine Carlin, and Octave Cornay, the husband of Hortense Carlin. Telesphore Carlin of New Orleans is also identified as one of the heirs of decedent.

1 July 1833. Buyers and sureties at sale: Michael Knight, Anthony Walker, Octave Cornay, Adelard Carlin, Richard Hungerford, William Sharp, Hilaire Carlin, Lufroy Carlin, Joseph Bryan, Jacob Haifleigh, Celestin T. Carlin, Sylvain Salles, Aimee Carlin, Alexis Carlin, Edwin L. Cockle, Jared Y. Sanders, John Long, Harris Tompkins, and Julien LeBlanc.

6 Jan. 1834. Buyers at another sale: Lufroy

Carlin, Urbain Carlin, William G. Sanders, Numa Cornay, Anthony Walker, Michael Hayes, Honore Carlin, Eugene Sennette, Celestin T. Carlin, Daniel P. Sparks, Octave Cornay, Ursin Demaret, Jacob Haifleigh, Thomas E. Bowles, Hilaire Carlin, Telesphore Carlin, Thomas Wallace, Joseph Gerbeau, Edwin L. Cockle, Ursin Carlin, Adelard Carlin, Milo F. M. C. ["Free man of color," term used to designate a freed negro], Godfroy Carlin, Sylvain Salles, Urbin Carlin, Henry C. Dwight, and Desire Carlin.

1 May 1852. Final settlement [This appears to be the final date.] Heirs of decedent: 1. Lufroi Carlin, 2. Adelard Carlin, 3. Celestin Theodule Carlin, 4. Aimee Carlin, wife of Desire Carlin, 5. Josephine Carlin, wife of Hilaire Carlin, 6. Hortense Carlin, wife of Octave Cornay, 7. Telesphore Carlin, deceased since his father and represented by his dative executor, Octave Cornay [since he is represented earlier as being "of New Orleans," his will and succession may be of record in Orleans or one of the surrounding Parishes.], and 8. William Frederick Haifleigh, representing his deceased mother, Celeste Carlin, wife of Jacob Haifleigh, deceased. [The heirs listed in this partition are given on page 289 of the book containing this succession in the Office of the Clerk of Court, St. Mary Parish, Franklin, La.]

Gen. note. Decedent was a son of Joseph Carlin [see Est. #1] and his wife, Francoise Lange [Est. #43]. He married Marie Therese Prevost in 1793. She was a daughter of Nicolas Prevost dit Blondin and widow of Pierre Provost. Her succession was opened in 1817 [Est. #61]. She had 3 children by her first husband. See her succession for details. According to Bodin I 113-114 and II 51, Celestin Carlin and Marie Therese Provost had 8 children, as follows: 1. Adelard, born 3 May 1802, married Marie Carmelite Carlin; 2. Amada [Aimee?], born 3 Aug. 1797; 3. Celeste, born ca. December of 1794, married Jacob Haifleigh in 1816; 4. Hortense, born 1 Jan. 1804; 5. Josephine, born 10 Apr. 1799; 6. Lufroy, married Henriette Carlin; 7. Telesphore, born 20 Feb. 1801; and 8. Euphrosius, born 12 Feb. 1796 [Celestin Theodule?].

Jacob Haifleigh remarried Elizabeth Riddle 20 Jan. 1825 [Marriage Book 1, page 287]. Lufroy Carlin married Harriet Carlin 12 Apr. 1825 [Marriage Book 1, page 300]. Adelard Carlin married Carmalite Carlin 11 Feb. 1831 [Marriage Book 2, page 12]. Aimee Carlin had a cattle brand registered in her name in 1833. She married Desire Carlin 17 July 1834 [Marriage Book 2, page 59. She died 6 Jan. 1847 at the age of 48 years, according to the Planters' Banner, 14 Jan. 1847, page 2, column 5. Her succession is Est. #608, opened in that year. Two successions were opened in the name of Desire Carlin: #889, opened in 1855, and #1021, opened in 1859.

Josephine married Hilaire Carlin 10 Jan. 1828 [Marriage Book 1, page 407]. Hortense married Octave Cornay 29 July 1828 [Marriage Book 1, page 431]. Her succession was opened in 1852, Est. #776. Octave Cornay remarried Caroline Lanoue in Baton Rouge [East Baton Rouge Parish] 13 June 1853 [Planters' Banner, 23 June 1853, page 3, col. 3]. Celestin Theodule Carlin married Henrietta Trowbridge, daughter of Isaac Trowbridge, in New Haven, Conn., 1 Sept. 1847 [Planters' Banner, 30 Sept. 1847, page 3, col. 2]. [Note: this could have been a second marriage for him, or even a later generation.]

#243. GROTIUS BLOSS, DEC. 9 APR. 1833

Will. Sgd. 26 Mar. 1833. Stated he had never been married. Mother, Mrs. Rowena Kellogg, widow first to James Bloss, father of decedent, and now of Andrew Patterson and who now resides in the State of Ohio. Brothers: James M. Bloss, Timothy R. Bloss, and Martin L. Patterson. Sisters: Eliza, wife of Kempshall, and Clarissa

Bloss. Estate to be euqally divided among them, share and share alike. Sister Eliza Kempshall and Judson Harmon to be executrix and executor. Witnesses: Hilary B. Cenas, William N. Hall, and Walter Finney. William Christy, Notary Public, New Orleans, La., notarized the document. Seals affixed in the presence of Anthony Hartman and John Martin. Deceased lately died in New Orleans. Apparently the deceased had a store in St. Mary Parish. Judson Harmon, clerk in the store, was made curator of the personal effects of decedent in the store.

17 Apr. 1833. Eliza Kempshall [sister] petitions for an inventory. Jesse E. Lacy, Thomas Wilcoxon and Andrew W. Dismuke appointed appraisers.

30 Apr. 1833. Open accounts: Christopher Bryan, John Smith, James Muggah, Estate of Lewis Moore, John Romel [?], Captain Harley Curtis, M. Carboulez, Franklin Wharton, M. H. Carroll, George W. Archer, John B. Bemiss, Edgar Demaret, Elam Patterson, Henry Knight, Hilaire Carlin, Numa Cornay, Thomas Wilcoxon, Robert B. Brashear, George Haydel, William Nimig [?], Andrew Bryan, E. P. Foust, James Andrews, Manuel Diluky, Conrad Hartman, Benjamin Hornsby, William H. Basherville, Charles M. Charpantier, George Bryan, Madame Margaret Rentrop, Marlin Chambers, Henry Brauman [?], Samuel Rice, James Owens, Joseph Berwick, Nathaniel M. Cochran, H. W. Farley, Charles Bryan, Michael Duval, Henry Knight, Jr., George Phipps, Estate of John Towles, Nicolas Broussard, Miss Hariette Knight, Daniel P. Sparks, William J. Nash, Anthony Coman [?], Adam Pitre, Pavy & Caillet, Walter B. Wilcoxon, Rowel [?] Vercin [?], Joseph Clement [?], William W. Wofford, Richard Hungerford, Robert C. Trimble, Joseph Gerbeau, Michael Davis, Raymond Lansalle [?], J. & P. Bryan, Ale----- Nash, Brashear & Barr, Henry J. Muggah, James Pamecy [?], Dr. Thomas Youngblood, Dr. Dismuke & Bain, Aler---

Hunnington, Alexander W. McClure, Samuel Ferguson, James Lynch, John Vining, Ursin Rowe, Captain William H. Basset, John Clayton, Ludger [?] Rowe, Benjamin Hudson, John B. Barks, William Waggoner, Madame Eliza Reels, Louis Daigle, Lewis Wofford, Lewis Moore, Jr., William Allen, Lorenzo Munson, Auguste Lapere, Pryor Bryan, Edmund Burke, Henry Pitree, Gilbert Sennett, Henry A. Thomas, Dr. A. M. Dismuke, Dr. John C. Bain, Hubert Bertrand, Richard Lynch, Robert Cook, Joel Vanoy.

Bad debts: Thomas C. Vines, Inman [?] & Root, John Hunnington, William Marcin [?], John Neilson, Thomas Vining, Cyrus Clark, John A. Chapman, William Shaver [?], Thomas Kirkham, Peyton T. Galesby, Jeremiah Munson.

Additional open accounts: Miss Eliza Petrie, E. H. Byrnes, William Jarvis, John O. Lacy, John Lay, William Michetree.

30 Apr. 1833. Alexander R. Splane appointed to represent the absent heirs.

20 May 1833. Buyers at sale: Ursin Rowe, Antoine Como, Jean Lanton, J. S. Norris [?], William J. Nash, Jean Lasslon [?], George Haydel, James Owens, Charles Theriot, Hilaire Carlin, Lacy [?] & Patterson, A. W. Dismuke, John Muggah, John & P. Bryan, William Vining, David Robbins, John Vining, Jacob Hartman, Arby Curtis, Harley Curtis, Placide Pulaski [?], Anthony Hartman, Bernard Migues, Auguste Lassere, James Andrus, Julien LeBlanc, John Smith, A. R. Splane, Bridges Sojourner, Martin Lenoue [?], Mrs. Kempshall, Octave Cornay, Thomas Wilcoxin, Michael Hartman, Pavy & Caillet, John Martin, Louis Daigle, Michael Charpantier, Placide [?] Carlin, Louis Wofford, J. B. Felteman, N. B. Cook, Michel Theriot, J. B. Broussard, John Wilcoxin, James McMurtrey, E. Doson [?], B. Sylvain, H. Brannon, H. A. Thomas, George Philips, Charles Trufort, N. Down [?], John Smith, A. Doiron, Louis Daigle, C. M. Charpantier, R. B. Royster, E. L. Cockle, John Martin. No final settlement shown.

#244. EMMA L. TAYLOR, WIFE OF JOHN B. MURPHY, DEC. 24 APR. 1833

John B. Murphy petitions; his wife, Emma L. Taylor, has lately died. She left these children by the petitioner, all minors: 1. Lydia, 2. Simon Taylor, 3. Donelson, 4. Martha, 5. Isaac Baker Murphy.

Fam. meeting for the minors: Donelson Caffery, paternal uncle by marriage; John Caffery, Seth Lewis, Jr., James Allison and Joseph W. Lyman, all friends in default of other relatives.

John B. Murphy was confirmed as the minors' natural tutor. Thomas H. Lewis, Esq., of St. Landry Parish, named undertutor. Joshua Baker and Henry Thompson witnessed.

25 Apr. 1833. Alexander Jackson and Henry Foote appointed appraisers. Thomas H. Lewis and Henry Thompson witnessed.

Gen. note. John B. Murphy was a son of John Murphy [Est. #146, opened in 1826]. He remarried Mrs. Lucy Brown 10 May 1833 [Marriage Book 2, page 38]. Donelson Caffery Murphy died 11 Oct. 1851 at the plantation of his father, aged 24 years [Planters' Banner, 18 Oct. 1851, page 3, col. 3.] His succession was opened in 1852, Est. #758.

Martha P. Murphy married Thomas J. Foster 20 Jan. 1848 [Planters' Banner, 27 Jan. 1848, page 3, col. 1].

#245. PEYTON LYNCH, DEC. 21 MAY 1833

James and Richard Lynch, sons of decedent, petition. Decedent has lately died. His widow and many co-heirs at present reside in the State of Virginia. Joshua Baker is appointed to represent the absent heirs.

23 May 1833. James Lynch is appointed administrator of the estate.

9 Oct. 1833. Alexander, Montgomery, Jane, and Ann Lynch are the minor children of decedent, absent from this state and resident in Petersburg, Virginia. George Lynch of St. Mary Parish is also

a son and heir of decedent, a minor over the age
of puberty; requests that James Lynch, his
brother, be appointed tutor to him. Ann Lynch is
the widow of the decedent.

15 Oct. 1833. Fam. meeting for all 5 minors:
Richard Lynch, their brother; in default of other
relations, James Sanders, James A. Anderson, John
Hartman, and John N. Field. James Lynch, brother,
is appointed tutor to all 5 minors. Joshua Baker
appointed undertutor to all 5.

16 Dec. 1833. Buyers at sale: James Lynch,
David Robbins, Richard Lynch, Joshua Baker, Joseph
Berwick, David Berwick, W. Rochel, William W.
Wofford, John Moore, Ursin Demaret, Nathaniel M.
Cochran, Honore Carlin, Michael Gordy, Ursin
Demaret, James Muggah, O. Cornay, George Haydel,
Daniel P. Sparks, Thomas Youngblood, C. M. Char-
pantier, M. H. Carroll, W. J. Nash, Pavy &
Caillet, Julien LeBlanc. Henry Branman [?] and
Edwin L. Cockle witnessed.

23 May 1833. John Smith and Bridges
Sojourner appointed appraisers. Daniel P. Sparks
and Harley Curtis witnessed.

6 Dec. 1834. Alexander Lynch is a major and
attended a family meeting for the other 4
minor children of decedent.

#246. BENJAMIN BUCHANAN, DEC. 24 MAY 1833
William G. Sanders petitions. Decedent of
Lafayette Parish, La., died 17 May 1833 in St.
Mary Parish. John Hartman and Watson McKerrall
appointed appraisers. Francois L. L. Boutie,
David Reid, and William G. Sanders witnessed.
Capt. Robert Perry of Lafayette Parish is
appointed curator of the estate.

Joseph H. Cole of Salem, Mass., gives
deposition; he is no blood relation to the
decedent.

No heirship indicated.

#247. PETER A. DE JARNATT, DEC. 30 APR. 1833
Watson McKerrall petitions. Decedent lately
died. Petitioner and decedent were business

partners.

4 May 1833. Watson McKerrall appointed curator of this estate.

25 May 1833. Winfrey Lockett and Gideon Boyce appointed appraisers. Victor Lataste and John Randlett witnessed. John P. McMillan is attorney for the absent heirs.

2 Mar. 1835. John Spickard of Montgomery Co., Va., and William Dunbar of Monroe Co., Va., appoint Doct. H. N. Saunders of Montgomery Co., Va., as lawful attorney to transact all business relative to the estate of the decedent, "being heirs and legal representatives of the same, by marriage with the sisters" of the decedent [names not given].

3 Mar. 1835. Richard Dejarnatt of Montgomery Co., Va., appoints same concerning the estate of his son, Peter, decedent.

#248. ISAAC BALDWIN, DEC. 7 MAY 1833

Authority from the judge in New Orleans to inventory the property of decedent in St. Mary Parish. Joshua Baker and David Bell appointed appraisers. Edwin L. Cockle and Henry Thompson witnessed.

This succession contains only the inventory. Decedent must have been a resident of New Orleans. No heirship is shown. His complete succession is probably of record in Orleans or one of the surrounding parishes.

Gen. note. Isaac Baldwin was married to Eliza _____. Her succession, Est. #324, was opened in St. Mary Parish in 1836.

#249. FREDERICK PELLERIN, DEC. 4 JULY 1833

Will. In French. Antoine Francois Solange Sorrel and Gabriel Laclair Fuselier witnessed the fact that the will was in the handwriting of the decedent. Jean Armelin and Laurent Sigur give deposition that decedent was of this parish and departed this life the 1st day of July, 1833. [Note: this is the first such document in these successions which compiler found.]

Mary Rose Angelique Desiree Coralie Pellerin petitions; decedent was her father. This petition is in French.

Seals affixed to personal effects of decedent.

Marie Anne Pecot is the widow of the decedent.

10 July 1833. Jean Armelin and Laurent Sigur are testamentary executors of the estate.

18 July 1833. Seals raised.

22 Jan. 1834. Marie Anne Pecot confirmed as natural tutrix to her minor son, Charles Frederick Pellerin. Laurent Sigur is appointed undertutor; Joseph Bacon, special undertutor [this is the only instance compiler found of a special undertutor].

2 Oct. 1837. Marie R. A. D. Coralie Pellerin now the wife of Martial Sorrel.

Gen. note. Decedent was a son of Gregoire Pellerin and his wife, Cecile Prejean, and he was born 10 Dec. 1770. He signed a Marriage Contract with Marie Anne Pecot in 1805 in St. Martin Parish. He is a brother to Marie-Joseph Pellerin, who married Alexander Frere [Est. #17]. [1774 Census, page 42, and St. Martin Parish OA 22, #201.] Marie Anne Pecot was a daughter of Francois Pecot and Rosalie Prejeant [1774 Census, page 42].

Another daughter, Cecile Rosalie Silenie Pellerin, wife of Antoine Francois Selange Sorrel, predeceased her father, without issue. See her succession, Est. #164, opened in 1828. The succession of Charles Frederick Pellerin was opened in 1835, Est. #317.

Bodin tells us [II 187] that Francois Pecot was of Mirabalais, Ile St. Domingue. See Est. #17.

#250. JAMES LACY, FAMILY MEETING FOR [NOT A SUCCESSION]

25 Apr. 1833. Fam. meeting for James Lacy, minor son of Susan Lacy and the late Jesse E. Lacy, deceased [see his succession, Est. #114, opened in 1821]. Susan Lacy petitions; she is natural tutrix of her minor son, James Lacy. The family meeting concerns the sale of 2 slaves.

Benjamin Lacy, Joseph Lacy, William Lacy, Jesse E. Lacy and Daniel Lacy, all his brothers, compose this family council. James Lacy is over 19 years of age at this time, heir to the late Jesse E. Lacy. He is emancipated.

10 June 1833. Another family meeting is held, this time composed of: Susan Lacy, the minor's mother; William, Benjamin, Daniel, Jesse E., and Joseph Lacy, his brothers. See Est. #114.

* #251. MARTIN M. CAMPBELL, DEC. 15 JULY 1833

Drusilla Campbell, the widow of decedent, petitions. Decedent lately died. Children born of their marriage were: 1. Martin, 2, Eliza, both minors over the age of puberty, 3. Caroline, and 4. Ann Campbell, both minors under the age of puberty. [Note: a 5th child, Emily Jane, was apparently a posthumous child. See Gen. Note, below.]

31 July 1833. Drusilla Campbell is the minors' natural tutrix and administratrix of the estate.

13 July 1835. Alexander R. Splane is administrator of the estate.

14 July 1835. Seth Lewis, Jr., and Ephriam P. Foust are appointed appraisers. Joshua Baker and Edwin L. Cockle witnessed.

2 Oct. 1835. John Hartman is appointed curator ad hoc to Alfred Thruston Perryman, an emancipated minor.

Gen. note. Decedent was married (1) to Mary Louise Ditch. For her background see Est. #31. Decedent married (2) Drusilla Highfield. Drusilla's first husband was Montford I. Perriman/Perryman, whom she married 28 Apr. 1814 [Marriage Book 1, page 43]. There were 2 children of this marriage: 1. Harriet Perryman, who married Jesse Hulick [see Est. #96] 8 Nov. 1832 [Marriage Book 2, page 33], and 2. Alfred Thruston Perryman, above referred to. Montford Perryman's succession [Est. #49] was opened in 1815. Drusilla Highfield Perryman married Martin M. Campbell, this decedent, 20 Mar. 1817 [Marriage Book 1, page 111].

Drusilla Campbell's succession was opened in 1848, Est. #647. Martin M. Campbell served in the War of 1812, and from Pension Application records in the National Archives, which Mrs. Clyde Alpha of Franklin generously shared with this compiler, we know of the 5th child. There is some discrepancy as to the exact date of this decedent's death. This succession was opened on 15 July 1833. In the pension records his death date is given variously as "on or about" the 7th, 13th, or 14th day of July in that year. A good educated guess, it would seem to compiler, would be the earlier date; it would be most unusual for a succession to be opened the day following a death, or even 2 days later.

On 24 Feb. 1851 Independence Alpha applied for a bounty land warrant on behalf of Martin M. Campbell's two minor children, "Louisa Ann Campbell, about 19 years of age, and Emily Jane Campbell, about 18 years of age," to which the "said Martin M. Campbell may be entitled under the Act of Congress passed September 28th, 1850."

Independence Alpha was at that time the minors' tutor, their mother having died. Emily Jane married John Alpha, brother of Independence.

Martin H. Campbell and Eliza Campbell, the 2 older children of decedent, had a cattle brand registered in their names in 1821. Martin married Mary Ann Johnson 5 Sept. 1843 [Marriage Book 3, page 62]. Eliza Campbell married Samuel Buniff. She was 26 in the 1850 census, he 36. [From the files of Mrs. Clyde Alpha of Franklin, La.]

#252. EUGENE BOREL, CONCERNING PROPERTY OF
11 July 1833. Fam. meeting called: Nicolas Loisel, half-brother; Eugene Borel fils, and Philogene Borel, sons; Bonin Clairville, son-in-law; Zenon Bourgeois, nephew; Jean Baptiste Bourgeois, brother-in-law, to compose council.

19 July 1833. Meeting held. Annette Prevost, wife, appointed curatrix.

20 July 1833. John G. Richardson and Godefroy Prevost appointed appraisers.

17 Mar. 1834. Fam. meeting held at the residence of Doralise Judice, widow of Lufroy Prevost: Eugene Borel fils, Philogene, and Valsain Borel, sons; Pierre and Benjamin Borel, nephews, composed council. Valsain Borel resides in the Parish of St. Martin. Nicolas Loisel appointed curator.

14 July 1834. Buyers at sale: Manette [Annette] Prevost, Nicolas Loisel, Camille Bonin, Valsain Borel, Simeon Patout, Lufroy Bonvilin, Dubreutil Soule, Dubreuil Olivier, Frederick Louviere, Eugene Borel fils, Pierre Bonin, L. Gonsoulin, Joseph Borel, Joshua Baker, Antoine Mendosa, Pedro Mendosa, Andy Nelson, George Singleton, William Kilgore, William Pumphrey, Regobert Verret, Pierre Arcenau, Reubin Doty, R. McCarty, Godfroy Verret, Philippe Verret, Zenon Boutte, Dezincourt Borel, Francois Louviere; Edwin L. Cockle and Joshua Baker witnessed.

28 Apr. 1839. Mrs. Victoire Etier is a sister of Eugene Borel pere. They, with others, are children of the late widow Loisel by her first marriage with Pierre Borel.

Madelaine Borel, widow of Francois Prevost, is another sister.

Marie Borel, wife of Jean Baptiste Bourgeois, is another sister. Some of these documents are in French. There are numerous inventories.

1 July 1850 [? This date is difficult to decipher.]. Dezancourt Borel; Cidalise Borel, wife of Cleoville Bonin [given as Bonin Clairville at the Fam. meeting on 11 July 1833, on the previous page]; and Doralise Borel, wife of Frederick Louviere, all residents of St. Mary Parish, are listed as heirs of Eugene Borel, deceased. [This document is on page 155 of the succession book containing this estate.] There were at least 3 other sons, listed in earlier Fam. meetings, though some of them may have been deceased at this time. There was no complete list of heirs or final settlement apparent to the compiler.

Apparent from these records are at least 6 children of Eugene Borel and Annette Prevost: 1. Eugene Borel fils, 2. Philogene Borel, 3. Valsain Borel of St. Martin Parish, 4. Dezincourt Borel, 5. Cidalise Borel, wife of Cleoville Bonin, and 6. Doralise Borel, wife of Frederick Louviere.

Gen. note. Jean Louis Loisel, of Paris, son of Adrien Loisel and Charlotte Chardin, signed a Marriage Contract with Catherine Tou[r]part, widow of Pierre Borel, 8 Apr. 1783 [St. Martin Parish OA 3, #66]. Nicolas Pelagie Loisel was their son [1774 Census, page 11]. Eugene Borel, son of Pierre and Catherine Toupart, and Manet [Annette] Prevost, daughter of Francois Prevost and Genevieve Bonain, signed a Marriage Contract 13 Nov. 1798 [ibid., page 26].

The 1774 Census further tells us [page 42] that Pierre Borel and Catherine Toupart evidently emigrated from the German Coast to Attakapas. His estate was opened in St. Martin Parish 18 June 1780. His heirs were his widow and 7 children (2 boys and 5 girls, the book says), but the children were not named.

The 1774 Census lists, on page 42, 3 of the 7 children of this couple:

1. Marie, who signed a Marriage Contract 18 July 1787 [St. Martin OA 5, #34] with Francois Pomet, son of Jean Baptiste Pomet and Francoise Barraillez, a native of German Coast. Marie secondly signed a Marriage Contract, on 26 July 1794 [St. Martin OA 15, #73] with Jean Baptiste Bourgeois, son of Jacques Bourgeois and Marie Anne Sauvagin.

2. Eugene, native of Attakapas, who signed a Marriage Contract 13 Nov. 1798 [St. Martin OA 18, #96] with Manet [Annette] Prevost, daughter of Francois Prevost [Est. #95, opened 1816] and Genevieve Bonin.

3. Philippe. [Compiler can find no information on him.]

4. Joseph. See Est. #55. It seems likely that this succession was opened for this Borel son. Joseph Borel is identified as a son of this couple on pages 23 and 27 of the 1774 Census.
5. Magdeleine, who married Francois Prevost.
6. Victoire, who married Pierre Etier [Est. # 110, opened in 1821].

Bodin gives us another daughter of this couple:
7. Louise, who married Joseph Bonin 6 Oct. 1794 [II 27].

These are the 7 children apparently specified in Pierre Borel's succession; but they are 3 boys and 4 girls, rather than 2 boys and 5 girls.

There is a document in French in the St. Martin Parish courthouse dated 30 April 1788 [OA 6, #70] which is listed in the Index as "Borrel Minors - Appointment of Tutors" which pertains to this family. A brother is assuming tutorship of the minors from the mother, who is identified as "Madame Loisel." Unfortunately, the brother is listed only as "Le Sieur Borel" and he signs his name - "Borel"!!!

The document reads in part: "il consent de ce jour etre le tuteur de Les freres et soeurs, mineurs" [the first part of this latter word is obliterated] - "he consents this day to be the tutor of his brothers and sisters, minors" [underscoring compiler's]. The plural of brothers is quite clear - which would seem to indicate that the tutor had at least 2 brothers; so perhaps there were, indeed, 3 boys and 4 girls, as above recorded, rather than 2 and 5, respectively.

#253. LOUIS LAVAN, DEC. 30 JULY 1833

Pierre Carboulez is curator of this estate. Jacob Haifleigh and Hilaire Carlin appointed appraisers. Sylvain Salles and Alphonse Carlin witnessed.

10 Aug. 1833. The estate was sold at public auction. Buyers not given. Edwin L. Cockle and Victor Lataste witnessed. No heirship given.

#254. JULIUS ROWE, DEC. 1 AUG. 1833
John Long gives deposition that decedent died 28 July 1833 at his house between 12 and 1 oclock in the afternoon.
16 Aug. 1833. Estate sold at public auction. Buyers: John Long, Peter Lyain [?], Daniel Lacy, James White, Capt. John DeHart, George Russell. Daniel Lacy and George Russell appointed appraisers. Edwin L. Cockle and Oliver Russell witnessed. No heirship shown.

#255. MARIE ALIX DEMARET, WIDOW OF JEFFERSON CAFFERY, DEC. 4 JUNE 1833
James Ferguson petitions. Decedent was the widow of Jefferson Caffery, lately died leaving 3 minor children: 1. Ralph Earl, 2. Clarissa Mary, and 3. Jefferson Jackson Caffery.
7 Aug. 1833. Fam. meeting for the minors: Martin Demaret, Ursin Demaret, Adelard Demaret, all maternal uncles; John Caffery, paternal uncle; and James Ferguson and Levi Foster, uncles-by-marriage. James Ferguson is appointed tutor to all 3; John Caffery, undertutor to Ralph Earl; Ursin Demaret, undertutor to Clarissa Mary; and Martin Demaret, undertutor to Jefferson Jackson.
13 Sept. 1833. George Royster and John Joshua Garrett are appointed appraisers. Inventory was made at the residence of James Ferguson. Eugene Sennette and Walter B. Wilcoxon witnessed.
23 Aug. 1847. Ralph E. Caffery is appointed dative tutor to **Jefferson Caffery** and **Clarissa Mary Caffery**.
12 Sept. 1848. Eugene Senette is appointed undertutor to Jefferson Caffery.
No final settlement is shown.
See Ests. #94 [Louis Demaret, decedent's father] and #180 [Jefferson Caffery, her husband].

*#256. BRIDGES SOJOURNER, DEC. 8 AUG. 1833
Petitioner is Mary (Bell) Sojourner, widow of the decedent. Her husband died 1 Aug. 1833, leaving her 4 minor children: 1. Charles, 2. Caroline Amanda, 3. Robert, and 4. Lenore Jane

Sojourner, all under the age of puberty. She is confirmed as their natural tutrix. William Sharp is undertutor to all 4.

22 Aug. 1833. Daniel Pierce Sparks and John Smith are appointed appraisers. John Lay and Nathan Berwick witnessed.

2 Feb. 1836. Mary Bell, widow of decedent, is about to contract a second marriage and prays for a family meeting. William J. Nash, Richard Lynch, John Smith, John Muggah, and William H. Baskerville, all friends, compose the council. Mary Bell is married to Matthew Rogers. He is co-tutor to the minors.

#257A. MATILDA JANE SIDNEY BAYLIES, WIDOW OF DAVID SMITH, DEC. 9 SEPT. 1833

Brice Elliot petitions. William Richardson and Jean Baptiste Perret are appointed appraisers. Brice Elliot and James Smith also sign the inventory. George Elliot and William Stewart witnessed.

18 June 1835. Decedent died "on or about 12 Aug. 1833." She left no known heirs in the state.

27 July 1835. William B. Lewis appointed curator of this vacant succession.

5 Aug. 1835. Henry Gibbons appointed attorney for the absent heirs. No heirship is shown. See also Est. #175, the succession of David Smith, her husband, opened in 1829.

*#257B. WILLIAM RICHARDSON, DEC. 5 OCT. 1833

Will. Signed 11 Nov. 1832, St. Mary Parish, La. Legatees: Newphew, Bryce Elliott. William Stewart to be paid. George Elliott [does not specify relationship] a legatee. Margaret Richardson, wife of William Elliott of the town of Anison [?], County of Dumfries, North Britain [does not state relationship, but she must be his sister, and the mother of Bryce and George] is mentioned; also, Hanislt [?] Richardson, unmarried [apparently another sister] of the same place, and Allen Richardson, unmarried, [a brother?] living as is supposed in the town of

Lees, County of Lancashire, South Britain. Jehu Wilkinson, John B. Murphy, and Brice Elliott, executors. James Smith, William Stewart, and James Campbell witnessed the will. Probated 5 Oct. 1833. Bryce Elliott petitions; decedent departed this life 23 Sept. 1833.

8 Oct. 1833. Bryce and George Elliott, both nephews of decedent, give deposition that the decedent departed this life on 23 Sept. 1833 between 9 and 10 oclock P. M. and that his remains were buried the next day on his plantation. George Elliott lived in the same house. Jean Baptiste Perret and William Stewart witnessed.

An undated deposition states that James Plaisted has been named attorney for the absent heirs.

8 Oct. 1833. Seals affixed to the personal belongings of the decedent. Jean Baptiste Perret and William Stewart witnessed.

14 Oct. 1833. Seals removed. James Campbell, Bryce Elliott and George Elliott signed the inventory. Jean Baptiste Perret and William Stewart witnessed. No final settlement shown.

Gen. note. Boyce or Bryce Elliott married (1) Madalin F. B. Gaw, 28 July 1828 [Marriage Book 2, page 428-1/2]; (2) Elizabeth R. Hamilton [see her succession, Est. #609, opened in 1847].(1) Her tombstone in Franklin, La., cemetery shows she was born in 1810 and died 6 Sept. 1835. Her full name was Madeline Frances Boys Gaw, and her succession was opened in 1837, Est. #343.

Decedent's birth year as shown on his tombstone in the same cemetery was 1774, and (2) Elizabeth R. Hamilton's was 1817. Her death date was shown to be 2 Sept. 1847.

George Elliott's succession was opened in 1856, Est. # 921.

#258. THOMAS J. ROYSTER, DEC. 11 OCT. 1833

Letter to Thomas L. Alexander dated 2 Sept. 1832 from the decedent served as his will, with the recipent to be executor. Decedent and executor were both lieutenants in the U. S. Army. The letter was written on decedent's death bed at a camp near Rock Island. He was in the 6th Infantry. Robert B. Royster was his brother; his father, in Louisiana, was unnamed in the letter; his younger sister was Ann Poindexter Royster; another sister was [Elizabeth] Virginia Royster. The letter was witnessed by L. Burbank or S. Burbank, lieutenant, 1st Infantry [appears to be 1st Infantry]. It was probated 11 Oct. 1833 as a will.

    6 Sept. 1832. Thomas L. Alexander, lieutenant, 5th Infantry [appears to be 5th Infantry] wrote Mr. George Royster that his son, the decedent, had died 5 Sept. 1832 about 7 oclock of cholera, having been ill for 3 days. The letter was mailed from Jefferson Barracks, postmarked St. Louis.

    11 Oct. 1833. George Royster petitions. Benjamin Hudson and John Hartman witnessed that the will [letter] was in the handwriting of the decedent.

    Gen. note. Decedent was a son of George Royster and Anna Bowes. See her succession, Est. #199, opened in 1831.

    #259. PIERRE VERDINE, DEC. 9 AUG. 1832

Petitioner is Melanie Robinette, wife of William Smith of St. Landry Parish, La. She is one of the legal heirs of the decedent, "who died sometime in the year 1823 in the Parish of St. Mary." Real estate is mentioned in Terre Bonne Parish. Decedent left no legal ascendants or descendants. Petitioner acts in right of her mother, Marie Verdine, now deceased, who was the wife of Nicolas Robinette, also deceased, she being the only sister of decedent. Petitioner, together with Nicolas Robinette, minor child and heir under the age of puberty of Pierre Robinette, late of the Parish of St. Mary, deceased, who was the only brother of petitioner, said minor being represented by his mother, Marie Zelwin Theriot; the said Widow Robinette resides in the Parish of

St. Mary, La.; these 2 and said Alexander R. Verdine of the Parish of Terre Bonne, brother of decedent, are the only legal heirs of said decedent.

10 Oct. 1832. Inventory ordered. Martin Demaret and Joshua Garrett are appointed appraisers. Edwin L. Cockle and Thomas P. Anderson witnessed. No final settlement is shown.

See also Ests. #197 and 260, below.

#260. JEAN BAPTISTE VERDINE, DEC. 9 AUG. 1832

This is a duplicate of Est. #259, except this decedent, a resident of St. Mary Parish, died in the year 1816. There is also real estate in Terre Bonne Parish. And no final settlement is shown.

See also Ests. #259, immediately above, and #197.

#261. THOMAS EDWARDS, DEC. 2 JAN. 1834

Margaret Smith, widow of decedent, is petitioner and natural tutrix of her minor child, Sarah Elizabeth Edwards. Decedent died "on or about 20 Oct. 1833."

23 July 1836. On 15 July 1834 a posthumous female child of her said husband was born, which she has named Julia Amanda; she is of right a legal heir of decedent equally with a former child of petitioner called Sarah Elizabeth.

16 May 1834. Fam. meeting: John Garrett, cousin to minor; Bennett A. Curtis, cousin by marriage; John J. Garrett, great uncle by marriage, and Henderson Crawford and Pryor Bryan, friends. Alfred Smith is named undertutor. Lucien Perret and John Smith witnessed.

18 Mar. 1837. Sarah and Amanda are the only heirs of decedent. John J. Garrett, John Garrett, Bennet A. Curtis and Nathan Wooster are the only relations of minors in this parish.

The Widow Edwards lived with Mrs. Phoebe Gordy [referred to also as Mrs. Phoebe Smith, widow of Benjamin Gordy; they were sisters].

John J. Garrett and Henderson Crawford appointed appraisers. George Schwing and Alfred Smith witnessed.

12 July 1851. Fa. meeting: Ralph D. Smith is tutor to Sarah and Amanda Edwards [No mention is made of their mother; but her succession was opened in 1846, Est. #584], minor children of Thomas Edwards, dec. Sarah now married to Spencer B. Roan of St. Mary Parish.

Fam. meeting: John Garrett and William Garrett, both second cousins; Julius Smith and Joshua Smith, maternal uncles, and Benjamin H. Gordy, first cousin; all referred to as "near relations of the blood."

Gen. note. Margaret Smith, wife of the decedent, was a daughter of Julius Smith and his wife, Sarah Armstrong. For her family background, see Ests. #171 and 227. They were married 21 Jan. 1833 [Marriage Book 2, page 13].

Sarah E. Edwards married Spencer B. Roan of Virginia 1 Aug. 1850 [Planters' Banner, 15 Aug. 1850, page 3, col. 3.]

#262. ROBERT P. ROGERS, DEC. 19 NOV. 1833

Petitioner is Rankin Rogers, brother and one of the heirs of decedent, who died "on or about 22 Oct. 1833" intestate.

30 Dec. 1833. Ranking Rogers appointed curator.

11 Jan. 1834. Watson McKerrall and Joseph T. Tarkington appointed appraisers. No final settlement is shown.

Gen. note. Robert Rogers, presumably this individual, married Elizabeth Hudson 9 Sept. 1823 [Marriage Book 1, page 262]. This is **Elizabeth Patterson, widow of Francis Hudson** [Est. #97, opened in 1817]. Her succession is Est. # 581, opened in 1846. Decedent apparently had no surviving children, since the petitioner, his brother, was one of his heirs.

#263. DOROTHY CARLIN, WIDOW BOWLES, CONCERN-
ING HER PROPERTY - NOT A SUCCESSION [HER
SUCCESSION WAS OPENED IN 1855, EST. #885]

#264. WINFREY LOCKETT, DEC. 29 JAN. 1834
Will. Signed at Franklin, La., 19 May 1832.
Wife, Jane Lockett; our 3 children: 1. Henry C.
Lockett; 2. John B. Lockett; and 3. Bartley C.
Lockett. Executors, Henry C. Lockett, Alexander
Jackson, and David Weeks. Pbt. 29 Jan. 1834.
Robert B. Brashear petitioned. Seals affixed to
personal belongings of decedent.
 22 Feb. 1834. Benjamin R. Garrett and Joshua
Baker witnessed that the will was in the hand-
writing of the decedent.
 11 Mar. 1834. John N. Field and John
Parkerson were appointed appraisers. Benjamin
R. Garrett and E. V. Davis witnessed.
 Gen. note. The succession of Mrs. Jane
Lockett was opened in 1839, Est. #397. Bartley
Lockett married Christina Knight 27 Aug. 1826
[Marriage Book 1, page 341]. His succession was
opened in 1835, Est. #310.

#265. CHARLES LEE, DEC. 20 MAR. 1834
By authority of the court in New Orleans,
dated 30 Dec. 1833, an inventory is ordered to
be made of property in St. Mary Parish belonging
to the estate of this decedent. Alexander R.
Splane and Edmund N. Sale are appointed
appraisers. Edwin L. Cockle and Seth Lewis, Jr.
witnessed. This file contains the inventory only.
No heirship is shown. Perhaps decedent's
succession is also of record in Orleans or one
of the surrounding parishes.

#266. JEAN BAPTISTE MILLER, DEC. 12 MAR.
1834 [SAME DECEDENT AS FOR EST. #182]
Petitioner is Mary Henry, wife of decedent.
Marie Rosalie Henry is her full name.
 19 Apr. 1834. She is natural tutrix to her
minor children: 1. Ursule, 2. Josephine, and 3.
Uranie Miller. Louis Daigle appointed undertutor.
 "Madam Miller received out her share of the

community with her former husband, Joseph Ring, for her minor duaghter, Rosalie Ring, from the succession of Joseph Ring 4 Sept. 1828." [Est. # 52, opened in 1816]

Fam. meeting: Jacob Miller, grandfather of the minors; Jean Baptiste Copel [married to Margaret Miller, decedent's sister], Jean Baptiste Felterman [married to Catherine Miller, another sister], Pierre Carrentine [married to Madeline Miller, another sister], and Hypolite Magnon [married to a fourth sister, Celeste Miller], all uncles-by-marriage; W. M. Carroll and _____ Clement were either friends at the family meeting or witnesses.

13 Sept. 1834. Julien LeBlanc and Charles Theriot were appointed appraisers. G. Haydel and F. D. Richardson witnessed. Final settlement not shown.

Gen. note. Decedent was the son of Jacob Miller and his wife, Sophie Hoffman. He was married to Mary Rosalie Henry, widow of Joseph Ring. See Est. #52, opened in 1816; she was a daughter of Jean Henry and Catherine Marguerite Nopper. See his succession, Est. #28, opened in 1813 for details of her family.

Jacob Miller's succession was Est. #356, opened in 1837. Sophia Hoffman's succession was Est. #144, opened in 1826.

Hypolite Magnon was the third husband of Celeste Miller. She married (1) Jean Baptiste Bertrand, Jr. See his succession, Est. #133, opened in 1824. She married (2) John Louis Felteman on 5 Sept. 1824 [Marriage Book 1, page 281]. He apparently died also, for she married Hypolite Magnon 1 Feb. 1834 [Marriage Book 2, page 49].

Uranie Miller was born 27 May 1822 [Bodin I 302].

#267. URSIN DEMARET, DEC. 23 APR. 1834

Eugenie Senette, widow of decedent, is the natural tutrix to her minor children: 1. Lavinia,

2. Lodviska, 3. Zeide, 4. Martin, 5. Azema, 6. Alsina, and 7. Ursule [female] Demaret, children and heirs of Ursin Demaret, deceased. Martin Demaret appointed undertutor.

Decedent departed this life 1 Apr. 1834 leaving 7 children by petitioner.

25 July 1834. Henderson Crawford and Honore Carlin appointed appraisers. Joseph Guidry, Edwin L. Cockle, and Martin Demaret witnessed.

27 Sept. 1834. Buyers at sale: Adelard Demaret, Edwin L. Cockle, for William Moore, Peter H. Rentrop. Edwin L. Cockle and Henry Gibbons witnessed.

22 Apr. 1848. Eugenie Senette and Martin Demaret both had departed this life. Joseph T. Hawkins appointed tutor of Azema and Alsina, still minors. John Moore is undertutor to Martin and Ursule [no record of their tutor; see below].

18 Apr. 1848. Mary Lavinia Demaret is married to John P. Murdock, Louisa Lodviska is married to Deaudrait Lamarandier and Adelaide Zeide is married to John F. C. Webb, all of St. Landry Parish, La. Ursule's dative tutor is Edgar Demaret of Vermilion Parish, La.; Martin's dative tutor is Adelard Demaret of St. Mary Parish, La.

19 May 1852. Azema is now the wife of James W. Murdock of St. Landry Parish, La.

No final settlement shown.

Gen. note. Decedent was a son of Louis Demaret and Adelaide Navarre. He was married to Eugenie Sennett 25 Aug. 1818 [Marriage Book 1, page 152]. She was a daughter of Eugene Sennett [Est. #99A]. Louis Demaret's succession is Est. #94, opened in 1815. Eugenie Sennett's succession was opened in 1836, Est. #323.

ADDENDA

#39. This decedent was a son of Nicolas Verret, Sr. and his wife, Marie Cantrelle. See also Ests. #117 and 188, Philip Verret [1822] and Henriette Verret [1830]. [From Mr. Sidney L. Villere.]

#42. A succession in the name of William S. or L. Brent was opened 21 Nov. 1816 in Wilkinson Co., Territory of Mississippi. Decedent, "late of Wilkinson Co.," died intestate. Duncan Stewart, Esq., was granted letters of administration as temporary administrator. [Inventory & Accounts Book 1, page 298, Wilkinson Co., Woodville, Miss.] There is no indication this is the same individual; it could have been.

#50. J. CHAREL. Margaret Cherett married Francois Gashe 29 Sept. 1817 [Marriage Book 1, page 120]. Mary Cheret married James McMurtry, son of Samuel McMurtry, 11 Oct. 1821 [Marriage Book 1, page 224].

#75. Decedent was probably a son of Hiram Knight or a brother of Jacob Knight. [Files of Mrs. Clyde Alpha of Franklin, La.] Rachel Hamilton, wife of Solomon Knight, was possibly a daughter of William S. Hamilton of Ascension Parish, La., and sister of Arthur and Charity Hamilton, wife of Michael Knight.

#80. Since the above was written, the compiler has learned of the existence of another son, Frederick, of the Rev. Charles Mynn Thruston, mentioned in his father's will. Frederick Thruston apparently died about this time. This could have been his succession, opened at the time of his mother's death. See her succession, Est. #140. Or this could be the succession of the daughter, Frances, also opened at the time of the mother's death on account of her children.

#94. Adelard.Demaret, son of decedent, was born ca. 1793; married Susan Carson 21 June 1831 [Marriage Book 2, page 18]; and died 6 Dec. 1853 at the age of 60 years [Planters' Banner, 8 Dec. 1853, page 3, col. 2]. Susan Carson was previously married to Thomas J. Foster, brother of Levi Foster. They were sons of Thomas Foster and Sarah Smith of Natchez, Miss., originally from South Carolina. Susan had 3 children by Foster: 1. Thomas Levi Foster, 2. Orlando Oscar Foster, and 3. Pamela Zeide Foster [from a petition dated 28 July 1834, of record in St. Mary Parish, La., in the files of Mrs. Clyde Alpha of Franklin, La.]

#95. Brown gives [page 4] this notation pertaining to the death of this decedent, Nicolas Provost:

"On September 12th, 1816, was buried Nicolas Provost living on Bayou Teche and native of Illinois, died the day before at the age of 67 years old." [St. Martin of Tours Catholic Church Death Register.]

This would place his birth ca. 1749. This death date also coincides with the earliest date I found in his succession - 16 Sept. 1816. Therefore it may be concluded that this succession was in fact opened on that date.

Brown also gives us the information [page 3] that decedent had a sister Felicite, born 1 Feb. 1772. Perrin states [page 127] that decedent married [probably a civil service, prior to the later church service] Marie Jeanne Provost in Santo Domingo, though she reputedly was born in Pointe Coupee, and that they arrived in Louisiana ca. 1780.

Nine children of this couple are given in this source, though only eight are listed in the succession: 1. Marie Louise, born 18 July 1778 [no further record]; 2. Marie Juliana (Julie), born 3 July 1788; 3. Godefroy, born ca. 1787; 4. Ursin, born ca. January of 1794; 5. Celeste Eleanore, baptized 12 Mar. 1797; 6. Hortense, born 15 May before 1798 [?]; 7. Lucie (Lucile), born 21 June 1797; 8. Leufroy, born in July of 1798; and 9. Nicolas Philemon Provost, born in November, 1802.

Brown gives this additional information on these children [pages 4-6]. There is no further record of the first child, Marie Louise Provost. Julie Provost married Hubert Pellerin. See her succession, Est. #129.

Godefroy Provost married Ann C. LeBlanc, daughter of Antoine LeBlanc and Marie Dupre, his wife. He died 30 June 1846. This source shows 7 children for this couple.

Ursin Provost, Sr., married Julie Provost, widow of Antoine Etier [Est. #36]. She was a daughter of Marie Therese Provost and her first husband, Pierre Provost. [See her succession, Est. #61. Thus brother and sister married brother and sister, for she was also a daughter of Nicolas Provost and Marie Francoise Quebedeau, and Pierre Provost was a son of Joseph Provost, dit Collet, and his wife, Jeanne Daublin, as was this decedent's wife, Marie Jeanne Provost.] Ursin Provost, Sr., died at Patoutville 14 May 1872. This couple had 4 children: 1. Nicolas Leclaire Provost, born 11 Dec. 1816; 2. Ursin Provost, Jr., born 12 Nov. 1819, died 11 June 1851; 3. Antionette Provost, married 28 Aug. 1858 Jean Baptiste Guiberteau, son of Francois and Marie Jeanne Guiberteau; and 4. Virginie Julie Provost. For Julie Provost's children by her first marriage, see Est. #36.

   Celeste Elenore Provost died 16 Nov. 1849, married 17 June 1816 Nicolas Loisel. He was born 4 Sept. 1781 and died 8 June 1856. He was son of Jean Louis Loisel and Catherine Toupart, widow of Pierre Borel. This couple had 5 daughters.

   Hortense Provost married (1) Hilaire Borel, son of Joseph Borel and Elizabeth Andres [Andrews?], and died before 1 Mar. 1851. They had 2 children: 1. Joseph Belisaire and 2. Hilaire Borel. See Est. #125, the succession of her first husband. This succession shows that this couple had 3 children. The second son, Elmore or Elmino, may have moved away or died in childhood. Hortense married (2) Philip Vigneaud, by whom she had 3 children.

   Lucile (Lucie) Provost, born in June of 1797, married Andrew Gauffreau. She died 1 Mar. 1851. They had 3 children, 2 of whom died unmarried, including their one son, Godefroy Gauffreau.

   Leufroy Provost, born in July of 1798, married (1) 1 Oct. 1812 Lucile Provost, daughter of Pierre Provost and Marie Therese Provost (and sister of

Julie, who married his brother, Ursin, above), his cousin. She died in 1822. They had 2 sons: 1. Edmond and 2. Leufroy Provost. See her succession, Est. #121. Leufroy married (2) Doralise Judice, widow of Francois Gustave de la Houssaye. They had 4 children. He died in 1832. See his succession, Est. #222. Her father was Jacques Judice.

Nicolas Philemon Provost, born 3 Nov. 1802, married Marie Amelia Judice, daughter of Santiago Jacques Judice and Marie Louise Hyacinthe Boutte. This couple had 9 children.

#96. The children of Julia Ann Hulick, daughter of this decedent, and her husband, Henry Randolph Nersen/Nurson, are given here because I did not have the information to include in the genealogical section of Vol. II, Records of Attakapas District, La.: St. Mary Parish, 1811-1860 [1963]. Julia Ann Hulick, born 30 Nov. 1806 in Ohio; died 18 Sept. 1867; Henry Randolph Nersen, born in Mississippi 6 June 1803 [one source says 1805]; died 6 Mar. 1870. They were married in St. Mary Parish 25 Oct. 1825. Their children were: Jared Isaac, born 29 July 1826, died 17 July 1843; Mary Eliza, born 5 Feb. 1828; Ellenor Ann, born 2 Nov. 1831, died 18 Jan. 1838 [?]; Catherine Ann & Mary Ann, twins, born 18 Jan. 1838; both apparently died in childhood; Henry Barnet, born 18 Jan. 1840, died 15 Sept. 1861; Alexander P., born 24 Mar. 1842; died 31 Dec. 1862; Nancy Josephine, born 16 May 1844; married Reuben Bennett Laws; died 31 Jan. 1918; and Henrietta Nersen, 5 [or 3] Mar. 1846; married the Rev. J. Fair Johnson 20 Nov. 1870; died 13 Oct. 1886 [1885]; he died 19 Jan. 1893.

#97. Gen. note. Decedent's widow remarried Robert P. Rogers 9 Sept. 1823 [Marriage Book 1, page 262]. See his succession, Est. #262. Her succession is Est. #581, opened in 1846. Mrs. Alpha, who has studied this family, tells us that Elizabeth Patterson was the mother of all decedent's children.They mar. 1799.See Civil Suit #147.

Francis Turner Hudson married Isabella Kemper,

daughter of Nathan Kemper, on 27 Jan. 1825 [Marriage Book 1, page 289]. He died 4 years later; see his succession, Est. #177. See also succession of Nathan Kemper, Est. #221, opened in 1832.

Elizabeth Hudson married Dr. Alfred Thruston on 13 Dec. 1818 [Marriage Book 1, page 161]. He was a son of the Rev. Charles Mynn Thruston and his second wife, Ann Alexander [Est. #140]. He died 4 years later; see his succession, Est. #122. Elizabeth remarried Thomas H. Thompson. In the 1850 St. Mary Parish Federal census she was 50 years of age, he was 66. The eldest child listed in their household at that time was Francis H. Thompson, 21, indicating his birth in 1829. Elizabeth must have married him no later than 1828; they were probably married earlier than that. Eveline E. Thompson, who married Dr. C. R. Fassitt 21 Dec. 1852 was his daughter [Planters' Banner, 1 Jan. 1853, page 3, col. 3]. Elizabeth Hudson may have been her mother.

Benjamin Hudson married (1) Julia Ann Reed on 6 May 1830 [Marriage Book 2, page 7]. She apparently died shortly thereafter, for he married (2) Mary Ann Gordy on 14 Mar. 1833 [Marriage Book 2, page 35]. These 2 grooms are probably the same man.

John P. Hudson married Alix Caroline Xavier Foster on 15 May 1839 [Marriage Book 3, page 27]. The bride is incorrectly listed in the Marriage Index as Alix C. Havier. She was a daughter of Levi Foster and Zeide Demaret. This groom is very likely the son of Francis Hudson, this decedent, and Elizabeth Patterson.

#100. After the above was written, I was able to obtain from the office of the Clerk of Court of West Feliciana Parish, St. Francisville, La., a certified photostatic copy of the will of this decedent, probated in Feliciana Parish [before it was split into East and West Feliciana]. It is in very bad condition. In it the decedent names himself as a native of Forfar, Angusshire, North Britain. He further states that Ann Alston was his lawful wife and the mother of his 7 children, whom he names as follows: 1. Henry, 2. Lewis, 3. Alexander, 4. William, 5. Ruffin, 6. Ann, and 7. John Sterling. He mentions his "only brother, Peter Sterling, residing in North Britain;" his brother's youngest daughter, Janet; his brother's 3 sons: Frederick, Alexander, and John Sterling; executors: John W. Johnson, Bryan McDermot, and his 2 sons Henry and Lewis Sterling; _____ Alston and James Perry named guardians of his minor children. Witnesses: John Harelson, Sam Barbour [?], Samuel O'Brien, Edmund Barker, James Black, Gideon Lowrey, and Isaac Tabor. The dates the will was signed and proved are not apparent. Decedent's wife had apparently predeceased him; other than being acknowledged as the mother of decedent's children, she is not mentioned in the document.

I am indebted to Mrs. Mabel Martin of St. Francisville, La., for helping me obtain this copy of the will, and to a descendant of the decedent, Mr. James Leake Stirling of West Feliciana Parish, who gives this additional information: Henry was born in 1785; Lewis, in 1786; Alexander, 1791; William, 1792; Ruffin Gray, 1795; Anne, 1797; and John, 1799. William Sterling was married in St. Mary Parish to Eppie Hall on 10 May 1825 [Marriage Book 1, page 305].

#101. Mr. Huey Henry Breaux of Lafayette, La., who has worked on this line, one of his wife's, tells me "Sellier" is really "Tellier" or "Le Tellier."

#106. This decedent was from Maryland and was married to Ann Waters [Bodin II 128]. Since the marriage record [Thomas Gates to Eliza R. Yates, 8 Feb. 1814, Marriage Book 1, page 37] shows that Thomas Gates married Eliza R. Yates, daughter of James Hennen, and this succession shows plainly that Eliza Hennen was married to Thomas Gates, it must be concluded that Eliza had previously been married to a Mr. Yates, by whom she apparently had no issue.

#108. Decedent was a son of Joseph Carlin, Est. #1.

#110. Eleocadie/Leocadie Etie married Bernard Migues; see her succession, Est. #870, opened in 1854.

#114. Martha Lacy married James F. Theall on 1 Feb. 1827 [Marriage Book 1, page 361]. See Ests. # 84, the succession of Hackeliah Theall, opened in 1820, and #230, succession of Joseph Theall, opened in 1832.

#117. This decedent was a son of Nicolas Verret, Sr., and Marie Marguerite Cantrelle, born 2 May 1759. The full name of his daughter, listed in this succession as "Manon," was Marie Anne. Her husband, Godefroy Verret, was also her first cousin, being a son of Louis Verret and Marie Patin. Louis Verret was a brother of this decedent. Their father, Nicolas Verret, Sr., was a son of Joseph Verret, a native of French Canada, born in Quebec in 1695. He came to Louisiana in 1724.

This information is from the files of Mr. Sidney L. Villere of New Orleans, who is a descendant of a third son of Nicolas Verret and Marie Cantrell, Jacques Verret. I am indebted to Mr. Villere for aiding in identifying the members of this family.

#122. Decedent refers to the will of his father. This will was probated in 1812 in Orleans Parish. See Est. #140, the succession of this decedent's mother, for this will in its entirety.

#123. Decedent was a son of Malachi Hays and his wife, Elizabeth Treet, of Pennsylvania. See Est. #92.

#126 & 129. One of the children of decedent, listed as "Julie" in Est. #126, is listed as "Jules" in Est. #129, the succession. Brown (page 6) identifies this individual as _Jules_ Pellerin. He died 7 May 1879 in Jeanerette at the age of 67, placing his birth at ca. 1812. His wife, Josephine Claire Landry, died 9 May 1883, also aged 67 years. This source shows 4 children of this couple. See this source for further information.

Brown also gives this additional information as

to these children (pages 6 & 7). **Caliste Pellerin** married Marie Virginia Provost 25 Dec. 1837. **She** was a daughter of N[icolas] Philemon Provost and Marie Amelia Judice, therefore his first cousin. See page 168. Brown shows 12 children for this couple.

Balthazar Pellerin married Marie Celina Judice, daughter of Maximillian Judice and Celestine Boutte. They had 7 children.

Marie Eleonide Pellerin married Francois Dolze Judice. **They** likewise had 7 children. See Est. # 222.

Hubert Pellerin fils married (1) Elina Moore, 15 July 1836. She was a daughter of Lewis Moore, Jr., and Modeste Hebert, and left 2 children. He married (2) Celestine Ernestine Dartes, 20 Dec. 1842, daughter of Pierre Dartes [t] and Julie Legnon. He had 4 children by this marriage.

There is no record in this source of Octave Pellerin.

#127. Peter Robert, this decedent, was a son of Peter Robert, born in Santee, South Carolina, ca. 1738 and died in Rapides Parish, La., in 1825, married Ann Grimball, born ca. 1749, daughter of Paul Grimball and his third wife, Mary Samms. He resided in Beaufort District, S. C., served with the South Carolina Militia in the Revolution and was known as "the captain." He came to Wilkinson Co., Mississippi Territory, in 1808 and moved on to Rapides Parish, La., between 1816 and 1820. He was the father of 12 children, 6 of whom were sons. This decedent is one of the sons, and was married to Elizabeth Jaudon, daughter of Elias Jaudon, Jr., and his wife, Mary H. Dixon. James, Joseph, Grimball, Paul Jabez, and Daniel were the other sons of Peter Robert. Joseph Robert was married to Mary Hyrne Jaudon, sister of Peter's first wife, Elizabeth. [Miss. D. A. R. book, page 250] Details on this family included in the Gen. note below the abstract of this succession on page 61, are from Mrs. Clyde Alpha of Franklin, La.

Mrs. Alpha found an unindexed marriage bond issued 9 Sept. 1820 [Marriage Book 1, page 206] for the marriage of Peter Robert, this decedent, and Mary Makin. Records elsewhere indicate she was a widow, but that her maiden name was Makin and that she was probably from Ohio. Her first husband's identity is not now known.

#136. The Mississippi D. A. R. book tells us [pages 302-304] that Edmund Taylor Thruston married in September of 1812 Sarah Terrell, born 6 Apr. 1790, a daughter and one of 11 children, of Micajah Terrell, born in Bladen Co., N. C. on 22 Apr. 1746, a son of Timothy Terrell and his wife, Mary Martin. Micajah Terrell died in Natchez, Miss., on 10 Oct. 1805. He married 7 May 1768 Hannah Goodman, born 7 Feb. 1751, died 27 Feb. 1824, a daughter of Samuel and Martha Goodman, apparently for whom Edmund Taylor Thruston's daughter, an only child, was named.

Micajah Terrell resided in Cumberland Co., N. C., during the Revolution. He signed the Cumberland Association in 1775 and also served in the military. He and his wife came to Mississippi in 1801 or 1802.

Sarah Terrell's younger sister, Mary Poiner Terrell, born in Fayetteville, N. C., 13 Aug. 1792, died 27 Apr. 1866, married Adams Co., Miss., 14 Feb. 1812, Charles Mynn Norton, born Fredericksburg, Va., 14 Feb. 1788, died Adams Co., Miss., 19 July 1824; he was president of Jefferson College. This individual appears to have been the nephew of Edmund Taylor Thruston, son of his sister Sarah A., apparently the wife of George Flowerdew Norton.

 The Nortons were the parents of 4 surviving children: 1. <u>Sidney</u> Ann Powell Norton, born 15 Dec. 1812, died 22 Jan. 1895, married Jilson Payne Harrison, born Mt. Sterling, Ky., 2 Mar. 1806; 2. <u>Louisa</u> Terrell Norton, born 25 Dec. 1814, died in November of 1887, married Shepherd Brown; 3. <u>Sarah</u> Claiborne Norton, born 26 Dec. 1822, died 1906, married in February of 1840, John Marshall Chilton; and 4. <u>Courtney</u> Mynn Norton, born 4 Nov. 1824, died 28 Mar. 1910, married William Hall Dameron.

 Edmund Taylor Thruston named his 2 nephews, John H. Norton and Charles M. Norton, among others to share in his estate should his only child, Martha Goodman Thruston, die before inheriting the estate. Apparently she did die, and as Charles M. Norton had died a year after his uncle, his 4 surviving children, above named, were his heirs to share in this estate. His brother, John Hatley Norton, also named by his uncle to share in his estate in the event of the death of his daughter, also apparently died shortly after his uncle, because the above 4 named Norton children were named heirs of Edmund T. Thruston in St. Mary Parish Probate suit #12, Nicholas Edgar of St. Landry Parish vs. Heirs of Edmund Taylor Thruston, filed 12 July 1826. Also named heirs to his estate in case of his daughter's death were Frances Elizabeth Conrad and her brother, Alfred T. Conrad "of the City of New Orleans." See below, Est. #140. The will of the Rev. Charles Mynn Thruston is included in its entirety.

 According to the Miss. D. A. R. book, Sarah and George F. Norton had one daughter in addition to the boys, John Hatley Norton and Charles Mynn Norton; however, she is unnamed therein; see page 178.

#140 In the name of God, Amen, I, Charles Mynn Thruston, residing in the Parish of the City of New Orleans, being feeble of body, but sound of mind, do make, constitute and ordain this my last will and testament, by these presents I do dispose of my estate, both real and personal, in manner and form following: I give and bequeath to my two sons Alfred Thruston and Edmund Taylor Thruston from and after their mother's death, all that of the tract of land which I purchased in partnership with my son-in-law, Henry Daingerfield, the contents of which I forget, situated lying and being one league and a half below the City of New Orleans, together with all my part of the trees, orchards and appurtenances whatsoever, contract for said lands and appurtenances having been having been entered into with Philip Grymes, Agent for the United States, which half, that is the whole of my tract purchased from said Grymes, I give and bequeath to my two said sons, Alfred Thruston and Edmund Taylor Thruston and their heirs forever, all my negroes to be equally divided between them on the demise of their mother, who is to retain the whole of them during her life, as she is, all my other property, real and personal. But in the event one of them only should survive my wife, then in that case, he shall succeed to and take the whole, provided the male have no lawful issue, then my wife shall dispose of them as she may think proper among my children and grandchildren, and not otherwise. The aforesaid negroes are notwithstanding, subject to such bequests as I shall hereafter make, and payments of such names as I shall herein direct. In case my above-mentioned sons or their lawful issue should survive my wife, Ann Thruston, then the said negroes are to be divided equally as practicable between my two sons or their issue, and in such manner as Gassier, his said wife and their children and their future increase and may if all to the share of Alfred Thruston, and all Judias family

except Lewis (who is to be Alfred's), are to fall
to the share of Edmund Taylor Thruston. If the
issue is to be taken into account, and to end that
same provision, may be made for my son, Frederick
Thruston, I give and bequeath an annual allowance
of one hundred and twenty dollars cash to my said
son, Frederick Thruston, to be paid him on any
first day of January from and after the demise of
my wife, Ann Thruston, by his brother Alfred
Edmund [?], charged upon the negroes above given
to them [brothers Alfred and Edmund?] and, further,
I give and bequeath to my son, Frederick, my new
coat and my best saddle and bridle, and further I
give and bequeath to my two sons, Alfred Thruston
and Edmund Taylor Thruston, all my plate, large or
small spoons, salt cellars, and other small silver
utensils, all my household furniture of every sort
and kind from and after the death of their mother.
And I further give and bequeath to my two sons,
Alfred Thruston and Edmund Taylor Thruston, all my
estate real and personal of what nature and
description soever in possession, remainder,
sanction or contingency to them and their heirs
forever. Subject, however, to the bequests herein
mentioned. I give and bequeath to my granddaughter,
Ann Conrad and her heirs forever, Aggy and her
child Dinah, with all her futrue increase, the said
Aggy being the same when a girl I gave to the said
Ann Conrad, by deed or gift, but which by accident
lost, which said gift I hereby confirm to the said
Ann Conrad, then hers forever. Item: I give,
bequeath to my two sons, Alfred Thruston and Edmund
Taylor Thruston, and Henry Daingerfield and their
survivors, for the use of my dear daughter Fanny,
the following negroes, to-wit: Caroline and her
children, James Martin, Addison, Harriet and Kitty,
also Milla, daughter of Hestor, and William, but
with this limitation, that William at the death of
my daughter Fanny, is to become the property of
Alfred Conrad, the son of Frederick Conrad [husband
of "dear daughter Fanny"]. And it may not be

necessary to note that for the said negroes, Caroline and her children, and Aggy, I have two separate deeds of trust of sale from Frederick Conrad while in Virginia. I give and bequeath to my wife, Ann Thruston, my carriage and two best horses, to be disposed as she shall think proper. And further, if it be not heretofore implicitely understood, I do hereby give and bequeath to my said wife, Ann Thruston, all my estate both real and personal, for her use and support during her natural life; except as heretofore mentioned should she survive my two sons, Alfred Thruston and Edmund Taylor Thruston without their having lawful issue, in which event she shall dispose of my negroes in the manner before-mentioned. Item: I give to my man Lewis my hat and my blue cassimese coat and two pairs of breeches. Also, to my man Gaston, all the rest of my wearing apparel of every description, my two pairs of boots and second-hand saddle, also to Philip and Collax, my other menservants, a good cloth coat each, and as soon as they can be conveniently purchased. Item: my wish is that all my just debts be paid as soon as practicable, and especially and amongst the first, that one to my daughter, Sarah Norton. Item: And wherever I have entered into a contract or agreement in partnership with Mr. Henry Daingerfield for the purchase of a tract of land from Philip Grymes as Agent of the United States, situated and lying one league and a half below the City of New Orleans in the Territory thereof. I, by these presents enable, empower and require my Executors hereinafter named to carry unto full effect the said Contract and any part thereof, according to the meaning and intention of the same in as full and ample a manner as I myself could do, were I alive. And further, a contract being shortly about to be entered into between the said Henry Daingerfield and myself touching the said partnership or joint purchase, I do by these presents enable, empower and require my Executors

hereinafter named, to carry into full effect the
said contract as will for the furtherance,
advantage, improvements and culture of the said
land, as the general benefit of the Estate, and
further I do appoint my son, Edmund Taylor
Thruston, hereinafter named as one of my Executors,
my Agent for management and conduct of the said
Estate. Finally, I do by these presents, appoint
my dearly beloved wife, Ann Thruston, and Edmund
Taylor Thruston, Executors of my last Will and
Testament. In testimony I have hereto signed my
own hand and affixed my own seal, this Fifteenth
day of March, in the Year of Our Lord, One
Thousand Eight Hundred and Twelve.
/S/ C. M. THRUSTON
Done, signed and published at the habitation and
residence of the Testator, in the presence of
Samuel Crowdson, P. R. Grymes, A. McIlhenny,
Samuel Nicholson, Joshua Lewis, Thomas B.
Robertson, A. W. Thornton, William Flood,
Courtney Ann Norton.
Ne Variteur /S/ Moreau Lislet
Judge

[Probate date not shown.]
[Testator had 2 granddaughters with Ann in their
names: Anne Alexander Conrad, who married Dr.
John Towles (see his succession, Est. #232); and
Sidney Ann Conrad, who married William Taylor
Palfrey (see her succession, Est. #532, opened
in 1844); both were daughters of this decedent's
"dear daughter Fanny" and her husband, Frederick
Conrad. I would think that the reference in his
will was to Anne Alexander Conrad, second wife
of Dr. John Thomas Towles.]
[The final witness to this will was Courtney Ann
Norton; this must be reference to the hitherto unnamed daughter of decedent's daughter, Sarah, and
her husband, George F. Norton (see pages 71A and
174); Courtney Mynn Norton, daughter of Charles
Mynn Norton and Mary Poiner Terrell who was an
heir of Edmund Taylor Thruston, was not born until

1824, after her father's death (page 174); this daughter is described in the D. A. R. book, page 309, as a daughter who "died unmarried in Louisiana."]

#158. I am notified by the Clerk of Court's Office of Iberville Parish, Plaquemine, Louisiana, that they are unable to find the will of this decedent. A succession is of record in that parish, but it is in such bad condition as to be almost illegible. [Please see page 184.]

#165. The succession of Lovinsky Dartest, Est. # 835, was opened in St. Mary Parish in 1854. This may be the individual called "Lovesgen" in this succession. The succession of Neville Dartest was opened in 1860, Est. #1058.

#167. Mr. Huey Henry Breaux of Lafayette, La., tells me Zenon Decuir's parents were Jean Paul Decuir and [Marie] Jeanne Legay/Legue. Mr. Breaux has studied this line, which is one of his wife's.

#171. Benjamin Gordy, this decedent; Michael Gordy; and Peter W. Gordy, brothers, were sons of Thomas Gordy, a prominent Methodist minister of Worcester Co., Md. A fourth brother, William, did not come to Louisiana, but his sons William Quinton Gordy and Dr. John C. Gordy did come to St. Mary Parish, La. [Files of Mrs. Clyde Alpha of Franklin, La.]

#176. Marie Antionette Pecot, the second wife of Gabriel Bouellet, was a daughter of Francois Pecot, the second husband of [Marie] Rosalie Prejean, the widow of Jean Baptiste Dupuis. Marie Antoinette Pecot was the mother of Joseph Sully Bouellet, this decedent, and Marie Rose Cecile Bouellet. This information is from Perrin, page 379-80. Perrin also tells us that Marie Rose Cecile Bouellet, whom he calls "Hermina," married Balthazar Martel. Also, that Francois Pecot, an Acadian, fled the British expulsion to San Domingo, where he and his wife were married. They fled that island when that Revolution there broke out, for Jamaica, and from there they came to Louisiana, stopping briefly in New Orleans before coming on to Attakapas.

Francois Pecot and [Marie] Rosalie Prejean had 7 children: 1. Luc [Louis?], the eldest, who died without children; 2. Jacques [who does not appear to have been in Attakapas], who had 4 sons [named therein]; 3. Marie Rose, who married Jean Armelin, the "uncle" of the minor, mentioned in this succession; this couple apparently had at least one son, Dr. Jean [John] Armelin, the minor's cousin mentioned herein; 4. Charles, who married Felicite Sigur 14 June 1814 [Marriage Book 1, page 44]; see Est. #153 for her background; 5. [Marie] Louise, who married Alexander Frere 17 July 1817 [Marriage Book 1, page 114] as his third wife; his succession was opened in 1841, Est. #452; hers was #379, opened in 1838; see also Ests. #17 and 59; 6. Marie Anne, who married Frederick Pellerin; see his succession, Est. #249; and 7. Marie Antionette, the mother of this decedent [Perrin, page 380].

Mrs. Alpha shared from her files the marriage bond of Marie Rose Pecot and Jean Armelin dated 25 Mar. 1799, Jamaica, parish of Kingston, recorded in St. Mary Parish, La., 6 June 1846 [Donation Book A, folio 99]. Jean Armelin is spoken of as "formerly of Port au Prince in the Island of Saint Domingo." Rosalie Prejean, her mother, is spoken of as a "widow." Apparently Francois Pecot died before the family arrived in Louisiana.

#179. George Marsh's succession was opened in 1860, Est. #1042.

#181. Rankin Rogers, husband of Eleanor Young Sanders, died 15 Aug. 1844. His succession is Est. #545, opened in that year.

#184. Decedent was survived at least by a widow, Susan, mentioned as a legatee in the will of Joseph Theall, Est. #230, page 133.

#185. The succession of Louise Armstrong, wife of Peter H. Robert, was opened in 1833, Est. #240.

#188. The husband of this decedent, Jean Baptiste Verret, was her first cousin. He was a son of

Auguste Verret, a fourth son of Nicolas Verret and
Marie Marguerite Cantrelle [see Est. #117]. Auguste
Verret and Marie Magdalen Bujol were married at
Donaldsonville 15 Feb. 1784 [Bodin I 389]. Marie
Bujol was a daughter of Joseph Bujol and Anne
LeBlanc [Bodin I 110].
#191. Henry Foote was born in Caswell Co., N. C.,
about 1783, a son of George Foote and Nancy
Williams. [From the files of Mrs. Clyde Alpha,
Franklin, La., and the 1850 St. Mary Parish
Federal census.]
   Perrin states (page 365) that Theodore
Dumesnil was born in France. His wife, Adele
Tenhold/Stanhope, was born in Lafourche Parish,
La. "Tenhold" in early records is translated as
our "Stanholt" or "Stanhope."
#197. Decedent married Marie Z. Theriot 29 Oct.
1827 [Marriage Book 1, page 389], a daughter of
Charles Theriot, who had at least 2 sons, Zepherin
and Marcelin, identified in this succession.
Michael Hartman married Leonise Theriot 8 Jan.
1827 [Marriage Book 1, page 351]. She may have
been another daughter of Charles Theriot.
Zepherin Theriot married Marguerite Rentrop,
daughter of Frederick William Rentrop and Marie
Marguerite Liqueur. See Est. #214. Her succession
was opened in 1855, Est. #880. Decedent's widow's
middle name is also spelled "Zelmire." She remarried Henry Knight, Jr. [From the files of Mrs.
Clyde Alpha, Franklin, La.]
#200. Decedent was a son of James Thomas, Est.
#142. See his succession for more details of this
family.
#202. According to the 1850 St. Mary Parish, La.,
Federal census, Lewis Moore, Jr., was born in
1795.
#207. According to Perrin, decedent had an only
son, by his second wife, Margaret Henry Crozier,
Monroe Baker of St. Martin Parish, but born in
St. Mary Parish in 1824. Decedent seems to have

moved to St. Martin Parish, St. Martinville; his principal succession is probably of record in St. Martin Parish. The St. Mary Parish succession seems incomplete, and perhaps that is why.

In 1845, Monroe Baker married Miss Mary L. Barrier of St. Martinville, daughter of Felix and Harriet Barrier [Perrin, page 310].

#220. [continued from page 122] they were married in St. Martinville 8 Oct. 1805 [Bodin I 99]. Their children were: 1. Claire, who married Charles Primeau/Primot; 2. Marie [Melite?], who married Aurelien/Orillon Broussard; and 3. Robert, Jr., who married in 1831 Carmelite Broussard.

Marie Evina/Elvina, decedent's daughter by his second wife, was born 11 Apr. 1832 [Bodin I 99] Melanie Materne married secondly John Arrington, 6 July 1835 [Marriage Book 2, page 74].

#221. Isabelle Kemper married (1) Francis Turner Hudson 27 Jan. 1825 [Marriage Book 1, page 289]; see his succession, Est. #177; (2) Hatton R. Fleetwood, 4 Feb. 1841 [Marriage Book 3, page 36]. Robert B. Royster was a son of George Royster and Anna Bowes. See her succession, Est. #199. Jane A. Kemper married Alexander R. Splane 19 Oct. 1830 [Marriage Book 2, page 8]. She died 9 Aug. 1853 [Planters' Banner, 11 Aug. 1853, page 3, col. 2], age 39, which places her birth in about 1814. Her succession was opened in that year, Est. #818. Alexander R. Splane died 27 Aug. 1851 [Planters' Banner, 30 Aug. 1851, page 3, col. 3], aged 47 years, which places his birth about 1804. Samuel Kemper married Rhoda Jane Vincent 22 Mar. 1838 [Marriage Book 3, page 4]. He died in 1854. See his succession of that year, Est. #843. Nancy Kemper was apparently married twice: (1) Edmund V. Davis, 3 Sept. 1839 [Marriage Book 3, page 30]; and (2) in 1842 to James Todd. See her succession, Est. #874, opened in 1855, and Perrin, page 385. Perrin also tells us she died in the 1854 Yellow Fever epidemic.

#222. Marie Doralise Judice was born 28 Apr. 1800,

daughter of Jacques Judice and his wife, Marie Louise [Hyacinth] Boutte, who were married in Attakapas 31 Jan. 1797 [St. Martin OA 18, page 36].

#223. Dr. Walter Brashier/Brashear married Margaret Barr 5 May 1803 [From the Kentucky Gazette, 10 May 1803. G. Glenn Cleft, Kentucky Marriages, 1797-1865.]

#230. Decedent was a son of Hackeliah/Heckeliah Theall [Est. #84] and Hannah Hughson [Est. #425]. Decedent was born in 1787 in Dutchess Co., N. Y., according to his tombstone in the Franklin, La., Methodist Church cemetery. This cemetery has been destroyed, but Mrs. Alpha had copied many of them, among them this one.

Decedent was married to Nancy Sanders on 3 Nov. 1814 [Marriage Book 1, page 54]. She was a daughter of James Sanders, Sr. According to Mrs. Alpha, this couple had an only son, who predeceased his father. Nancy Sanders Theall remarried (2) Joseph S. Tarkington 11 Aug. 1833 [Marriage Book 2, page 42].

#251. Louisa Ann Campbell married B. F. Harris on 28 Mar. 1850 [Planters' Banner, 4 Apr. 1850, page 3, col. 2].

#256. Mary Bell Sojourner and Mathew Rogers were married 2 Feb. 1836 [Marriage Book 2, page 79]. Her succession was opened in 1853, Est. #822. Another succession in the name of Mary Bell, Est. #915, was opened in 1856. These could have been the same succession. The succession of Mathew Rogers was opened in 1854, Est. #849. Amanda Sojourner married William Rochel, Jr. See her succession, Est. #970, opened in 1857. The succession of Robert N. Sojourner, Est. #983, was also opened in 1857.

#257B. Elizabeth R. Hamilton was previously married to Alfred Brown. She and Bryce Elliott were married 6 Oct. 1836 in St. Martin Parish. [Files of Mrs. Clyde Alpha, Franklin, La.]

SUPPLEMENTARY ADDENDA SECTION

#37. Conveyance Book D, page 197, entry no. 2020 of the Parish of St. Mary, La., dated 6 Sept. 1832, recorded 1 Sept. 1834, is an instrument which sets forth the fact that the partition of Louis Thibeau's succession was dated 21 Feb. 1814; that decedent was survived by his widow and 4 children and that the widow was the mother of all the children; that one of the children died after the father but before the final partition. Unfortunately, none of these heirs or widow is named in this document, but it does confirm that this decedent's succession was opened in St. Mary Parish; this was, undoubtedly, the succession of Louis Thibeau.

#68. Mrs. Clyde Alpha found an unindexed marriage bond [Marriage Book 1, page 169] and license issued 18 June 1818 for John Lewis and Mary Walker, daughter of Jane Walker. Possibly this is the Mary Walker for whom Robert Trousdale was appointed Curator in this year. There is no mention of her father.

#158. #3. **Marie Therese Boutte**, who signed a marriage contract with Samuel Charles Meyer in St. Martin Parish, La., 3 July 1806 [OA 23, folio 126] was a native of Attakapas and a "legitimate daughter of Francois Cesar Boutte and Marie Therese DeGruy," his wife. Samuel Charles Meyer was a native of Paris, a son of Jean Daniel Meyer and Catherine Salomee Baer. See the succession of Marie Therese Boutte, Est. #166.

Andre Claude Boutte and his wife had at least 5 children: 1. Philippe; 2. Francois Cezar, this decedent; 3. Louis Hilaire, husband of Marie Lucile Decuir, who may be decedent of Est. #69 herein; 4. Antoine, husband of Hyacinth DeGruis, sister of this decedent's wife, married also on 12 July 1778; and 5. Jean Baptiste, who signed a marriage contract with Marie Louise LeMelle, a daughter of Francois LeMelle and Charlotte L'Abbe on 18 Dec. 1789 [1774 Census, page 44].

#172. Bodin tells us [II 56] that Elizabeth Clark, the widow of John Stien, this decedent, was a daughter of Francis Clark and Rachel Melon. They were from Maryland. Apparently Francis Clark was her first husband, her second being Joshua Garret, Est. #12. Rachel and Joshua Garret were the parents of William Garret, who married Agatha DeRouan [Bodin II 103]. Joshua Garret may have had a previous marriage also, so that his 2 sons, John Joshua and William Garret, may have been half-brothers.

#174. Decedent, Julien Lesassier, is probably the son of Julien LeSassier, who was deceased by 7 Feb. 1803, and Sara Collins, who signed a marriage contract in Opelousas 26 Oct. 1786. This Julien LeSassier was a son of Charles LeSassier and Genevieve Galard, and he was a native of New Orleans. Sara Collins was a daughter of Luke Collins, Sr., and Sarah White of Opelousas, formerly of Hampshire Co., Va. [now West Va.]. [See DeVille, Opelousas Marriage Contracts, pages 11, 22, 23.]

#195. Mrs. Alpha checked the marriage record of Louis Parquin and Miriam Thompson, 2 Dec. 1818 [Marriage Book 1, #158, page 186] and found that Louis Parquin was a native of Paris, France, a son of Louis Francois Parquin and Mary Ester Frere; that Miriam Thompson, widow of the late Jeremiah Tinker, was a native of Nassau, Island of Providence, and a daughter of the late James Thompson and Mary Kemp. Thomas Thomson was a witness to this marriage.

#232. Mrs. Alpha found an unindexed marriage bond [Marriage Book 1, page 182] dated 24 Oct. 1818 for marriage between John Towles and Ann A. Haslet - indicating that Ann Alexander Conrad had previously been married, perhaps in East Baton Rouge Parish, to a Mr. Haslet. It is not known if there were children of this marriage.

INDEX

*Also included in Supplementary Index, pages 230-1

ADAMS, Thomas A. [or
 H.] - 125, 126
ADDISON, J. W. - 17, 27
 Julia W. - 17
 William - 17
AILLAIN - See Allen
AILLIAN, Joseph - 119
 Malain - 119
AL----, James - 140
ALEXANDER,* Ann - 71, 71A
 Thomas L. - 158, 159
ALIN - See Allen
ALLAIN - See Allen
ALLEN, Claire [See also
 Carlin] - 115
 D. - 18
 David - 18
 Ethan - 87
 George - 64, 110
 Hiram - 41, 42
 James - 42
 Jeremiah H. - 139
 Joseph [Allain, Alin]
 50, 64, 67, 74, 78,
 110, 115, 126 [Mrs.]
 Mary - 42
 Mary Ann - 41
 Nesbett - 42
 Rebecca - 42
 Sarah - 42
 William P[orter] -
 39, 146
ALLIRIE [?], William -
 127
ALLISON, J[ames] - 125,
 132, 135, 147
 R. P. - 125
ALPHA,* Mrs. Clyde - 1, 8,
 13, 28, 33, 34, 46,
 66. 102, 129, 152,
 165, 166, 168, 172
 Independence - 152
 John - 152
ALSTON, _____ - 170
 Ann - 43, 169
AMY, Mary Ropela - 21
 [See Mary Rosalie
 Henry]
ANDEE, John M. - 67
ANDERSON, David - 98,
 99
 James [A.] - 43,
 142, 148
 Samuel - 127
 Thomas P. - 160
ANDREWS [ANDRES(S),
ANDRUS], Ann - 65, 78
 Benjamin - 23, 53,
 66
 Elizabeth - 23, 59,
 66, 103, 167
 Emilia [Rosela?] -
 22, 23
 James - 43, 65, 78,
 103, 104, 145, 146
 Jean Baptiste - 66
 Joseph - 23, 65, 66,
 67, 78, 103, 104,
 112, 113, 114, 126,
 135
 Lavinia - 65
 Rachel N. - 65, 66,
 102, 103, 113
 Rosela [Emilia?] -
 22, 23
 Samuel - 43
 Sarah [wid. of
 Solomon; see also

    Sarah Moore] - 23
    Solomon - 23, 65, 66, 103, 108, 114
    Susan - 33, 53, 66, 106
ANSELEN, Jacob - 139
ANTOINE, Charles Joseph 51, 57
ARCENEAU(X), Herbert - 127
    Pierre - 153
ARCHER, George W. - 125, 145
ARMAND, Ann Felicite - 69
    Augustine - 119
    Jean Baptiste - 69
ARMELIN, Jean [John] - 83, 89, 149, 150, 180
ARMSTRONG,
    Elizabeth - 95, 96
    John - 86, 95, 96, 97, 127, 140
    Louise/Louisa - 61, 96, 97, 141, 180
    Margaret - 61, 87, 95, 96, 131, 140, 141
    Phoebe - 5, 87, 95, 96, 97, 141
    Sarah [See also Sarah Smith] - 86, 96, 97, 131, 161
    William [A.] - 54, 96, 97, 127

ARRIEUX, Pierre - 41
ARRINGTON, John - 182
ATKINSON & Gilliam - 127
    Dr. - 127
    H. [Dr.?] - 128
AUKMAN, A. - 22

    Andre/Andrew - 22
    Mary - 22
AUSTIN, F[rancis] - 109, 110, 126

BABARINO - See Barabino
BACON, Joseph - 150
BAER, Catherine Salomee 184
BAILES, Matilda J. [See also Matilda Smith] - 88, 157
BAIN [BEIN?], Dr. John C. - 145, 146
BAIRD, Robinson - 8B
BAKER & ST. JONES - 7
    Amelia Villers [Evalina] - 8A
    Anthony W[ayne] - 7, 8A, 94
    Elizabeth - 85
    Evalina [Amelia Villers] - 8, 8A
    Isaac L[ewis] - 7, 8, 8A, 42, 58, 72, 73, 75, 80, 84, 85, 90, 94, 95, 103, 126 [I. L.], 181
    J. - 6, 120, 126
    John W. - 8B, 73, 94
    Joshua [G.] - 6, 7, 8, 8A, 74, 85, 94, 95, 97, 111, 112, 119, 121, 125, 128, 136, 139, 147, 148, 149, 151, 153, 162
    Lewis/Louis - 7, 8A, 74, 84, 85, 94, 111
    Louisa R[ussell] - 8A, 111
    Lucy L. [see also

Myswonger] - 84, 85
Mary [Howard] - 8, 8A
Monroe - 181, 182
Nancy - 68, 69
Sarah W[illiams] - 8, 8A
Solomon - 64, 68
Susan E[valina?] - 8, 8A
BALDWIN, Eliza - 149
  Isaac - 149
BARBOUR [?], Sam - 170
BARKER, Edmund - 170
  William H. - 104
BARKS, John B. - 146
BARR & BRASHEAR - 127, 145
  Eliza - 129
  Margaret [See also Margaret Brashear] - 129, 183
  Maria - 129
  Nancy - 129
  Robb [Robert?] R. - 126, 129
  William S. - 106, 125
BAR[R]ABINO, John - 126
  Maximillian - 127
  Stephen [Esteve, Stefano] - 37, 43, 48, 51, 55, 78, 126, 128
BARRAILLEZ, Francoise - 22, 154
BARRAS, Marie Celine - 57, 84
BARRIER, Felix - 182
  Harriet - 182
  Mary L. - 182
BARROW, Martha - 137
BASKER[VILLE], BASHER-VILLE, William [H.] - 104, 145, 157
BASSETT, Capt. William H. - 126, 146
BASTINE, J. William - 29
BATEMAN, John M[ills] - 39, 110, 115, 120, 121, 127
BAUDOIN, Catharine - 14, 52
BAUVELIN, Jean Baptiste 1
BAYARD, Benoit Bar[r]on 34A, 79, 80
BAYLIES - See Bailes
BEEKLEY, I. or J. - 14
BEIN & HALL - 127, 128
  [Also Bien]
  Archibald B. - 111, 125, 133
BELAIR, Marie Marthe Hubert - 112
BELL, Mrs. - 127
  Claire - 122, 182
  *David - 39, 95, 99, 109, 127, 135, 149
  [Marie] Elvina - 121, 122, 182

  John - 110, 122
  John Adam [s] - 121, 122
  Mary - 156, 157, 183
  *Melite [Marie?] - 122
  Robert - 121, 122, 182
  *Samuel [E.] - 99, 109
  *Thomas - 59, 122, 125
BEMISS, John B. -145
BENDY, W. - 110, 112, 127
BENGRUREL [?], George - 90

BENOIT, Genevieve - See
  Genevieve Bonin
BENRISS [?], John B. -
  127
BERARD - See also Bernard, Achil[l]e - 19,
  34A, 35, 80
  Achile Camille - 34A,
    35
  Antoine - See Antoine
    Bertrand
  Christine - 69
  Hortense - 34 A
  [Jean][Baptiste]
  [Known by either or
    both names] - 34A,
    35, 44, 69
BERNARD - See also
  Berard, Francois
  Xavier - 18
  Hervillian - 18
  Hyacinthe - 18
  P. H. - 18
  Pierre - 18
  Pierre Hervillien -
    18
  Pierre Hiacinthe -
    18, 19, 34 A
  Raymond - 88, 89
BERTRAND, Antoine - 63
  Calice/Calista - 63,
    64, 118
  Hebert/Hubert - 63,
    146
  Jean Baptiste - 63,
    118, 163
  Lastie - 63
  Marguerite - 117
BERWICK, David - 148
  Joseph - 63, 112,
    120, 145, 148
  Nathan - 157

BIGGS, Andrew - 54, 55
  Ann [See also Nancy
    Biggs] - 55
  Charlotte H. - 54,
    55
  Edith - 54, 55
  Jane - 54, 55
  Louisiana - 55, 56
  Nancy - 54, 55, 82,
    126
  Susan - 54, 55
  William - 45, 54,
    55, 56, 82, 129
BIGSON, J. W. - 128
BIMUS [?], John B. -
  130
BIRD, Abraham - 34
BIRDSALL, Mrs. Ann -
  127
  F[irmin] G. [B.] -
    125, 127, 128
  M[att] - 110, 125
BISHOF, MARIE ANN - 21
BLACK, James - 170
BLANCHARD, Marguerite-
  122
BLONDIN - See Nicolas
  Provost
BLOSS, Clarissa - 145
  Eliza - 144 [See
    also Eliza Kempshall]
  Grotius - 144
  James - 144
  James M. - 144
  Timothy - 144
BODEN/BODIN, Francois
  [dit Miragrouin] -
    27, 79
  Gregoire/Grigured -
    125, 126
  Lenore - 125
BONHEUR, Abram - 67

BONIN, Antoine - 44, 45
   Camille - 153
   Cleoville - 153, 154
   Genevieve [also Bonain, Benoit] - 44, 84, 154
   Joseph - 155
   Pierre - 153
BONNEMAILER [?], Jean Baptiste - 52, 61
BONMAISON, MR. - 53
BONNEY, Ann C. - 48
BONVILLIAN, BONVILLAIN
   Lufroy - 153
   Pierre - 3, 43
BOR[R]EL[L][E], [Joseph]
   Belliza/Belisaire - 59, 167
   Benjamin - 22, 23, 59, 67, 78, 103, 113, 153
   Cidalise - 153, 154
   Dezancourt/Dezincourt 153, 154
   Doralise - 153, 154
   Elizabeth [Lise] - 23, 66
   Elmore/Elmino - 59, 167
   Eugene - 23, 44, 45, 53, 59, 67, 103, 152, 153, 154
   Francois [See also Joseph Francois] - 67
   Henrietta - 75
   Hilaire - 23, 37, 44, 59, 60, 62, 167
   J. - 22
   Joseph [Francois] - 22, 59, 60, 66, 103, 153, 155, 167
   Lise [Elizabeth] - 23
   Louis - 23

   Louise - 23, 155
   Madeline/Magdeleine - 44, 45, 52, 53, 119, 153, 155
   Marie - 21, 22, 23, 153, 154
   Marie I./**Marie** Eurasie 23, 103
   Pelagie [Louise?] - 23
   Philippe - 154
   Philogene - 152, 153, 154
   Pierre - 22, 23, 45, 52, 59, 62, 66, 153, 154, **167**
   Valsin/Valsain - 153, 154
   Victoire - 14, 51, 52, 57, 155
BORGIA, Angelo - 109
BOUELLET, Gabriel - 89, **179**
   Hermina - See Marie Rose Cecile
   [Joseph] Sully - 89, **179**
   Marie Rose Cecile - 89, **179**
BOULERICE, BOULERISSE, BOULORICE, Jean Balthazar [Jean Baptiste] - 78
BOURDON, Marie Jeanne - 36
BOURG, BOURQUE, Edmond - 116, 118
   Honorine - 116, 118
   Maxil/Maximilian - 116, 117, 118
   Rosalie - 116, 117,

BOURGEOIS, Hortense - 23
   Jacques - 3, 22, 154
   Jean Baptiste - 22, 23,
     152, 153, 154
   Jean Marie - 3
   Marguerite - 3
   Modeste - 22
   Ursin - 59
   Zenon - 44, 152
BOUTA [BOUTTE?], Henry
  L. - 141
BOUTIE [BOUTTE?],
  Francois L. L. - 148
BOUTON [BANTON?], Nathan
  65
BOUTTE, Andre Claude -
  27, 79, 90, 184
   Antoine - 90, 184
   Celestine - 172
   Cezare Francois - See
    Francois Cezar
   Francois - 90
   Francois Cezar [Cassar]
    34A, 79, 80, 84, 179, 184
   Francois Zennon - 13
   Hortense Marie/Marie
    Hortense - 34A, 35,
    80
   Jean Baptiste - 184
   Joseph V. - 34A
   Leon - 90
   Leontine - 90
   Louis Hilaire/Hylaire
    26, 27, 77, 184
   Louis Leopold - 90
   Magdelene - 90
   Marguerite - 90
   Marie Louise - 168,
    183
   Marie Therese - 83,
    184
   Philippe - 184
   Phillepot - 77
   Pierre - 77
   Z. - 13
   Zenon - 153
BOWEN/BOWERS, William
  B. [W.] - 88, 109
BOWES, Ann[a] - 105,
  159, 182
BOWIE, Resin - 34
BOWLES, Eleanor - 132,
  133
   Eliza - 133
   Evan - 3, 37, 43, 46,
    47, 55, 66, 74, 78,
    103, 113, 114, 125,
    126, 131
   John - 131
   Louisa - 132
   Matilda - 132, 133
   Polly - 132
   Susan A. - 132, 133
   Thomas E. - 132, 143
BOWMAN, Mary - 43
BOYCE, E[lijah] - 125,
  128
   Gideon - 149
   William - 72
BRADLEY, Henry [Harry] -
  101, 126, 128
BRANNER, William - 79
BRANNON, BRANMAN, H[enry]
  146, 148
BRASHEAR & BARR - 127,
  145
   Charles D. - 73
   J[eremiah] - 46, 47,
    49, 51, 126
   Lucy Cross [Brashier]
    74
   Mrs. Margaret - 129

Marie Anne - 36
Nancy P. [See also
 Ann Poindexter
 Royster] - 128
R[obert] B[arr] - 106,
 120, 125, 126, 128,
 129, 145, 162
Stephen - 41
Dr. Walter - 48, 126,
 128, 129, 183
BREAUX, *Huey Henry - 170
 Hypolite [Braud] - 127
BRAUMAN [BRANMAN?], Henry
 145
BRENT, Richard - 16, 17
 Dr. William L. - 16,
 165
 William Leigh - 16, 17,
 26, 43
 William S. [?] - 165
BRIAN, BRIEN - SEE BRYAN
BRIDGEFORE [?], A. - 140
BROUSSARD, Adelle Julie -
 73
 Alexandre - 53
 Angelica Julie - 122
 Anne - 35, 69
 Belisaire - 109
 Carmelite - 182
 Catherine - 9
 Drousin [R.] - 109
 Edward A. - 108
 J[ean] B[aptiste] -
 78, 146
 Joseph - 53
 Leon - 109
 Nicolas - 53, 61, 63,
 77, 145
 Orillon/Aurelion -
 122, 182
 Simon - 122

BROWN, Capt. - 126
 Daniel W. - 74
 Elizabeth J. - See
 Elizabeth J. Knight
 John - 46
 Mrs. Lucy - 74, 147
 Shepherd - 174
BROWNSON, Mrs. Anne -
 33
 John - 76, 81, 115,
 134, 136
BRUNET/BRUNOT, Louis
 Luli del - 57
BRYAN[T], Andrew - 130,
 145
 Charles - 145
 Christopher - 145
 G[eorge] [Philippe] -
 120, 145
 John - 146
 Joseph - 111, 112,
 127, 136, 142, 145
 Luke - 45, 54, 55,
 111, 127
 P[ierre] P[aul] - 114
 130
 P[rior]/Pryor - 127,
 145, 146, 160
BUCHANAN, Benjamin - 148
BUCKNER, Mary - 71
 Col. Samuel - 71
BUELLY, Lewis - 18
BUFORD, Albert - 94
 Catherine - 8B
 Henry [?] - 9
 James - 8B, 9, 95, 96
 James A[rmstrong] -
 95
 Mary - 8B, 9, 10, 96
 Thomas - 9, 126
 W. - 40
 Warren - 8B, 9, 37,

48, 96
William - 9
BUJOL, Joseph - 181
  Marie/Magdalen - 98, 181
BULLE, A. - 18
BULLOCK, J. B. - 128
BULRICE, Fifi - 114
  John B. [See also Boulerice, etc.] - 114
BURBANK, L. or S. - 159
BURELL, Joseph - 22
BURKE, Edmund [See also Bourg, Bourque] - 146
BURNEUR, Abram - 67
BURNS, E. H. - 109, 146
  [Also Byrnes]
BYRNE, James W. - 111

CAFFERY, Mrs. - 127
  Clarissa Mary or Mary Clarissa - 35, 91, 156
  Donelson - 15, 35, 42, 46, 48, 49, 58, 74, 81, 85, 91, 111, 127, 128, 136, 147
  Jefferson - 35, 67, 78, 91, 156
  Jefferson [Jackson] - 35, 91, 156
  John - 140, 147, 156
  Ralph Earl - 35, 91, 156
CAFFIER, Jacques - 31
CAILLET & PAVY - 145, 146, 148
CALOMAL - SEE CALUMET
CALUMET, Bartholemy - 41
CAMPBELL - 125
  Alfred - 135
  Caroline - 151
  Mrs. Drusilla [S.] - 151, 152
  Eliza[beth] - 151, 152
  Emily Jane - 151, 152
  F. - 34
  Farquard - 34, 37, 41
  James - 48, 53, 99, 103, 115, 125, 126, 134, 135, 158
  John - 34
  [Louisa] Ann - 151, 152, 183
  M. M. [or W.?] - 48
  Martin [H.] - 151, 152
  Martin M. - 12, 13, 19, 34, 47, 54, 55, 72, 110, 135, 151, 152, 183
  T[helender] - 111
  William - 41, 42
CANTRELLE, Carmelite - 69
  Marie Marguerite - 56, 164, 171, 181
CARBOULEZ, M. - 145
  Pierre - 155
CAREY, Joshua B. - 87
CARLIN, _____ - 37
  Adelard(e) - 100, 115, 128, 142, 143
  Aimee - 142, 143, 144
  Alexis - 2, 27, 47, 50, 55, 59, 110, 126, 140, 142
  Alphonse - 50, 155
  Amada [Aimee?] - 143
  Amarant/Emertiana - 50
  Carmalita - 143
  Carmiselle - [See also

Victoire Carmesille]
50, 115
Celeste - 66, 142, 143
Celestin - 2, 3, 14,
25, 26, 37, 41, 49,
59, 60, 62, 66, 78,
126, 132, 142, 143
Celestin T[heodule] -
136, 142, 143, 144
Claire - 50, 115
Denis - 2, 35, 41, 43,
47, 49, 50, 54, 55,
72, 114, 115, 116
Desire - 127, 143, 144
Dorothea/Dorothy - 3,
115, 131, 132, 133,
162
Dorothy S[uzanne] - 50
Edward/Edouard - 50,
115, 116
Emma - 50, 115
Eugene - 3
Eulalie - 50, 115
Eufroisie/Euphrasy -
100, 126, 144
F. - 1, 17
Fils Fils - 37
God[e]froy - 50, 115,
127, 143
H. - 3, 4, 13
H. I. - 128
Harriet/Hariette - 144
Hilaire - 64, 72, 73,
88, 100, 115, 120,
126, 128, 141, 142,
143, 144, 145, 146,
155
Honore - 1, 2, 3, 25,
37, 47, 49, 54, 59,
62, 78, 84, 88, 102,
107, 115, 120, 132,
134, 136, 142, 143,
148, 164
Hortense - 142, 143,
144
Hyacinth - 27
Joseph - 1, 2, 3, 4,
13, 17, 66, 133,
143, 170
Josephine - 142, 143,
144
Lufroi/Lufroy - 61,
63, 73, 78, 104, 111,
127, 136, 138, 142,
143, 144
Oream [?] - 126
Patrick - 54
Placide - 125, 146
S. - 112
Mrs. Susan - 126
Susanne [See also
Susanne Labaterie]
50, 114
Telesphore - 142,
143, 144
Terrence - 50, 115,
125
Theodore - 50, 115,
127
Theolin [Theoliste?]
50, 115, 126
Theotiste - 50
Therese - 3
Urb[a]in - 50, 115,
127, 143
Ursin - 43, 50, 78,
98, 99, 115, 122,
143
Victoire Carmesile -
See Carmesile Carlin
CARLINI, Joseph - 1
CARLYLE, John - 40
CARMOZEL, Mrs. - 125
CARNAY - SEE CORNAY

CARRANTINE/CARRENTINE,
  Pierre - 73, 130, 163
CARROLL, Charles "Bar-
  rister" - 17
  Charles of Carroll-
    ton - 17
  Charles Hobart - 17
  Daniel - 17
  M[ishaux] [H.] - 88,
    107, 108, 116, 130,
    145, 148, 163
CARSON, Mrs. - 126
  John [E.] - 81, 97,
    125, 128, 136
  Robert S. - 125, 126
  Susan - 165
CASSAR [BOUTTE?], Fran-
  cois - 34
CASSON, J. [John Carson
  ?] - 111
CASTAGNIER [?], [Joseph]
  122, 135
CAULFIELD, Ada - 102
  Charlotte [Thwaites] -
    102, 107
  Eliza Frederica - 102
  Emma Stratford - 102
  Madeleine - 102
  William Austin - 102
  William G. - 33, 102
CAVALIER, Celeste - 62
  Constance - 62
  Constant - 62
  Marcelin - 62
  Ursin - 62
  Valsin - 62
CENAS, Hilary B. - 145
CHACHERE, Constant - 90
  Julien Lile - 90
  Lise - 90
  Louis - 90, 101

CHAMBERS, Marlin - 145
CHAPMAN, John A. - 146
CHARDIN, Charlotte - 154
CHAREL, CHARET, CHERET,
CHARITE, JARRED
  J. - 21, 78, 165
  Jacob - 21, 78
  Margaret - 21, 165
  Mary - 21, 165
CHARPANTIER, Charles
  Michael/Michel - 28,
    37, 41, 61, 73, 104,
    105, 126, 136, 145,
    146, 148
  Joseph H. - 28, 37,
    38, 41, 63, 82
CHASTANT, John - 69
CHILTON, John Marshall -
  174
CHO[A]T[E], David - 4
  John/Jean - 40
  Mary/Marie - 40
CHRETIEN/CHRITIEN,
  Gerard - 98
CHRISTY, William - 145
CLAIRVILLE, Bonin -
  See Cleoville Bonin
CLARK & LEWIS - 71
  Cyrus - 146
  Daniel - 43
  Eliza[beth] - 87,184A
  Frances Eleanor - 71A
  Francis - 184A
  George Rogers - 71A
  James - 127
  John [C.] - 58, 65,
    70, 71A, 78
  William - 71A
CLAYTON, John - 146
CLEMEN[T][S],_____ -
  94, 163

Joseph - 61, 107, 130, 145
COCHRAN/COCKRAN, Jane - 131
  Nathaniel M[artin] - 61 [N. M.], 63, 116, 117, 145, 148
  S[amuel] - 61, 63, 78
  William - 130
COCK, Z. - 34
COCKLE, Edwin L. - 86, 109, 112, 120, 125, 128 [L. E.], 132, 133, 134, 135, 136, 141, 142, 143, 146, 148, 149, 151, 153, 155, 156, 160, 162, 164
COE, Joel - 101, 110, 128, 136
  John [Joel?] - 141
  Mary Jane - 124
COFFIN, E. - 126
COLE, Joseph H. - 148
COLEMAN - 110
COLLETE - See Joseph Provost
COLLINS, L[loyd] - 37, 43, 55, 64, 110, 126
  Luke - 184A
  Phrosine - 139
  Sarah - 184A
  William - 78, 111
COMAN [?], Anthony [See also Antoine Comeaux] - 145
COM[E]AU[X], Antoine - 146
  Constance - 130
CONNER, Henry [L.] - 8, 8A

CONRAD, Alfred T[hruston] - 30, 67, 68, 70, 174, 176
  Ann[e] [Alexander] - 30, 135, 137, 176, 178, 184A
  Charles Mynn - 29, 136
  Elizabeth Frances - See Frances Elizabeth
  Frances [See also Frances Thruston] - 68
  Frances E[lizabeth] 30, 68, 70, 174
  Frederick - 29, 68, 71A, 108, 137, 176, 177, 178
  Frederick D. - 30, 67, 68, 135, 136
  Glenn R. - 20
  Mary Clara/Clare - 30, 68, 108
  Sidney Ann - 30, 70, 178
CONSTANCE - 110
CONSTANT, Madame [See also Marie (Joseph) Saunie (Sonnier)] - 62
COOK, F. C. - 128
  J. - 11
  J. M. - 128
  John [C.] - 11, 125, 126, 140, 141
  Martha - 131
  N[orman] B. - 146
  Robert - 127, 146
  Samuel - 11
  William [H.] [P.] - 120, 127

COPEL[L][E], Jean
 Baptiste - 73, 130, 163
CORNAY/CARNAY & Haydel -
 126
   Henry - 53
   Numa - 101, 111, 143,
    145
   Octave - 110, 115, 125,
    126, 132, 142, 143,
    144, 146, 148
COSBY, Garland - 50, 53,
 72, 115
COUART, Ann - 9
COVINGTON, Charles F. -
 43
COWEN, George - 69
COWHERD, Sarah - 137
COX, Sempson - 72
CRAIG, Eliza Ann [See
 also Eliza Marsh] - 91
   Euphemie - 76, 77, 91
CRAWFORD, Henderson - 100,
 127, 136, 138, 160, 161,
 164
   John - 111
CROW, Adam - 126
   Ann [Nancy] - 36
   Basil - 40
CROWDSON, Samuel - 178
CROZIER, Margaret Henry -
 8A, 181
CURTIS, Arby [Bennett?] -
 146
   Bennett A[rby?] - 86,
    123, 125, 128, 135,
    141, 160
   Harley - 145, 146, 148
CYPRIAR - 127

DAD [?], Randel - 126
DAGOBERT, Father - 1, 2

DAIGLE, Louis - 78, 146,
 162
DA[I]NGERFIELD, [William]
 Henry - 71B, 175, 176,
 177
DAMERON, William Hall -
 174
DANCEY, Col. [Francis] -
 112, 126
D'ARBY, Francois - 62
   John - 62
   St. Marc - 69
   Ursin - 44, 53
DARLING, William - 43
DARTES[T] - 37
   Alexander - 31, 32
   Celestine Ernestine -
    83, 172
   Eugenie - 32
   Euphemie/Uphumie -
    62, 83
   Evars - 31
   Lovesgen/Lovinsky -
    83, 179
   Neuville/Nevell - 83,
    179
   Pierre - 32, 83, 172
   [Pierre] Adrien - 83
DARTICE [DARTES?],
 Madame - 125
DAUBLIN, Jeanne - 25,
 37, 167
DAVIS, Miss - 137
   E[dmond] V. - 162,
    182
   Joseph - 88
   Michael - 145
   P. - 113
   Rev. Stephen J. - 82
   T. - 4
   Thomas - 4

William - 110
DAVISON, Ann - 48
DAWSON, John R. - 43
DEBARR, Paul - 126
DEBLANC, Celeste Matilda 5, 20
   Louis Charles - 5, 20, 34A, 57, 62, 79
   Louis E[loi] - 57, 78, 84, 124
DEBORE, Therese - 2
DECOUX, Julie - 112
DECUIR, Francois - 13
   Jean Paul - 179
   M. A. - 13
   Marie Aspasie - 13
   M. L. - 27
   Marie Lucile - 27, 184
   Maximilian - 77
   Zenon - 57, 84, 90, 136, 179
DEFAZENDA, Jeanne Henriette - 5
DEFERIET, Louis - 112
DEFORCELLE - See Olivier
DEGRUY/DEGRUIS, Hyacinthe 184
   Marie Therese - 79, 80, 84, 184
DEHART, Cornelia S. - 140
   John [Capt.] - 128, 139, 140, 156
   John Evans - 139
   Margaret E. - 139
   Sarah Ann - 140
DEJARNETTE/DEJOURNATT & McKerral - 126, 128
   Peter A. - 126, 148, 149
   Richard - 149

DEJEAN, Honore - 56
DE LA COURET, J. - 22
DE LA GAUTRAIS, Marie Louise Celeste - 80
DE LA HOUSSAYE, Francois Gustave - 168
   Lepelletier/Pelletier 115
   Octave - 5
   St. Cyr - 5
   Terrance - 53
DE LA THULE, Dorothea - 115
   Robert F. G.[H.] - 50, 115
DEL BRUNET, Louis Luli 57
DELCAMBRE, Charles - 52
DEMANDEVILLE - See De Marigny de Mandeville
DEMARET, Adelaide - 35, 108
   Adelaide Zeide - 164
   Adelarde - 35, 55, 91, 125, 156, 164, 165
   [Marie] Alix - 35, 36, 91, 156
   Alsina - 164
   Andre George - 36
   Ann - See Ann Crow
   Azema - 164
   Clarice/Clarissa - 35
   Edgar/Edouard - 35, 36, 126, 145, 164
   [Marie] Lavinia - 163, 164
   Louis [George] - 35, 36, 41, 108, 156, 164

Lodviska/Louisa - 164
Martin [F.] - 35, 36,
 40, 41, 84, 88, 91,
 102, 105, 107, 123,
 127, 132, 136, 142,
 156, 160, 164
Ursin - 35, 41, 91,
 127, 143, 148, 156,
 163, 164
Ursule - 164
[Marie] Zade/Zeide -
 35, 36, 169
DEMARIGNY, Francoise - 3
DEMARIGNY DE MANDEVILLE,
 Marie Madeleine Philippe
 19
DEMONTIGNY, Marguerite -
 3
DENNETT, Daniel - 138
DENSON, Joseph W. - 120
DERICHEBOURG, Marie - 1
D'ERNEVILLE, Elizabeth
 Pouponne - 5, 20
DEROUAN/DEROUEN, Agathe -
 4, 87, 184A
 Genevieve - 2, 27
 Jacques - 59
 Joseph - 2
 Rosalie - 58
DESK, William - 48, 57
DETRAVAME, M. A. G. - 28
DETRAVANE, Marie Adelaide
 Guerne - 28
DEVEZIN [See also
 Olivier De Vezin],
 Joseph O. - 112
DEVINCE BIENVENU,
 Alexandre - 20
 Jeanne Aspasie - 20
DILUKY, Manuel - 145
DINEINA [?], Theodore [?]
 [See Devina Theodum] - 128

DISMUKE[S], Andrew W.
 [M.] - 130, 145, 146
DITCH, John - 12, 13,
 99, 127, 135
 Louise - 13
 Mary [Louise] - 12,
 151
 Rebecca - 13
DIXON, Mary H. - 172
 William George - 91,
 93
DIZLANDE, Martha - 2, 116
DOHERTY, George - 46
DOIRON, A[uguste] - 146
DOLLY [DOOLEY?], Caesar
 67
DOSON [?], E. - 146
DOTY, R[euben] - 23, 48,
 103, 114, 136, 153
DOUGH, [Capt.] John W. -
 86, 101, 110, 125, 128,
 135
DOUGHERTY, James - 134
DOWN, Abigail - See
 Abigail Prindle
 Andrew - 101
 Calvin - 101
 Eliza L. - 101
 John - 101
 N. - 146
 Sarah - 101
 Sarah W. - See Sarah
 W. Summers/Semmes
DUBAY, Marie - 30
DUBLAUGH, Edward - 111
DUBRAUEL [?], Solie [?]
 114
DUBRIEL, Ambroise Colerin
 77
DUCROS, Joseph Marcel - 5
DUGAS/DUGAT, Aurelin -
 109

Desire - 109
Joseph - 127
Louis - 108
DUMAIN [DUMINEL?],
  Theodore - 48
DUMARTRAIT, Adrien - 53, 69
  Louise - 69
DUMENEL, DUMINEL, DUMESNIL, DUMINEY, DUMISNIL, Adelaide - 100, 101
  Francois - 99, 100
  [Jean Baptiste] Hyacinth - 99, 100
  Joseph [Hiacinthe] - 99, 100, 101
  Theodore - 99, 100, 181
DUNBAR, William - 149
DUNN, Azariah C. - 26
DUPERIER, Frederick H. - 34 A
DUPLESSIS [See also Gatineau], Francois Armerautt - 84
  Marie-Josephine Gatineau - 19
DUPRE[E], DUPRE, DUPUIS, James - 43, 48, 55, 64
  Jean Baptiste - 179
  Marie - 166
DURAND, Julien - 62
DURRI [?], A. - 26
DUVAL, Michael - 145
DWIGHT & Hartman - 101, 127
  Edmund P. - 128
  H[enry] - 142, 143
  J. A. - 128

EADS, Estate of - 111

EAGLESON, Martha - 53
EASTIN, Herbert - 91
  Ranson - 90
EBERT - See Hebert
EDELEMER, Henry - 30
EDGAR, Ann - 78
  Nicholas - 65, 67, 68, 70, 78, 174
EDWARDS, Julia Amanda - 160, 161
  Sarah E[lizabeth] - 160, 161
  Thomas - 120, 131, 138, 140, 160, 161
ELLIOT[T], Mrs. - 126
  B[oyce]/Bryce - 33, 110, 120, 126, 157, 158, 183
  Elizabeth R. - See Elizabeth R. Hamilton
  George - 157, 158
  William - 157
ELLISON, James - 8B
ELY, H. - 110
EMAR, E. - 28
EMBRIE [?], Elisha - 136
ENFEEL, ENFILE, INFILE, Christine - 45, 46
  Michel - 45, 46, 117
ERMAN, Catherine - See Catherine Hennen
ESKRIDGE, Frances Peyton - 137
ETIE[R], A. - 14
  Antoine - 14, 25, 52, 167
  Constance - 52
  Drusin - 52
  [E]leocadie - 52, 171

    Joachem - 52
    Julia [See also Julie
      Prevost] - 14, 36
    Julie Antionette - 14
    Marcellite - 52
    Pierre - 14, 43, 44,
      51, 52, 53, 57, 155
    Pierre Guillaume/
      Peter William - 51,
      57
    Selesie - 52
    Victoire [See also
      Victoire Borel] - 153
EUMEL, C. - 4
EVANS, Capt. - 6
    Cornelia S./ Louisa
      Cornelia - 11, 139
    David - 11
    J. - 11, 140
    John - 11, 140
    John M. - 140
    Louisa Cornelia [See
      also Cornelia
      Louisa] - 140

FARIE [?], Charles - 73,
  78
FARK - See Faulk
FARLEY, H[enry] [W.] -
  130, 145
FAULK, Mary - 27, 29
    Richard - 111
FAUST/FOUST, E[phriam]
  P. - 101, 145, 151
FAY, Claire Elodie - 89
    Theodore - 9, 67, 77,
      90, 99, 136
FELT[E][R]MAN, J[ohn]
    B[aptiste] - 73, 130,
    146, 163
    John [Louis] - 63, 64,
    73, 130, 163
FENISTER, Wesley - 101
FENNESSY [?], Richard -
  48
FERGUSON, James - 35,
    46, 54, 55, 72,
    91, 125, 127, 128,
    131, 138, 156
    Joseph - 59
    Samuel - 146
    Thomas L. - 38
FIELD[S], Dr. - 109
    Alexander [L.] - 132,
    133
    J[ohn] [N.][W.] - 110,
    127, 148, 162
FINCH, Ann [See also Ann
    Tinker, Ann Smith,
    Ann Watson] - 46,
    47, 102
    William - 10, 42, 43,
    46, 47
FINNEY, Walter - 145
FLAGG, William H. - 109,
  126
FLEETWOOD, Hatton R. -
  89, 182
FLOOD, William - 178
FLOYD, Richard - 43
FONTINETTE, Jacques -
  34A, 44
FOOT[E], Henry - 78, 99,
    100, 101, 127, 128,
    133, 147, 181
    John M. - 138
    Perryman/Berryman -
    43
FOREST, Ephriam P. - 97,
  101 [Faust, Foust?]
FORK - See Faulk
FORTIER, Faustin - 53

FORTIN, [Jean] Julian
FOSTER, James - 73, 75, 111
  Levi - 35, 46, 48, 64, 67, 73, 75, 88, 91, 92, 97, 102, 106, 110, 125, 128, 133, 134, 138, 156, 165, 169
  Thomas J. - 147, 165
  Mrs. Zeide - See [Marie] Zeide Demaret
FOURMY, Joseph V. - 152
FOWLER, John - 111
FRANKLIN, Corp. of - 111
FRASER, James - 33
  Malcolm A. - 33, 135
FREME, Alexander - 57, 58
FRENCH, Josiah - 87
  Thomas - 69
FRERE, A. - 24
  Alexander - 9, 24, 25, 48, 67, 128, 150, 180
  Caroline - 24, 48
  Frederick Adrien - 69
  Joseph Alexander - 9
  Marie Elizabeth Iphigenie - 9
  Rene - 9
  W. H. - 139 [Fere]
FRILOT, Claude - 79
  J. N. - 128 [Frilo]
FUSELIER, A[gricole] - 48, 69, 74, 76, 77, 98, 99, 111, 112, 122, 128, 134, 136, 140
  Aimee - 69
  [Elizabeth Anne] Aspasie/Aspudie - 69
  Coralie - 69
  Gabriel [de la Claire or L.] - 9, 48, 69, 75, 76, 83, 98, 111, 128, 136, 149
  Gabriel Agricole - 69
  Leclair - 48, 136
  Marie Louise - 69
FVETS [?], Thomas - 126

GACHE[R] - See Gashe
GALARD, Genevieve - 184A
GALTNEY - See Waltney, Goultenetyt
GALVEZ - 19
GANT [GARRET?], Benjamin R. - 133, 135
GARDEN, Joseph - 52
GARETZEN, Jeanne - 100
GARRET[T], B[enjamin] R[ush] - 127, 132, 162
  Celeste [Sarah] - 4
  J. - 4, 10
  John - 86, 160, 161
  John Joshua - 4, 54, 69, 86, 87, 89, 95, 96, 97, 104, 111, 119, 120, 140, 141, 142, 156, 160, 161, 184A
  Joshua - 4, 96, 126, 131, 140, 160, 184A
  Phoebe - See Phoebe Armstrong
  Rachel [See also Rachel Melon] - 4
  Sally/Sarah Ann - 87
  William - 4, 87, 127, 161, 184A
GASHE, Alexander - 11

Francois - 21, 165
Jacob - 11
Jacques - 11
Louis [Alexander?] - 11
GATES, Eliza [Hennon] - 16, 47, 48
T. - 15
Thomas - 15, 16, 47, 170
GATINEAU DUPLESSIS, Marie Josephine - 19
GAUDET, Marguerite - 9
GAUFFREAU, Andre/Andrew 36, 37, 53, 167
Godefroy - 167
GAW, Madaline F[rances] B[oys] - 158
GAYOSO DE LEMOS, Adelaide 36
Gov. - 36
GEOGE, Celestin - 111
GERBEAU, Joseph - 136, 143, 145
GERHARDSTEIN, Joseph - 63
GIBBONS, Henry [J.] - 141, 157, 164
GIBSON & GILLIAM - 126
Dr. - 110, 135
J[ohn] W. - 110, 127, 133, 140
Joshua - 74
Martha Powell - 76
GIL, William - 90
GILBERT, Mr. - 127
GILLIAM & ATKINSON - 127
& GIBSON - 126
J. P. - 127
GIROUD, Marie - 27
GODFREY, B. - 110
GONSOULIN, Jean Francois 80

L. - 153
Marie Louise Celeste - 79, 80
Ursin - 84
GOODMAN, Hannah - 173
Martha - 173
Samuel - 173
GOODRICH, Henry - 133
GORDY, Mr. - 125
Mrs. - 140
Archibald - 97
Benjamin - 47, 86, 96, 97, 98, 131, 160, 179
Benjamin H. - 86, 161
Caroline E[lizabeth] 97
Eleanor/Elender - 86, 87
John C. - 86, 179
Mary Ann - 70, 169
Michael - 47, 60, 61, 86, 97, 120, 121, 125, 128, 141, 148, 179
Peter - 97
Peter W. - 47, 86, 97
Phoebe [See also Phoebe Smith] - 86, 160
Samuel E. - 86
Sarah A. - 47
William - 97, 179
William Quinton - 179
William Smith - 97

GOULTENETYT [See also Galtney, Waltney], Elizabeth - 29
GOYNEAU, Pierre - 111
GRAY, Joseph [J. or G.] 31
GREAVES, Justus/Joseph - 54, 127

GREVEMBERG, Charles - 48,
    53, 98, 112, 136
  Louise Pouponne - 69
GRIMBALL, Ann - 172
  Paul - 172
GRYMES. P[hilip] R. - 175,
    177, 178
GUENON/GUEDON, P[ierre] -
    26
GUIBERTEAU, Francois -
    167
  Jean Baptiste - 167
  Marie Jeanne - 167
GUIDRY/GUEDRY, Herene -
    101
  Joseph - 55, 62, 100,
    164
  Marguerite Adelaide -
    100
  Modeste - 118
GUILBEAU, Joseph - 52
GULICK - See Hulick
GWINBALL [?], John D. -
    86

HAIFLEIGH, Frederick - 66
  Jacob - 55,
    55, 66, 75, 125, 142,
    143, 144, 155
  William Frederick -
    66, 142, 143
HALL & BEIN - 127, 128
  Mrs. - 110, 126
  Catherine - 93
  Eppie - 170
  James - 93
  Rebecca - 93
  William N. - 145
HAMBLETON/HAMILTON, A. -
    34
  Arthur - 165
  Charity - 46, 165
  Elizabeth R. - 34, 158

  Rachel - 28, 165
  William S. - 165
HARANEDER [?], Charles -
    53
HARDING, Mrs. - 48
  Elizabeth - 49
  Lyman - 49
  Winthrop S[argent] -
    30, 49, 64, 67, 68,
    73, 110, 135, 136
HARDY, _____ - 31
  Clark[e] - 37, 55
  Polly [Mary] - 96
HARELSON, John - 170
HARGRAVES/HARTGREVE/
HARGROVE, Benjamin - 29
  James [H.] - 27, 29,
    111
  Marie - 23, 53, 66
  William [D.] - 111,
    121
HARGROIDER/HERGROIDER,
    Michel - 26
HARMON, Judson - 145
HARPER, Mason - 80, 110,
    111, 120
HARRINGTON, Charles - 43
HARRIS, B. F. - 183
HARRISON, Jilson Payne -
    174
HARTMAN & DWIGHT - 101,
    127
  Anthony - 78, 116,
    145, 146
  [Edward] Conrad - 55,
    61 [Mrs.], 145
  Jacob - 146
  John [Peter] - 73, 85,
    97, 127, 133, 148,
    151, 159
  Michael - 105, 146,
    181

Peter - 61, 78
HATFIELD, William W. - 126
HAVENS, Capt. John S. - 126
HAVIER, Alix C. - [See Foster]
HAWKINS, John - 32, 83
  Dr. Joseph T. - 164
HAYDEL/HEYDEL & CORNAY - 126
  G[eorge] - 78, 107, 111, 115, 130, 136, 145, 146, 148, 163
HAY[E]S, Mrs. - 126
  Agathe - 58, 59
  David - 34, 58, 59, 76, 127
  Delezin - 59
  Eliza[beth] - 34, 59
  Jacob - 111
  James - 126, 138, 139, 140 [Jacques Haze]
  John - 58, 59, 76, 127
  Legure - 127
  Marcelite - 58
  Marie Caroline - 59
  Mary [Ann] - 59, 137, 138, 139
  Michael - 34, 43, 55, 58, 143, 171
  Onezime - 59
  Polly/Mary - 58
  Wade - 40
HAYME - See Haynie, M. L.
HA[Y]NIE, M[artin] L. - 21, 42
HEBERT, Alexander [N.] - 57, 84, 130
  Charles - 78, 108, 114
  Elizabeth - 57, 84
  Francois - 57, 84
  Genevieve - 2
  J. B. - 4
  Jean Baptiste - 4, 56, 98
  J. L. - 6
  Jean Louis - 6, 59
  Joseph - 57, 84
  Julie - 57, 84
  Marie - 56, 98
  Modest - 57, 84, 107, 172
  Nicolas - 44, 57, 84, 107
  Rosaline - 59
HEMPHILL, Jane - 81
  Joseph - 81
  Matthew - 82
  Samuel - 82
HENDERSON, G. - 34
  George - 34
HENDLEY, Samuel - 75
HENNEN, Alfred - 47, 48
  Mrs. Ann - 16, 24, 47, 48 [See also Ann Waters]
  Catherine - 10, 24, 48
  Eliza - 16, 47, 170
  Dr. James - 16, 24, 47, 48, 170
HENRY, Elizabeth - 11
  Hannah - 11
  Jean/John - 11, 12, 21, 163
  Jean Baptiste - 12
  Margaret - 11
  Martin Adam - 12
  Mary Ropela/Rosalie - 12, 21, 73, 94, 162, 163
HENSHAW, Rebecca - 30, 107, 108

HERON, James - 125
HIGGINS, J. & W. J. - 18
  John - 18
  W. J. & J. - 18
HIGH, John - 28
  M. - 27
  Michael - 27
HIGHFIELD, Drusilla - 13, 19, 151
HIMEL/HYMEL, Charles - 4
  Christopher - 4
  E. - 28
HINES, Homer - 117
HOBBY, Joseph - 99, 103, 113, 114
HOFFMAN/OFFMAN, Sophia - 63, 64, 73, 94, 163
HOLBERT, N. - 110
HOLMES, Gov. David of the Mississippi Territory - 6
  Lucile Barbour - 8, 75
HOLSTEIN, Sarah - 40
HOOVY/HUFFY [?], John - 110
HORNER, Christine - 45
  John - 45
HORNSBY, Benjamin - 125, 126, 145
HOURY, Jean - 11
HOWE, J. - 11
HUBBERT - 125
HUDSON, Benjamin - 40, 70, 89, 97, 102, 104, 105, 110, 127, 136, 146, 159, 169
  Caroline - 40
  Elizabeth - 40, 54 [Mrs. E. Hudson, possibly referring to the mother], 58, 71B, 161, 169
  Francis - 40, 58, 70, 71B, 89, 161, 169
  Francis T[urner] - 40, 43, 51, 89, 122, 168, 182
  Isabelle/Isabella [See also Isabella Kemper] 89
  John [P.] - 40, 112, 128, 131, 136, 169
  Thomas Thompson - 89
  Virginia - 40
  William F[rancis] - 89, 114
HUGHES, T[errence] - 99, 110, 126
HUGHSON, Hannah - 33, 183
HULICK, Barnet - 37, 38, 93
  Caroline - 37, 39
  Eliza [J.] - 37, 38, 39, 123, 124
  Hendrick - 38
  Jesse [W.] - 37, 39, 121, 127, 135, 151
  Jochem - 38
  Julie Ann/Julia Ann - 37, 38, 39, 168
  Mary Vance - 37, 39
  Peter - 38
  Rachel N[ixon] - 37, 38, 39, 93, 123
HUNGERFORD, R[ichard] - 125, 126, 128, 142, 145
HUNNINGTON/HUNTINGTON, Aler_____ - 146
  John - 146
  Samuel - 37

HUTCHESON, H. B. - 140
HUTCHINSON, Lewis C. - 51
HYDER, Benjamin - 32
    Catherine - 32
HYMEL - See Himel

INFIL - See Enfeel/Enfile
IRWIN, D. W. - 18
    Joseph - 18
INMAN [?] & ROOT - 146

JACKSON, Alexander - 109,
    140, 147, 162
    John F. [J.] - 138, 139
    Louise - 12, 13
    Washington - 15, 81,
    136
JANUARY, Janette - 71A
    Peter - 71A
JARRED/JARRET - See
CHAREL, ETC.
JARVIS, [William] - 99,
    101, 127, 135, 146
JAUDON, Elias - 172
    Elizabeth [See also
    Elizabeth Robert] -
    61, 96, 141, 172
    Mary Hyrne - 172
JEANERETTE, J[ohn] W. -
    90, 103, 113, 114
JOHNS, Helve - 34
    James - 34
    L. - 34
JOHNSON, Catherine/
    Caroline - 103, 104,
    113, 114
    Eliza - 102, 104, 113,
    114
    Henry - 103, 104, 113,
    114
    Rev. J. Fair - 168
    James L[yons] - 48, 59,
    65, 66, 70, 75, 78,
    81, 102, 113, 114
    James S. [See also
    James L.] - 43
    John [H.] [F. E.?] -
    42, 43, 127, 128, 135
    John W. - 170
    Joseph [E.] - 81, 103,
    104, 113, 114, 126
    Julius A. - 127
    Margaret [A.] - 102,
    103, 104, 113
    Mary - 103, 104, 113,
    114
    Mary Ann - 152
    Milton - 127
    Nancy - 103, 113
    Nicholson - 38
    P. - 15
    Patrick - 15
    Rachel - 102, 104,
    113, 114
    Rachel Andrus Johnson
    [See also Rachel
    Andrus] - 103
    Robert [E.] - 138
    Sarah/Sally - 102,
    103, 104, 113, 114,
    127
    Solomon - 102, 103,
    104, 113, 114, 125,
    127
    Thomas - 126
    Willemptige - 38
JOLLY - 113
    Philip[pe] A[ugustin]
    108
JONES, S. - 28
    Samuel - 26, 28
    T. - 26
    Thomas - 26
JOSEPH - 127

JUDICE, Alexander - 124
   Drozel [?] - 115
   Francois Doleze - 124, 172
   Jacques/Santiago - 119, 124, 168, 183
   Louis - 43
   Marie Amelia - 168, 172
   Marie Celina - 172
   Marie Doralise - 124, 153, 168, 182
   Maximillian - 172
JUPITER [?], Peter - 126

KEBLE - See Kible
KELLOGG, Mrs. Rowena - 144
KEMPER, E[liza] [See also Eliza J. Hulick] 127
   Elizabeth F. - 123
   Isabella/Isabelle [See also Isabelle Hudson] 89, 122, 168, 182
   Jane A. - 122, 182
   John M. - 89, 110, 122
   Nancy/Ann - 122, 123, 182
   Nathan - 48, 51, 70, 85, 89, 106, 111, 122, 123, 169, 178
   Peter - 123
   Reuben - 123
   Samuel - 122, 123, 138, 182
   Sarah - 106, 122
   Thomas Jefferson - 123
   William [Peter] - 39, 69, 123, 124
KEMPSHALL, Mrs. [Eliza] 144, 145, 146

KENSHAW - See Kershaw
KER[R], David - 8A
   McG. - 11
   John - 8, 8A
KERSHAW, Elizabeth Grace [Also Betsy] - 64
   John [N.] - 18, 23, 55, 59, 64, 111, 126, 128, 137, 138
   Mary Ann - 18, 64, 138
   Nedham V./Vardelle N. - 64
   Samuel [A.][K.] - 64, 125, 138
   Thomas B. - 23, 64, 112, 125, 127, 138
KEY, A[llen] J. - 48, 72, 128
   L. - 126
KIBBE - See Kible
KIBLE, Benjamin - 51
   Charles - 51, 134
   Francis - 51
   Gains - 51
   George - 51, 54
   Henry - 51
   Isaac - 51, 53
   Lucy - 51
   Margaret - 51, 53
   Mary - 51
   Nancy - 51, 54
   Sarah - 53, 54
   William - 51
KILGORE, Dr. - 111
   Raniels [?] - 127
   William - 153
KIMBERLY, Catherine F. - 133
KING, Mrs. - 126

G[eorge] W. - 40, 52, 72
Jacob W. - 110, 111, 125, 138
KIRKHAM, Thomas - 133, 146
KNIGHT, Abel - 28
  Catherine - 54
  Christina - 162
  Elizabeth J. [See also Elizabeth J. Brown] - 45, 46
  Hariet [C.] - 118, 145
  Henry - 45, 46, 63, 116, 117, 145, 181
  Hiram - 165
  Jacob - 45, 46, 117, 126, 165
  Madeleine Liqueur/Siqueur - See Madeleine Liqueur
  M[ichael] - 45, 46, 111, 125, 127, 128, 135, 142, 165
  Philip - 45
  S. - 28
  Solomon - 28, 165
  William - 45, 46, 52

LABARTHE, Jacques - 27
  John - 15, 27
LABATERIE/LABATRE, John 2, 116
  Suzanne - 2, 49, 50, 51, 114, 116
LABAUVE, Olduf - 113, 114
L'ABBE, Charlotte - 184
  Marie - 13
LABLASAN, Julian - 63
LACOMB, Jonathan - 17
LACOEUR - See Liqueur

LAC[E]Y & PATTERSON - 146
  Benjamin - 48, 53, 66, 81, 103, 104, 112, 114, 134, 151
  Daniel - 53, 104, 128, 134, 151, 156
  James - 53, 127, 128, 150, 151
  Jesse E[agleson] - 21, 43, 48, 53, 66, 75, 99, 104, 106, 109, 114, 125, 145, 150, 151,
  John O. - 110, 112, 125, 126, 131, 138, 146
  Joseph A. - 48, 53, 76, 104, 122, 134, 135, 151
  Martha - 33, 53, 171
  Susan - 53, 75, 126, 150, 151
  Theodosia H. - 53
  William [Eagelson] - 53, 66, 103, 104, 134, 151
LAGATRIE, Modist - 23
LAMAR, John - 111
LAMARANDIER, Deaudrait 164
LANANAY/LANAWAY, T[homas] H. - 25
LANDRY, Josephine Claire 171
LANGE, Francoise - 1, 3, 17, 143
  Jean Baptiste - 1, 2
  Pierre - 1
LANGSTAFF/LONGSTAFF, Dr. Ogden D. - 55, 109, 110, 125, 127, 136, 140

208

LANLON/LAULON/LANTON,
 Jean - 105, 130, 146
LANOUE, Caroline - 144
 Martin - 146
LANSALLE [?], Raymond -
 145
LAPERE, Auguste - 146
LASSERE, [Jean Marie]
 Auguste - 146
LASSLON [?], Jean - 146
LATASTE, Victor - 149,
 155
LATIL DE TIMECOUR,
 Louise - 20
LATIOLAIS, Joseph - 20
 Marie Joseph - 20
LATOUR, C. - 110
LAURENCE - See Lawrence
LAURENDINY, Catherine -
 18, 19, 34A
LAVAN, Louis - 155
LAWIENDING, C. - 34A
LAWRENCE, Dr. James -
 109, 110
LAWS, Reuben Bennett -
 168
LAY, John - 136, 146,
 157
LEASE - See Lees[e]
LE BLANC, Ann[e][C.] -
 36, 166, 181
 Antoine - 76, 166
 Clite - 76
 Edouard - 76
 Judge J. - 1
 Julien - 48, 61, 73,
  104, 105, 111, 116,
  117, 128, 130, 136,
  142, 146, 148, 163
 Norbert - 76
LE CANN, Anne-Marie - 6,
 20

LE COEUR - See Liqueur
LEE, Charles - 162
LEE[S][E], Mrs. Esther/
 Easter/Hester - 79,
 125
 James - 79
 John - 43, 48, 54,
  55, 79, 110
 Maria - 79
 Rosanne/Rosanna - 79
LEFORT/LUFERT, Francois
 64, 78, 110
 H. - 142
LEGAY, Marie Jean - 179
LEGNON/LOIGNON/LEGRON,
 Arthemize - 32
 Emelie - 31
 Eugene - 32, 83
 Eugenie - 31, 32, 83
 Francois - 30, 79
 Frederic Louis - 32
 Joseph - 32, 37, 55,
  83
 Julie Anne/Julienne
  32, 83, 172
 L. - 30
 Laurent - 83
 Louis - 10, 30, 31,
  37, 83
 M. J. - 10
 Marie Alexandrine -
  30
 Marie Louise - 31
LEGUIER - See Liqueur
LELAND, M. J. - 34
LE MELLE, Francois -184
 Marie Louise - 184
LENO, F. M. C. [Free
 man of color] - 14
LENORE, Martin - 11
LEON, F. M. C. - 14

LE SASSIER, Charles -184A
   Julien - 88, 108, 184A
   Rebecca L[ouisa] - 88
LE TELLIER - 170
LEWIS & CLARK - 71
   Alexander - 28, 29
   Charlotte - 8A
   Isaac - 6
   Isam [Isaac?] - 110
   Joshua - 178
   Mary Eliza Angela - 29
   Seth - 88, 95, 97, 98, 99, 101, 102, 109, 110, 111, 112, 114, 125, 130, 134, 135, 141, 142, 147, 151, 162
   Susannah - 6
   Thomas H. - 147
   William B. - 97, 157
LINIER, Widow - 19
LINTON, John - 136
LIQUEUR, Jean - 46, 117
   Mary Madeleine - 46, 117
   Marie Marguerite - 64, 116, 117, 118, 181
LISLET, Moreau - 175
LOCKETT, B[artley]/B[arthelot] - 110, 120, 127, 128, 162
   Henry C. - 72, 162
   Mrs. Jane - 162
   John B. - 99, 125, 140, 162
   W[infrey] - 35, 40, 43, 47, 48, 52, 55, 72, 73, 74, 78, 80, 88, 97, 101, 109, 110, 111, 120, 121, 125, 127, 128, 129, 140, 149, 162

LOIGNON - See Legnon
LOIRET, Jeanne - 4
LOISEL, Widow [See also Catherine Toupart] 153
   Adrien - 154
   Jean Louis - 154, 167
   Nicolas [Pelagie] - 36, 44, 52, 53, 59, 62, 67, 77, 79, 114, 152, 153, 154, 167
LONG, John - 115, 135, 142, 156
   William - 53, 54
LONGSTAFF - See Langstaff
LOURI, J. - 4
LOUVIERE, Francois - 153
   Frederic - 153, 154
LOWREY, Gideon - 170
LUALE [?], Charles - 114
LYAIN [?], Peter - 156
LYMAN, Dr. J[oseph] W. - 109, 127, 128, 133, 147
LYNCH, Alexander - 147, 148
   Ann - 147, 148
   George - 147
   James - 125, 146, 147, 148
   Jane - 147
   Montgomery - 147
   Peyton - 103, 147
   Richard - 136, 146, 147, 148, 157
LYON[S], Able - 111
   David M. - 31
   Henry - 29
   William - 80

MC CALE [MC CALL?], Milledge - 76

MC CARTY, Bartholomew/
  Barthelemy - 139
  Edmund - 139
  Jean Baptiste - 139
  R[obert] - 103, 119,
    124, 153
  William M. - 126
MC CLAIN/MC CLEAN,
  Andrew W. - 37, 46,
    55
  Kentucky - 37
MC CLERKIN, Eleanor/
  Elender - 92
  James - 92
MC CLOED/MCLOED, Duncan
  [J.] - 110, 126
MC CLURE, Alexander W. -
  146
MC DANIEL, Dennis - 42
  John - 42
MC DERMOT, Bryan - 170
MC FARROW [?], John -
  128
MC FENNEN - 110
MC FHADON, W. - 4
MC ILHENNY, A. - 178
MC INTOSH, D. S. - 110,
  125, 126
MC KERRAL & DEJARNATT -
  126, 128
  Watson - 127, 128,
    148, 149, 161
MC LEAN - See McClain
MC MILLEN, John P. - 125,
  134, 138, 149
MC MURTRY, James - 21,
  78, 146, 165
  Nancy Alzira - 32
  Samuel - 32, 165
MC NAMAR[A], J. B. - 128
  W[illiam] B. - 99, 125,
    127, 141

MADISON, President - 16
MAGILL, Charles - 71A
MAGNON, Hypolite - 63,
  64, 78, 163
MAHE[A]----, George -
  53, 126

MAKIN, Thomas - 40, 54,
  61
MALBROOK, Benjamin -
  117, 118
MALBROU, Marie Anne -
  46, 117
MANDEVILLE - See De
  Marigny
MARCIN [?], William -
  146
MARDEN, William - 141
MARSH, Eliza Ann - 90
  George - 34, 90, 180
  Helen McKay - 90
  John C. - 76, 77, 90,
    91
  Margaret H. - 90
  Sarah Craig - 90
MARTEL, Balthazar - 179
MARTIN, Carmelite - 12
  John - 78, 94, 130,
    145, 146
  Joseph - 59
  Joseph Voltair - 59
  Mrs. Mabel - 170
  Marguerite - 122
  Mary - 173
MASKELL, Thomas - 134
MASSICOT, Augustin - 52
  Charles - 51, 52, 57
  Eulalie - 51, 52, 57
  Jean Baptiste - 52,
    53
  Marie Francoise - 52
  Theophile - 52

MAT[H]ERN[E], Adam - 122
  Gustin [?] - 122
  Jean Baptiste - 122
  Melanie - 121, 122, 182
  Nicolas - 122
MATHISON, Capt. Simon
  C. - 133
MAXENT, Marcelite - 112
MAYEAUX, Magdalen - 44
MAYER/MEYER/MYER[S],
  Charles Christian - 84
  Emelie - 84
  Euphemie Ida - 84
  Jean Daniel - 184
  [Samuel] Charles - 53, 84, 184
MEAD, John - 42
MELON, Rachel - 4, 10, 184
MENDOSA, Antoine - 153
  Pierre/Pedro - 153
MERELL, Amos - 63
MERRIMAN/MERRYMAN,
  Edward - 111
  John - 12, 111
MESTAYER - 111
  Francis - 84
METCALF[E], James - 8, 8A
MEUILLON, Edmond - 4
MICHETREE, William - 146
MIGUES/MIGUEZ, Bernard - 146, 171
  Salvador - 52
MILLER, Catherine - 12, 73, 163
  Celeste - 63, 64, 73, 118, 163
  Jacob - 63, 64, 73, 78, 94, 129, 130, 163
  Jean Baptiste - 12, 21, 63, 73, 94, 162
  Josephine - 162
  Madeline - 73, 163
  Margaret/Marguerite 63, 73, 163
  Marie - 73
  Patten [Peter?] - 128
  Sophia [See also Sophia Hoffman] - 63, 73, 129, 130
  Uranie - 162, 163
  Ursule - 162
MILLS, Joseph - 111
MILO, F. M. C. [Freeman of color] - 143
MIRAGROUIN - See Bodin
MITCHETTESEE [?], George - 125
MIX[T]ER, Frances - 33
MONNIER, Jacques - 36
MOORE, Elina - 172
  Israel - 127, 128
  John - 30, 35, 107, 148, 164
  Joseph Andrews - 41, 54, 107
  L. - 10
  Lewis - 23, 30, 42, 57, 58, 59, 65, 66, 67, 70, 78, 81, 84, 88, 90, 94, 107, 110, 114, 139, 145, 146, 172, 181
  Mrs. Lewis - 61, 108
  Louisa - 88, 107, 108
  Louise Camille - 108
  Mrs. Sarah - 65, 108, 114
  William - 11, 56, 107, 108, 164

MORISON, Daniel [David?] - 126
MORRIS, Dr. J[ames] G[ardner] - 12, 37
MOSS, Alfred P. - 134
MOUNTAINE [?], A. - 128
MOUTON, Marin - 111
   Olesime - 111
MUGGAH, Charles [R.] - 82
   David - 82
   Henry [J.] - 82, 145
   James - 45, 55, 56, 61, 73, 77, 82, 126, 136, 145, 148
   John - 82, 146, 157
   Julia/Julie Ann - 82
   Mrs. Nancy [see also Nancy Biggs, Nancy Robbins] - 56
   Samuel - 82
   Mrs. Sarah - 82
   Thomas - 56, 82
MULLIAN, Auguste - 119
   Francoise - 119
   Marie Louise - 119
   Nicolas - 119
   Palmice - 119
   Teups [?] - 119
MUNSON, Jeremiah - 146
   Lorenzo - 146
MURDOCK, James [W.] - 164
   John P. - 164
MURPHY, Donaldson/Donelson Caffery - 147
   Isaac Baker - 147
   John - 74, 147
   John B[arrett] - 48, 64, 73, 74, 75, 99, 115, 126, 128, 136, 147, 158
   Levinia - 74
   Lydia - 74, 147
   Martha P. - 147
   Sarah Ann - 74
   Simon Taylor - 147
   Thomas - 74
MUSE, Eliza Carlin - 50, 116
   Sampson - 50
MYERS [See also Mayer, etc.], William - 76
MYSWONGER, Lucy - 8A

NASH, Ale____ - 145
   William J[unius] - 120, 136, 145, 146, 148, 157
NAVARRO, A[delaide] [See also Demaret] - 36, 164
   Don Martin - 36
NEILSON, John - 146
NELSON, Andy - 153
NERSON/NURSEN, Alexander P. - 168
   Catherine Ann - 168
   Ellenor Ann - 168
   Henrietta - 168
   Henry Barnet - 168
   Henry Randolph - 38, 39, 115, 126, 168
   Jared Isaac - 168
   Mary Ann - 168
   Mary Eliza - 168
   Nancy Josephine - 168
NETTELTON/NETTLETON, Dr. [Col.] Clark - 111, 120, 128, 136, 138, 140
NEWMAN, James - 111
NEXON - See Nixon
NEZAT, Francoise - 20

NICHOLS, Benjamin - 114, 135
NICKELSON/NICHOLSON,
  Rachel - 66
  Rufus - 40, 48, 53, 54, 69
  Samuel - 178
NIMIG [?], William - 145
NIMMO, Eliza Ellen - 39
  Henry - 73
  M[athew] - 37, 39, 79, 88, 111, 126
NIXON, Abby Ann - 39
  Alexander [Nexon] - 40
  Ann/Nancy - 40
  Caroline P. - 39, 127
  Emily Sofeah - 39, 122
  Henry R[obert?] - 40
  Jackson Robert - 39
  Jediah/Judiah - 37, 38, 39
  Joshua - 40
  Rachel - 38, 39
  Robert - 38, 39
  Sarah - 38, 39
  Thomas R[obert?] - 40
  Woodson [?][Nixin?] - 40
NOBAN, E. - 4
NOPPER, Adelaide - 21, 77, 78
  Augustine - 77, 78
  Catherine Margaret/Marguerite - 11, 12, 21, 163
  Jacob - 77
  John - 21, 77, 78
  Marcellin - 77, 78
NORRIS, James S. [L.] - 135, 146
NORTON, Charles M[ynn] - 67, 68, 71A, 173, 174, 178
  Courtney Ann - 178
  Courtney [Mynn] - 68, 174, 178
  Daniel S. - 89
  George F[lowerdew] - 8A, 71A, 174, 178
  John H[atley] - 68, 71A, 174
  Louisa [Terrell] - 68, 174
  Philo - 4
  Sarah [A.] [See also Sarah A. Thruston] - 68, 174, 177, 178
  Sarah [Claiborne] - 68, 174
  Sidney [Ann Powell] - 68, 174
  William - 8A

O'BRIEN [See also Brian, Bryant, etc.],
  Samuel - 170
ODILLE, Catherine - 100
  Nicolas Theodore - 100
OFFMAN [See also Hoffman], Marie Barbe - 12
OGDEN, Frederick N. - 99, 109
  Robert Nash - 50, 72, 74, 88
OLIVIER [See also De Vezin], Adelaide Dugue - 20
  C. - 5
  C. A. - 19, 20
  Celeste [Mathilde] - 5

Charles [Barromee] - 5,
6, 19, 34A, 52, 53,
57, 59, 62, 77, 79,
90, 108
[Hugues] Charles
  Honoree - 6, 19, 20
Dubreuil - 153
Elina - 5
Francoise Emelie - 19
Joseph - 5, 99
Laure - 5
Marie-Perle - 5
Pierre [Olivier
  Duclosel DeVezin] -
  20
Pierre Charles - 5
Pierre Francois Marie
  [Olivier, Sieur de
  Vezin] - 19, 20
OUDUM [?], Pierre - 41
OWENS, James - 88, 145,
  146

PALASKI, Placide - 78
PALFREY, William T[aylor]
  30, 136, 140, 178
PAMECY [?], James - 145
PAMPHLEU, Robert - 29
PAMPTON, R. - 28
PAR[R]IS - 114
  Lemuel - 54
PARKERSON/PARKINSON,
  John N. - 111, 127, 140,
  162
PARKINS [PARKERSON?],
  John - 125
PARQUIN[S], Louis - 46,
  47, 88, 102, 126,
  128, 184A
  Miriam [See also
    Miriam Thompson] -
  19, 46, 47, 88, 102
PATIN, Marie - 15, 27,
  171
PATOUT, Simon/Simeon -
  113, 153
PATTEE/PATTIE, John -
  42, 127
  Marie - 12
  R. - 12
  Roland [Patti] - 12
PATTERSON & LACY - 146
  Andrew - 144
  Capt. E. - 127
  Elam - 145
  Elizabeth [W.]/Betty
    40, 58, 70, 71B, 89,
    161, 168, 169
  Martin L. - 144
PAVY & CAILLET - 145,
  146, 148
  Caroline - See
    Rentrop
  P. J. - 118
PECOT, Charles - 57, 67,
  77, 180
  Francois - 150, 179, 180
  Jacques - 180
  Luc [Louis?] - 180
  Marie Anne - 82, 150,
    180
  Marie Antionette -
    89, 179, 180
  [Marie] Louise - 10,
    25, 180
  Marie Rose - 180
PELLERIN, Alex. - 112
  Baltezar/Badthazar -
    60, 61, 172
  Bartholome Valsin -
    112
  Bernard - 9

    Calice/Calista - 60, 61, 172
    Cecile Rosalie Selinie 82, 150
    Charles Frederick - 82, 150
    Coralie - 82
    Edmond - 112
    Emelie - 77
    Eugene - 112
    Frederick [B.] - 52, 58, 69, 75, 79, 82, 83, 88, 112, 124, 134, 149, 180
    George - 112
    Gregoire - 9, 77, 150
    Hubert/Herbert - 37, 53, 60, 61, 62, 83, 166, 172
    Jacques Louis - 112
    Jules - 61, 171
    Julie [See Jules] - 60, 171
    Louis - 112
    Louis Alexandre - 113
    Louis Gerard - 112
    M. - 9
    Marie - 112
    Marie Eleonide - 60, 61, 172
    Marie-Joseph - 9, 77
    Marie/Mary Rose Angelique Desire Coralie - 150
    [Don] Martin - 112
    Nicolas [Louis] - 60, 61, 62, 83, 102
    Octave - 60, 61, 172
PENN[E], Henry - 114
PENNEL, John B. - See Jean B. Perrett
PERL, J. - 110
PERRAULT, Anne Wilhelmina - 6, 20
    Jean Baptiste - 6, 20
PERRET[T], Jean B[aptiste] - 34A, 111, 127, 128, 157, 158
    Lucien - 160
    Ursin - 111
PERRIE, James - 42
PERRIMAN - See Perryman
PERRY - 111
    Burton - 127
    James - 170
    Capt. Robert - 148
PERRYMAN, Alfred J. - 19, 151
    Drusilla Highfield [See also Highfield] 19, 151
    Harriet - 19, 39, 151
    J. M. - 26
    Montford/Munford J./I. - 13, 19, 27, 151
PETER, Frederick - 89
PETOT [PITOT?], Armand - 139
PETR[I]E/PETR[E]Y, Miss Eliza - 146
    George - 31
    George Washington - 31
    Henry - 31
    Louis - 31
    Mary - 31
    Selina/Celina [see also Wofford] - 31
PHIL[L]IP[P]S, George - 146
    J. - 24
    John - 24

PHIPPS, George - 145
PICKETT, James B. - 88
   Reuben - 87
PILLENARY [?], H. - 52
PITRE, Adam - 145
   Henry [see also Petre, etc.] - 146 [Pitree]
PLAISTED, James - 85, 104, 114, 120, 132, 158
POMEL, F. - See Pomet
POMET[T][E], Francois - 21, 154
   Jean Baptiste - 22, 154
POOLEY, Jane - 133
PORTER, Alexander - 8, 8A, 74, 75, 85, 111
   James - 8
   James A[lexander] - 74
POWELL, Capt. - 110, 112
   Elizabeth - 76
   John - 76
   Martha - See Martha Powell Gibson
   Rachel - 76
   Squire - 75, 76
   Walker - 76
   William Green - 76
PREJEAN[T], Cecile/Cecelia - 9, 77, 150
   Charles - 9
   [Marie] Rosalie - 150, 179, 180
PREVOST - See Provost
PRIMEAU/PRIMOT, Charles - 122, 182
PRINDLE, Abigale D[own?] 101
   Lyman - 101
PROVOST/PREVOST, Alexander Luke - 124
   Annette/Manette - 44, 45, 152, 153, 154
   Antionette - 167
   B. - 4
   Baptiste - 4
   Celeste Elenore - 36, 166, 167
   Celestine - 124
   Claire Emma - 124
   Edouard/Edmond - 58, 124, 168
   Eleanor [see also Celeste Elenore Provost] - 62
   Eliza - 44, 119
   Eugenie - 26
   Felicite - 166
   Francois - 44, 57, 84, 119, 153, 154, 155
   Godfroi/Godefroy - 36, 37, 57, 60, 62, 63, 84, 119, 124, 152, 166
   Hortense - 59, 60, 62, 166, 167
   Hyacinthe - 44
   Jean Baptiste - 44, 119
   Joseph [Alias Collet] 1, 25, 37, 44, 75, 98, 119, 126, 167
   Julie - 13, 14, 25, 37, 44, 57, 60, 61, 83, 84, 166, 167, 168
   Lenfroi [see also Lufroy Provost] - 36, 37
   Lucil[l]e [also Lucie] 26, 36, 37, 58, 124, 166, 167

Lufroy [see also Lenfroi Provost] - 26, 53, 58, 59, 60, 62, 119, 124, 153, 166, 167, 168, 178
  Madelaine - 44, 119
  Marie - 45, 60, 62
  Marie Jeanne - 14, 36, 37, 60, 166, 167
  Marie Juliana - See Julie Provost
  Marie Louisa - 124, 166
  [Marie] Therese - 2, 14, 25, 66, 143, 167
  Mary Virginia - 172
  Nicolas - 14, 25, 36, 37, 59, 60, 62, 143, 166, 167
  Nicolas LeClaire - 167
  Nicolas Philemon - 36, 60, 119, 124, 166, 168, 172
  Philemon - [see also Nicolas Philemon Provost] - 36, 59, 62
  Pierre - 2, 14, 25, 143, 167
  T. - 25
  Ursin/Ursant - 14, 25, 36, 44, 51, 60, 62, 63, 114, 119, 124, 166, 167, 168
  Virginie Julie - 167
PUGH, Thomas - 43
PULASKI [?][See also Palaski], Placide - 146
PUMPHREY, William - 136, 138, 153

QUEBEDEAU, Marie Francoise 25, 37, 167

QUIN, Justin - 52

RAGNEY, August - 67
RAMAY, G. B. - 10
RANDALL, Samuel B. - 99
RANDLETT, John - 149
RANDOLPH, Isaac - 76
RAPHALL, Morris - 137
RAWLS, Daniel - 113, 114
  Job. B. - 113
  Philip A[lston] - 113
  Silas - 113
RAY, James - 42
REAVES - See Reeves
REDDICK, Purnel J. - 55
READ/REED, Isaac - 37, 69
  Juliann - 69, 70, 169
  Leticia - 69
  Mrs. Sarah Towles - 137
REELS, Madame Eliza [see also Elizabeth J. Brown & Elizabeth J. Knight] - 146
  Patrick - 46
REEVES, Edmund - 74
  John [Rieves] - 37, 95, 133, 180
  Joseph - 95
  Susan - 133, 180
REGNIER/RUGNIER, Peter - 86
REGNOIR, Dr. - 53
REID [see also, Read/Reed], David - 148
RENTON, Alexander - 13, 22, 34
RENT[H]ROP[E], Auguste F[rederick] - 64, 116, 117, 118

[Sara Charlotte Juanita] Caroline - 116, 117, 118
Celeste Sarah - 116, 117, 118
Detour - 118
Dorsino L. - 118
Eliza[beth] - 116, 117, 118
Frederick [William] - 45, 64, 116, 117, 118, 181
Henry - 63, 64, 116, 117
Henry M[aurice] - 116, 118
Madame Margaret - 145
[Teville?] Marguerite 117, 118, 181
Marguerite Liqueur - See Marguerite Liqueur
Octave - 118
Pamela - 118
Peter H[enry] - 44, 63, 78, 82, 88, 103, 111, 116, 117, 119, 136, 164
Sarah Celeste - See Celeste Sarah Rentrop
Tarquile - 116, 117, 118
Valsan/Valsin - 116, 118
RICE & SEAY - 125, 126
John - 48, 61, 126, 128, 141
Samuel R[ussell] - 51, 145
RICHARD[S], James - 110
Marie - 12
RICHARDSON, Col. 114

Allen - 157
F[rancis] D. - 163
Hanislt [?] - 157
John W. [G?] - 54, 55, 114, 133, 136, 138, 139, 152
Margaret - 157
Samuel - 70
William - 43, 47, 111, 126, 157
RIDDLE, Elizabeth - 66, 144
RIGAUD, Gov. Pierre [Marquis de Vaudreuil] 19
RIGGS, Eli - 136
RIGUES, Andre - 12
Jean A. - 12
RILEY, James - 126
RING[UET][T][E], Andre - 21
J. - 21
Joseph - 12, 21, 73, 163
Margaret - 77, 78
Rosalie - 21, 163
ROAN, Spencer B. - 161
ROB[B]IN[S], Ann/Nancy - 56, 82
David - 55, 61, 63, 78, 82, 126, 130, 146, 148
Julie Ann - 56, 82
ROBERT[S], Bay[n]ard C. 60, 61, 86, 121, 141
Benjamin C. - 86
Daniel - 172
Dianna - 141
Elizabeth [see also Elizabeth Jaudon] - 60

Elizabeth J[audon?] - 60
Grimball - 172
Harriet - 60
James - 172
Jo Ann - 141
Joseph - 111, 172
Louisa [see also Louisa Armstrong] - 141
Martha E. - 60, 141
Mary - 60, 61
Mary Ann - 60
P. W. - 111, 126
Paul Jabez - 172
Peter - 60, 61, 96, 141, 172, 173
Peter H[ickock] - 60, 61, 86, 95, 96, 97, 126, 141, 180 [Hilkiah]
Peter W[ilkinson] - 60, 61
Peter William [Wilkinson?] - 141
P. Y. [W?] - 125
Sarah A. - 47, 60, 141
Solathost [?] - 141
ROBERTSON, Thomas B. - 178
ROBICHAUD, Claire - 56, 98
ROBIN [See also Robbins], A. - 67
ROBINET[T][E], Melanie - 159
   Nicolas - 104, 105, 159
   Peter [also Robin] - 104, 105, 159, 181
ROCHE, Anne - 77
ROCHEL[L][E], W[illiam] -
63, 78, 127, 148, 183
ROGERS, Mrs. - 127
   Mrs. Elizabeth - 111
   Joshua - 55
   Mary Monica Reynolds 124
   Mathew - 116, 157, 183
   R[ankin] - 94, 136, 161, 180
   R[obert] [P.] - 127, 135, 161, **168**
ROMAN, Jeanne - 69
ROMEL [?], John - 145
ROOT & INMAN [?] - 146
   Benjamin - 126
ROSE, E. - 34
   Edmund/Edouard - 34
   Elizabeth Judd - 139
ROWE, Julius - 156
   Ludger [?] - 146
   Ursin - 146
ROYSTER, **Ann/Nancy** P[oindexter] - 105, 106, 159
   Anna [see also Anna Bowes] - 40
   Elizabeth Virginia - 105, 106, 159
   George - 40, 46, 48, 51, 53, 54, 69, 70, 89, 95, 105, 123, 125, 131, 136, 156, 159, **182**
   Robert B. - 95, 105, 106, 114, 122, 123, 126, 146, 159, 182
   Robert M. [B?] - 106
   Sarah Kemper [see also Sarah Kemper] 106

Thomas J. - 105, 106, 158
ROWLAND/ROWLING, Joshua/Josiah - 23
RUCKER, Catherine - 44, 136, 137
  Peter - 137
RUMAL, John - 127
RUSS, Catherine - 46
  William - 46
RUSSELL, George - 126, 156
  Oliver - 156
RUTLAND, John S. - 121

SALE, Edmund/Edwin N. [M.] - 92, 97, 111, 121, 125, 126, 130, 135, 162
  J. N. [?] - 110
SALLES, Sylvain - 67, 115, 128, 142, 143, 155
SAMMS, Mary - 172
SA[U]NDERS, Mrs. Abby Ann [see also Abby Ann Nixon] - 126
  Davis H. - 91, 94
  Miss E. - 126
  Elender/Eleanor - 91, 94, 180
  Eliza - 126
  Elizabeth - 94
  Dr. H. N. - 149
  James - 35, 37, 38, 39, 49, 54, 55, 73, 79, 85, 91, 92, 93, 97, 100, 105, 106, 109, 120, 123, 125, 126 [Mrs.], 127, 130, 148, 183
  Jared Young - 28, 38, 39, 43, 48, 49, 52, 53, 54, 61, 72, 91, 93, 105, 111, 115, 121, 123, 127, 129, 130, 134, 135, 142
  Mary [see also Mary Young] - 91, 93
  Nancy - 91, 93, 183
  Thomas Young - 91, 94
  William G[unnell] - 48, 49, 91, 92, 93, 120, 127, 128, 143, 148
SANDY, Uriah - 110
SANFORD, William - 120
SAUNIE - Sonnier
SAUVAGIN, Jean Baptiste 3
  Marie Anne - 3, 22, 154
SAUVE, Pierre - 1
SAVOIE, Anastasie - 66
SCANLON, Jeremiah - 69
SCHNEXAYDER, Marguerite 63
SCHWING, George - 125, 161
SCOTT, S[amuel] E. - 37, 40, 47, 54, 60, 61, 86, 111, 126
SCUDDER, Mary Jane - 82
SEAY & RICE - 125, 126
  W[illiam] A. - 101, 105, 109, 125, 126, 128, 130, 135
SEGUR - See Sigur
SELLIER/TELLIER/LE TELLIER, Marie Marguerite - 45, 170
SEMMES - See Summers
SEMPLE, Robert - 136

SEN[N]ET[T][E], Aurore –
  41
  Azelie – 41
  Charlotte – 41
  Charlotte Delphine –
  41
  E. – 10
  Eugene – 4, 10, 41,
  126, 143, 156, 164
  Eugenie – 41, 163,
  164
  George – 125
  Gilbert – 146
  Hugere Silvanie – 41
  John [see also John
  Baptiste] – 125
  J[ohn] B[aptiste] –
  4, 11, 41
SENEQUER/SINEQUIRE/
SINITIERE/SIMIKER,
  Francois – 98, 99,
  100
  Marie L. – 56
  Rosaline – 13
  Rosemond – 100
SERRA, G[aytavae] – 111,
  126
SHARP, William – 103,
  104, 111, 114, 125, 128,
  134, 142, 157
SHAVER, William – 146
SHAW, Jones – 43, 48, 55
  William – 74
SHIELD[S], Benjamin –
  132, 133
SIGUEUR – See Liqueur
SIGUR/SEGUR, Adelaide –
  77
  Alexander – 77, 83
  Amemaide – 77
  Edouard/Edward – 77

Elagie [?] – 77
[Emelia] Felicite –
  77, 180
Francois Pierre – 77
Laurent – 77, 83, 89,
  149, 150
Numa – 77
Treville [?] – 77
SIMON, _____ – 115
  Edward – 86
SINGLETON, G[eorge] –
  43, 58, 70, 81, 114,
  153
  Jefferson – 81
  John W[esley?] – 81,
  114
  Owen – 81
  Sidney – 81, 114
  Washington – 81
  Wesley – 81
SITTIG [?], Dominque C.
  90
SKILLMAN, Andrew – 21,
  42, 43
  Ann [see also Ann
  Sterling] – 43
SLAUGHTER, Robert – 137
SMITH Plantation – 125,
  126
  Mrs. – 126
  Alfred – 86, 128,
  131, 140, 141, 160,
  161
  Andrew [C.] – 138,
  139
  Ann – See Ann Tinker
  Ann Tinker – 102
  Archibald – 97
  Boyd – 109
  D. – 10
  Daniel – 18

David – 10, 26, 46, 47, 88, 102, 157
Elijah – 86, 125, 126, 131
Elizabeth – 97
George – 18
Harriet – 97
Capt. J. – 127
Jacob – 18
Dr. James [Y.] – 10, 46, 47, 88, 99, 102, 107, 120, 125, 128, 136, 157, 158
Jesse – 37
John – 18, 32, 54, 55, 81, 99, 111, 112, 127, 136, 138, 139, 145, 146, 148, 157, 160
Jonathan – 17, 18, 55, 64, 127, 138, 140,
Joshua – 131, 161
Jules – 86
Julia [Ann] – 18, 95
Julien/Julian – 131
Julius – 54, 86, 89, 96, 97, 131, 161
L. – 28
Lebanon – 18
Lucius – 28
Margaret – 131, 160, 161
Matilda [see also Matilda Bailes] – 88, 125
Phoebe – 86, 96, 131, 160
Ralph – 131, 161
Sarah – 95, 96, 131, 165
William – 95, 120, 131, 159
SNIPES, Dempsey – 27

SOJOURNER, B[ridges] – 126, 146, 148, 156, 179
 [Caroline] Amanda – 156, 183
 Charles [Bell] – 156
 Lenore Jane – 156
 Mary Bell – 156, 183
 Robert [N.] – 156, 183
SOLANGE, Dr. – 111
SONNIER/SAUNIE, Celeste 78
 Jean Baptiste – 62, 78
 Marguerite – 12
 Marie Eroin [?] – 62
 Marie [Joseph][alias Madame Constant] – 62
SORREL, Antoine Francois Solange/Selange – 82, 149, 150
 C[ontamine?] J. – 24, 33
 Francois – 24
 J. – 24
 Jacques/Santiago – See Joseph Sorrel
 Joseph – 24, 41
 Martial – 150
 Santiago/Jacques – See Joseph Sorrel
 Solange – 76, 89
 Tom – 112
SOULE, Dubreutil – 153
S[O]UTHERLAND, Alexander S[mith] – 85
 Ann – 85
 Jane – 85
 Mary – 85
 William – 85

SPARKS, Daniel P[ierce] - 43, 48, 53, 61, 65, 78, 101, 136, 143, 145, 148, 157
SPAULDING, Daniel - 54
  Sarah - 51, 54
SPEARS, Abigail E. - 131
SPENCER, Thomas - 114
SPICKARD, John - 149
SPLAN[N][E], A[lexander] R. - 81, 85, 87, 88, 97, 99, 101, 109, 121, 122, 123, 126, 128, 129, 130, 135, 137, 138, 140, 146, 151, 162, 182
  Peyton [R.] - 69, 75, 110
  Susan Lacy [see also Susan Lacy] - 75
SPRADLEY, Lucy - 31
ST. AMANT, Antoine - 52
ST. JULIEN, Cleonide - 112
  Marie Zoe - 112
ST. PIERRE, Charles - 78
STANBROUGH, Anson - 37
STANHOPE [see also Tenhold], Caroline - 100
STANSBURY, Albert - 111
STEELE, Frances A. - 8A
  James - 101, 109, 110, 111, 112, 114
STEER, Samuel - 49
STEPHENS, William - 111
STEPHENSON, Wendell Holmes - 75
STERLING/STIRLING, Alexander - 42, 43, 169, 170
  Ann [see also Ann Alston] - 21, 43, 170
  Frederick - 170
  Henry - 28, 42, 170
  James Leake - 170
  Janet - 170
  John - 42, 170
  Lewis - 28, 42, 43, 125, 126, 136, 170
  Peter - 170
  Ruffin [Gray] - 42, 43, 170
  William - 42, 43, 72, 75, 88, 111, 170
STEWART, Duncan - 165
  William - 157, 158
STEIN/STINE/STAIN, Edmond - 87
  J. - 114
  James - 87
  John - 87, 184A
  Marie/Mary - 87
  Philip - 87
  William - 87
STONE & MARSH - 91
  Davis A. Craig - 76
  Samuel - 76, 90, 91
  William - 76, 91
SUBLETTE, Mrs. M. A. - 124
SUMMERS/SEMMES, Enoch - 101
  Sarah W. - 101
SUMNER, D. - 18
  Dorothy/Dorothea - 15, 18
  Duke W[illiam] - 15, 18

Ecum/Exum - 15, 18
J. J. - 15
John - 15
Joseph J[ohn] - 15, 18
William Henry - 15
SURRIL, Amos - 126
SWAYZE, Lucretia - 93
SYLVAIN, B. - 146

TABOR, Isaac - 170
TANNER, Joshua - 109, 110
TARKINGTON, Joseph S. [T.] - 127, 134, 161, 183
TATE, Joseph - 42
TAYLOR, Emma L. - 74, 147
  John J. - 74
TELLIER - 170
TEMPLETON, Samuel - 131
TENHOLD [See also Stanholt, Stanhope], Claire Adelaide/Adele - 100, 181
  Frederick - 100
  Jean Henry - 100
TENNANT, Bazelie - 98
TERRELL, Mary Poiner - 71A, 173, 178
  Micajah - 71B, 173
  Sarah - 71B, 173
  Timothy - 173
TEVIS, Noah - 40
THAYER, W. C. - 125
THEALL, Miss Fannie - 127
  H. - 33
  Hackeliah - 33, 171, 183

Hannah [see also Hannah Hughson] - 127, 134
Henry [Mixter] - 33, 134
James F. - 33, 48, 111, 125, 126, 128 133, 134, 135, 171
John B. - 33, 40, 43, 48, 81, 111, 126, 134
Mrs. John - 111
Joseph - 32, 33, 37, 43, 48, 55, 66, 72, 73, 80, 88, 92, 111, 127, 133, 171, 180, 183
Nancy [see also Nancy Sanders] - 33, 133, 134, 135, 183
Ruffin - 33, 134
THEODUM [?], Devina [?] [see Theodore Dineina] 128
THERIOT/TERRIO, Charles 63, 94, 104, 105, 117, 118, 130, 146, 163, 181
  Leonise - 181
  Marcellin - 104, 181
  Marie Zelwin - 104, 105, 159, 181
  Michel - 146
  Zepherin - 105, 117, 118, 181
THIBEAU/THIBAUD, L. - 15
  Louis - 15, 184
  Louis D. - 15
  Marie Joseph - 10, 30
THIBODEAU[X], Anne - 108, 109

Rose - 4
THOMAS, Alexander - 72
  Elizabeth - 120
  G[reenbury] B. - 111,
    120, 125, 126
  H[enry] A. - 141, 146
  James - 72, 106, 120,
    121, 181
  James L[yons] - 104
  John L. - 104, 120
  Martha - 120
  Martin - 104, 120
  Mary Elizabeth - 104
  Mary J[ane] - 72, 106,
    121
  Owen - 72, 99, 106,
    121, 126
  Peyton - 72, 106, 121,
    181
  Sophia W[ardlaw] - 72,
    106, 121
  T. - 38
THOMPSON, Drury - 41, 42
  Henry - 86, 133, 147,
    149
  John - 42
  Miriam [also Miriam
    Tinker, Parquin,
    Parkin(s)] - 33, 47,
    102, 184A
  Thomas H. - 58, 71B
THORNTON, A. W. - 178
THRUSTON, Miss - 171
  Dr. Alfred - 37, 58,
    68, 70, 71B, 169,
    171, 175, 176,
    177
  Mrs. Ann [see also
    Ann Alexander] - 68,
    70, 175, 176, 177,
    178

  Buckner - 71
  Charles Mynn - 58,
    70, 71, 71A, 71B,
    165, 174, 175, 178
  Edmond Taylor - 58,
    67, 68, 70, 71A,
    71B, 173, 174, 175,
    176, 177, 178
  Elizabeth [see also
    Elizabeth Hudson] -
    58
  F. - 29
  Frances [see also
    Frances Conrad] -
    29, 68, 71A, 108,
    137, 165, 176, 178
  Frederick - 71A,
    165, 176, 178
  Martha [Goodman] -
    67, 68, 71B, 174
  Mary Buckner [see
    also Mary Buckner]
    71, 71A
  Sarah A[lexander] -
    8B, 71A, 174, 175
THURSTON - See Thruston
THWAITES, _____ - 33
  C. - 32
  Charlotte - 33, 102
  Charlotte Frederica
    33, 102
THWEATT/THEWEATT,
  Micajah W. - 72, 106,
    121
TINKER, Ann - 10, 26,
    47, 102
  Charlotte - 32, 33,
    102
  Jeremiah - 33, 47,
    102, 184 A
TODD, David - 129

James - 182
TOMLINSON, Catherine - 129, 130
  James - 129, 130
  Jesse - 63, 73, 129, 130
TOMPKINS, Harris - 142
TOU[R]PART, Catherine - 22, 45, 66, 154, 167
TOUPS, Ambroise - 111
  Paul - 31
TOWLES, Ann Frances - 135
  Charles Mynn - 135
  Gertrude Elizabeth - 135
  Dr. John T[homas] - 30, 35, 46, 48, 53, 73, 74, 84, 85, 105, 112, 135, 137, 145, **178, 184A**
  John Turnbull - 105, 135, 136, 137, 139
  Mary Elizabeth - 135
  Philip Slaughter - 135
  Susan Turnbull [see also Susan Turnbull] 137
  Thomas - 135
TRAUGHAN, Charles - 111
TRAPPE, Anne Catherine Elizabeth - 117
TREULLIER, Marie Anne - 18
TRIMBLE, Robert [C.] - 101, 103, 114, 127, 145
TRIPLOT [?], Coleman - 112
TROUSDALE, R. - 27
  Robert [C.] - 27, 48, 54, 55, 80, 92, 125, 139, 184

TROWBRIDGE, Henrietta - 144
  Isaac - 144
TRUFER [?]/TRUFORT, Charles - 62, 146
TURELLA, L. - 10
TURNBULL, Daniel - 136, 137, 139
  Isabella - 136
  John - 43, 136, 137
  Sarah - 43, 136
  Susan - 135, 136
  Walter - 137, 139
TURREYA - 10
TWILEY - 111
TYSON, C[ornelius] C. - 126

VAMOIX [?], Joel - 127
VAN NESS - 38
VANOY, Joel - 146
VAN PELT - 38
VAN SALEE - 38
VAN SICKLIN - 38
VAN VOORHEES - 38
VARNIER, Victor Edward 99
VEEDER, Nicolas - 135
  P[eter] - 111, 127
VERCIN [?], Rowel [?] - 145
VERDEN/VERDIN[E]/VERDUN, Alexander - 105, 160
  Jean Baptiste - 105, 160
  Marie/Mary - 105, 160
  Pierre - 105, 159
  Romain - 125, 127
VER[R]ET[T][E], Arcisse [?] - 98
  Auguste - 98, 181

Carmelite - 56, 98
Eloise - 56, 108
Francoise - 98
Godefroi - 56, 98, 153, 171
Henriette - 56, 98, 164, 180
Jacques - 171
Jean Baptiste - 56, 98, 115, 180
Joseph - 171
Josephine [Dometille] 98
Louis - 15, 27, 171
Lucien - 122
Manon/Marie Anne - 56, 171
Marcelin - 117, 118
Marguerite Clarisse - 28
Marie - 15, 27
Marie Celeste - 98
N[icolas] - 43, 48, 56, 98, 115, 121, 122, 135, 164, 171, 181
Philippe - 56, 98, 108, 153, 164
Regobert/Rigobert - 37, 153
VERNICE, Philip - 59, 78
VERNO [?], T. C. - 112
VIDRINE, Mrs. Drouet W. - 21
VIGN[E]AUD, Philip - 113, 167
VILLERE, Gov. Jacques Philippe - 5
Jules - 5
Sidney L. - 6, 20, 71B, 164, 171

VINCENT, A[dolph?] [G.] 109, 135
Francois - 113
VINES, Thomas C. - 146
VINING, John - 146
Thomas - 146
William - 146
VINSON, Rhoda Jane - 178
WADDLE, John A. - 127
WAGGONER, William [W.] - 146
WALKER, Anthony - 37, 43, 48, 55, 64, 125, 128, 138, 142, 143
Gideon - 27, 29
James [H.] - 126
Mary - 27, 184
Moses - 126
Sarah [Celeste] - 27, 29
William [W.] - 48, 55, 64, 112, 127
WALL, James - 73
Rev. Spencer - 126, 134
WALLACE, Thomas - 111, 126, 143
WALTNEY - See Goultenetyt, Galtney
WALTON, E. H. - 126
WARFIELD, Elisha - 129
WASHINGTON, George - 70, 71
WATERS, Ann - 170
WATKINS, John - 91, 93
WATSON, Ann - See Ann Tinker
Dexter - 127, 128
John M. - 10, 26, 47, 102

Susan - 26
Zorabel - 26
WEBB, Jane - 85
  John F. C. - 164
WEEKS, David - 30, 67, 68, 90, 108, 109, 135, 136, 162
WELLMAN & PHILLIPS - 24
  A. W. - 24
WELLS, Dr. B[uckingham] F. - 48, 72, 73, 75, 109, 126
  Edmund - 109
  Judith - 109
  Lydia - 109, 110
  Nathan A. - 110
  Persis - 109
  Samuel - 109, 110
  Sarah - 109, 110
  Thayler - 109
  William A. - 109
WESSON, John - 125
WEST, Winifred - 46
WESTREM [?], George - 127
WHALEY & LEES - 43
  William - 43, 55
WHARTON, F[ranklin] - 125, 127, 128, 140, 142, 145
WHITAKER, Ann/Nancy - 106, 122, 123
WHITE, James - 156
  John - 127
  Joseph - 111
  Peter - 29
  Sarah - 184A
WHITING, G. & CO. - 126, 128
WHITING or WHITNEY, William - 142
WHITTINGTON - See Withington
WILCOXON/WILCOXEN, John 146
  Lloyd - 11, 48, 61, 69, 75, 127
  Nancy - 134
  Thomas [B.] - 51, 65, 78, 121, 126, 145, 146
  W[alter] [B.] - 55, 119, 120, 123, 125, 128, 145, 156
WILKINS, John D. - 113
WILKINSON, Jehu - 28, 37, 43, 48, 64, 78, 132, 134, 136, 158
  P. - 121
  Samuel - 37, 48, 55, 112, 127, 139
WILLIAMSON, Ann N. - 8B
  Elizabeth - 8B
  Esther A. - 8B
  Mary B[uford?] - 8B
  William - 8B
WILLSON, James - 82
WILSON, Mr. - 109
  D. W. - 125
  Joseph G. - 121
  S. A. - 125
  S[ingleton] W. - 95, 127
  Thomas - 99, 127
WING, Samuel W. - 133
WITHINGTON/WORTHINGTON, Benjamin B. - 140
  William L. - 140
WOFFORD, Celina [Selina] E[ugenie?] - 31
  Louis [Hamilton] - 31, 32, 146

William [Nathaniel] - 31
William W[ashington] 31, 32, 38, 128, 145, 148
WOOLFOLK, Mary Sowell - 121
  Sowel[l] - 106, 107, 121
WOOSTER, Nathan - 86, 131, 136, 138, 160
WORTHINGTON - See Withington
WRIGHT, Alva - 75
WYCKOFF - 38
  Antje - 38

YATES, Eliza R. [see also Eliza R. Hennen] - 16, 170
YOUNG, Mary - 91, 92
  Notley - 111, 134
  William - 92
YOUNGBLOOD, A. [C.?] - 141
  Eliza - 120
  Gen. C. William - 120
  Joseph Alston Moore 120
  Mary Rebecca - 120
  Dr. Thomas - 112, 120, 121, 141, 142, 145, 148
YOUNGER, Mrs. - 126
  James - 111
YO YA, Joseph - 126

ZADIG, Samuel - 42
ZERBINATI, Marie - 1

SUPPLEMENTARY INDEX

ALEXANDER, Col. - 71
  Ann - 169
  David - 71
ALPHA, Mrs. Clyde - 34A, 122, 173, 179, 180, 181, 183, 184, 184A

BELL, Agatha - 122
  David - 122
  Melite [Marie?] - 182
  Samuel [E.] - 122
  Thomas - 128
BIRDSALL, Ann Theall [See also Ann Theall] - 34
  Benjamin M. - 33
BREAUX, Huey Henry - 179
BROWN, Alfred - 34, 183
BUCKNER, Ann - 71
  John - 71
  Philip - 71
  Thomas - 71
BUNIFF, Samuel - 152

CANBROUGH, William - 34

DOOLEY, William - 34

FASSITT, Dr. C. R. - 169
FOOT, George - 181
FOSTER, Alix Caroline Xavier - 169
  Orlando Oscar - 165
  Pamela Zeide - 165
  Thomas - 165
  Thomas L. - 165
FRERE, Mary Ester - 184A

GORDY, Peter W. - 179
  Thomas - 179

HAMILTON, Alexander - 34
   Elizabeth R. - 183
   Rebecca - 34
HANES, Sarah [See also
   Sarah Mynn] - 70
HASLET, Mr. - 184 A
   Ann A. [See also Ann
     lexander Conrad] -
     184 A
HAYS, John - 34
   Malachi - 34, 171
   Mary - 34

KEMP, Mary - 184 A

LACY, Jesse Eagleson - 33
LEWIS, John - 184

MAKIN, Mary [See also
   Mary Robert] - 173
MYNN, Sarah [See also
   Sarah Hanes] - 70

O'FALLON, Dr. James - 71A

PARQUIN, Louis Francois -
   184 A
POWELL, Alfred - 71B

ROSE, John - 34A
   William P. - 34A

TAYLOR, Edmund H. - 71B
THEALL, Ann [See also
   Ann Theall Birdsall]
   33
THOMPSON, Eveline E. -
   169
   Francis H. - 169
   James - 184A
   Thomas H. - 114, 169,
     184 A

THRUSTON, Edward - 70
   Elizabeth Mynn - 71B
   John - 70, 71
   Louisa - 71B
   Sydney Ann - 71B
TREET, Elizabeth - 34,
   171

VINCENT, Rhoda Jane -
   182

WALKER, Jane - 184
WHITING, Elizabeth J. -
   71
WILLIAMS, Nancy - 181

YATES, Mr. - 170

www.ingramcontent.com/pod-product-compliance
Lightning Source LLC
Chambersburg PA
CBHW022110150426
43195CB00008B/342